# Fundamental Written Chinese

# About the Authors

NORA YAO has been teaching Chinese to tertiary students for over twenty years since receiving an MA (Hons) in language teaching from the University of Auckland. Currently, she is a senior tutor in the School of Asian Studies and is the director of the Confucius Institute at the University of Auckland. Her research interest is foreign-language teaching methodology, particularly teaching Chinese as a foreign language. She is the recipient of the Distinguished Teaching Award from the University of Auckland and the Good Citizen Award and Medal for Distinguished Women from the Mayor of Auckland.

MARGARET SOO KIAK LEE is a senior tutor at the University of Auckland with over twenty years' experience in teaching Chinese as a foreign language at the tertiary level, having previously taught at the Victoria University of Wellington and the Auckland Institute of Studies. She graduated with a BCA from the Victoria University of Wellington and an MA (Hons) in Chinese from the University of Auckland. Her areas of research are teaching Chinese as a foreign language and computer-assisted language learning.

ROBERT SANDERS, who has over twenty years' experience teaching Chinese language and Chinese linguistics at the tertiary level, is currently a senior lecturer in Chinese at the University of Auckland, having previously taught at Tohoku University, the Ohio State University, and the University of Hawai'i. He has studied at both National Taiwan University and Peking University in addition to receiving an MA in Chinese from the University of Hawai'i and a PhD in linguistics from the University of California at Berkeley. His area of research interest is the comparison of Beijing and Taiwan Mandarin, and he has served as a co-editor of the *ABC Chinese-English Dictionary* and the *ABC Chinese-English Comprehensive Dictionary,* both published by University of Hawai'i Press.

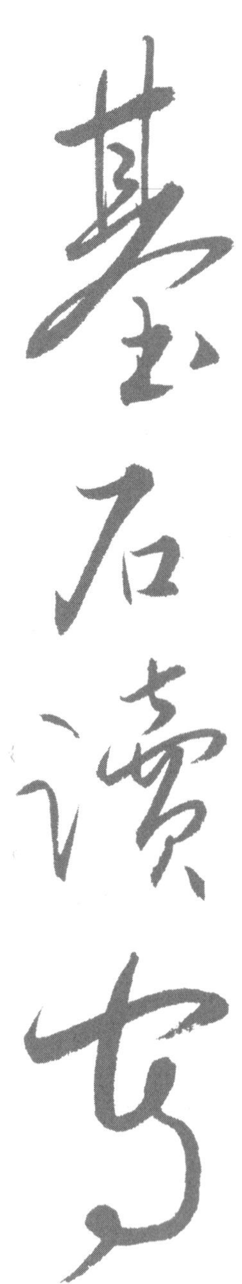

# Fundamental Written Chinese

基石读写

Simplified Character Version

Nora Yao, Margaret Lee, and Robert Sanders

UNIVERSITY OF HAWAI'I PRESS
HONOLULU

Printed in the United States of America

14 13 12 11 10 09     6 5 4 3 2 1

**Library of Congress Cataloging-in-Publication Data**

Yao, Nora.
Fundamental written Chinese : simplified character version / Nora Yao, Margaret Lee, and Robert Sanders.
p. cm.
Includes indexes.
ISBN 978-0-8248-3157-8 (paper back : alk. paper)
1. Chinese language—Writing. I. Lee, Margaret Soo Kiak. II. Sanders, Robert, 1955- III. Title.
PL1171.Y345 2009
495.1'11—dc22
2008055802

University of Hawai'i Press books are printed on acid-free paper and meet the guidelines for permanence and durability of the Council on Library Resources

Designed by the University of Hawai'i Press production staff
Printed by The Maple-Vail Book Manufacturing Group

# Contents

# Preface

## Approach

Three core assumptions underlie the design of *Fundamental Written Chinese* and its relationship with *Fundamental Spoken Chinese*. The first assumption is that oral and written language represent two different but related systems that are most effectively taught by delinking the sequence in which the particulars of each system are taught, while ensuring that the instruction of reading and writing skills is firmly grounded in the spoken vocabulary and grammar that the learner has already acquired. A consequence of this principle is that instruction in vocabulary and grammar takes place exclusively in *Fundamental Spoken Chinese*. The role of *Fundamental Written Chinese* is clearly defined as providing instruction in reading and writing what users have already learned how to say.

The second core underlying principle is that the unit of the individual written character should not be confused with the concept of a word, as many words in modern Chinese comprise more than one syllable and as such are written as a combination of two or more different characters. A consequence of this is that quite a number of characters in modern Chinese can never stand alone as independent words. Instead they must always combine with another character before they can be considered linguistically whole. For example, the underlying meaning of the character 汉 is "China; Chinese," but in fact, it can never stand alone as an independent word. Instead, it must always combine with another character, for example, 汉语, "Chinese language"; 汉字, "Chinese character(s)"; and 汉人, "person of Chinese Han ethnicity."

The third core assumption is that the optimum way to teach the mastery of the written system is by focusing on structural regularities such as radicals, phonetic components, shared graphic components, stroke order, and principles of proportion, and to sequence the introduction of characters according to a principle of graduated structural complexity from simple independent characters to more complex compound characters. This is best carried out by avoiding the distraction of teaching too many different radicals or too many structurally unrelated characters in any one chapter. In this way, a sufficient number of characters sharing the newly introduced radical can appear simultaneously, allowing the saliency of that particular radical to be generously reinforced. From a practical standpoint this can only be accomplished after a sufficient number of spoken words have already appeared in *Fundamental Spoken Chinese* that, when written, happen to use at least one character constructed with the targeted radical. Before a sufficient number of spoken vocabulary of this type have been learned, it is often more appropriate simply to use Hanyu Pinyin romanization rather than a Chinese character to represent a particular syllable in a *Fundamental Written Chinese* text.

For example, the word *shuō*, "to speak," first appears in Chapter 4 of *Fundamental Spoken Chinese*. In Chapter 4 of *Fundamental Written Chinese*, it appears in the written text in Hanyu Pinyin romanization only. In Chapter 5 of *Fundamental Spoken Chinese*, three different syllables, 词 *cí*, "word," 话 *huà*, "speech," and 语 *yǔ*, "language," all of which share the speech radical 讠 in their character composition, appear in vocabulary words for the first time. The speech radical is then introduced in Chapter 5 of *Fundamental Written Chinese*, together with all four characters that illustrate the speech radical's use. Because the speech radical has been systematically taught in Chapter 5, it is then possible in the remainder of *Fundamental Written Chinese* to introduce without need for further explanation another thirteen examples of speech radical characters as soon as each character first appears in a spoken word in the corresponding chapter of *Fundamental Spoken Chinese*.

Beyond our core assumptions, we wish to make two other points about Chinese characters. One is the importance of practicing them in linguistic context. The other involves our decision to include a limited number of extended character combinations in our supplementary reading exercises.

It is our firm belief that one should avoid writing Chinese characters over and over as isolated symbols. Rather, individual characters should always be treated as functioning as parts of larger words and phrases. Therefore, when practicing the character 汉, in addition to learning to write it as an isolated character, one should also practice writing it as a part of real words one can already say, such as 汉语, 汉字, and 汉人. And a word such as 汉字 or 汉语 can be further inserted into larger, already learned spoken phrases for further writing practice, regardless of whether or not every character in that known spoken phrase has already been learned. For example, one might write "*xiě* 汉字" (write Chinese characters) or "他 huì 说汉语。" (He is able to speak Chinese).

Finally, an individual Chinese character often exhibits a range of meanings that can vary from its core meaning, depending on the specific word in which the character is embedded. One such example is 商人, a new combination not included in the vocabulary list of either textbook but comprising two known characters with known meanings: 商, "commerce," and 人, "person." It doesn't take too much head scratching to realize that 商人 means "business person." In contrast, another example of a word composed of two characters is 书房 *shūfáng*, "study," which combines the character 书 *shū*, whose core meaning is "book," with the character 房 *fáng*, whose core meaning is "room/building." However, the meaning of 书房 *shūfáng* is not simply a room or building where books are placed (i.e., a library). Rather, it is primarily a room where people read and study. It is common in written Chinese for known characters to see their core meanings extended as they combine with other characters to form new words. A limited number of examples of such vocabulary extension are included in the supplementary readings in this text, although the main purpose of these readings is to reinforce previously taught vocabulary and grammar in natural written contexts.

## Chapter Format

The first three chapters of *Fundamental Written Chinese* are designed to educate users about the Chinese writing system, preparing them to embark upon their study of this aspect of the language starting in Chapter 4. At this point the student is well equipped with essential knowledge and understanding of the intrinsic nature of Chinese characters, what they are and what they are not, how they are constructed, and how native speakers and advanced non-native learners go about looking up written characters and words in a dictionary. As such, each of the first three chapters presents selected information about Chinese characters, including illustrative examples, which is then reinforced by hands-on exercises at the end of the chapter. It is not our expectation that users master all the skills and knowledge introduced in these first three chapters before they begin their actual study of Chinese characters in Chapter 4. Rather, we believe that the experience of going through the chapter exercises will help users to familiarize themselves with the general nature of the task that they are about to undertake, thus allowing them to be more knowledgeable and at ease with what lies ahead.

Starting with Chapter 4, then, every chapter of *Fundamental Written Chinese* is organized as follows:

1. a long written text
2. a list of vocabulary items being used for the first time in the textbook with
   romanized pronunciation
   English meaning
   part of speech label
3. exercises related to the reading passage
4. a chart introducing the chapter's independent characters (graphically minimal autonomous characters), including
   romanized pronunciation
   traditional form in parentheses[1]
   an asterisk when the character is not an independent word in modern Chinese[2]
   basic underlying meaning
   total number of strokes and stroke order
   classificatory radical
   the character's inventory of identifiable graphic components
   a box schema indicating character's proper balance and proportion
5. a chart introducing the chapter's new compound characters constructed using radicals that have already been taught, including
   romanized pronunciation
   an asterisk when the character is not an independent word in modern Chinese
   basic underlying meaning
   total number of strokes and stroke order
   classificatory radical
   a composite meaning clue (if present)
   all identifiable graphic components used to construct the character
   a box schema indicating the character's proper balance and proportion
   a composite phonetic clue (if present)

1. This information is provided for reference purposes only and only appears when the traditional and simplified forms of the character differ from one another.

2. According to John DeFrancis, ed., *ABC Chinese-English Comprehensive Dictionary* (Honolulu: University of Hawai'i Press, 2003).

6. the chapter's new radicals and example characters, presented in informational chart form
7. suggested mnemonics and other clues for remembering how certain characters are put together[3]
8. character exercises, vocabulary exercises, and structure exercises
9. one or two short supplementary texts[4]
10. eight empty squares next to each new character for writing practice[5]

## Distinctive Features

*Fundamental Written Chinese* has many of the same features as its companion volume *Fundamental Spoken Chinese*. It is designed not only to teach the content of each lesson, but also to inculcate habits that are essential for further learning in later years.[6]

1. **Systematic Introduction of Characters.** The emphasis on explaining characters explicitly in terms of radicals and phonetics is one such example. Every character is described in terms of regularities that will make it easier to remember and raise awareness of the organizational principles of the written lexicon as a whole. Emphasis is placed on proper stroke order. The importance of stroke order is demonstrated by teaching students to look up characters in the dictionary. Specific exercises are devised to be sure that the students are able, for example, to "write the fourth stroke of this character." Because many characters cannot stand alone as independent words in modern Chinese, those that cannot are marked as such with an asterisk when they are initially introduced.
2. **Pinyin-plus-Character Writing.** In order to adhere to our vision that written language is composed of words, not characters, and at the same time to carefully control the sequence and manner in which individual characters are introduced, it has been necessary to make limited use of a Pinyin-plus-character system of writing in the written texts in this volume. This hybrid method of representing written language is more prevalent in the earlier chapters of *Fundamental Written Chinese* than it is in the later chapters.
3. **Separate Dialogues.** A deliberate decision has been made that the dialogues in the two texts not be identical. Thus students must actually read and understand the dialogues and texts in *Fundamental Written Chinese* rather than refer to the Hanyu Pinyin in *Fundamental Spoken Chinese.*

---

3. These clues are not always historically or linguistically correct, but they offer a strategy that may be useful for remembering how the charcter in question is constructed.
4. The purpose of these supplementary texts is both to reinforce previously learned vocabulary, grammatical structures, and characters through additional readings as well as to provide opportunities for students to expand their knowledge of vocabulary through new combinations of known characters embedded in linguistictically natural sentences and longer passages. Some passages in the later chapters also give students brief introductions to aspects of Chinese culture.
5. Although we have noted above that writing practice should largely take the form of using characters in actual words and phrases, learning how to write a new character is a lot like learning how to play a musical instrument or mastering a new sport. All require considerable repetitive practice in order to develop the unconscious muscle memory necessary to perform required movements smoothly and effortlessly. For beginning students of Chinese, writing a new character just eight times will not provide the muscle memory necessary to produce it smoothly from memory. Therefore these eight squares are intended only as a starting point for writing practice.
6. Portions of this section are based heavily on written comments by an anonymous reviewer of the original manuscript proposal for this text.

4. **Meets the Needs of Heritage Learners.** *Fundamental Written Chinese* can be used independently of *Fundamental Spoken Chinese* by heritage learners and other semi-fluent speakers of Mandarin who do not require instruction in spoken skills but are in earnest need of support in acquiring a solid foundation in reading and writing.
5. **Flexible Coordination of the Two Textbooks.** There is a sizable controversy in Chinese-teaching circles about whether one should introduce characters from the beginning of study or wait until the spoken language has progressed to a certain level and then introduce them, following the pattern of literacy acquisition in children, who learn to speak before they learn to write. We have designed *Fundamental Written Chinese* in such a way that it can be used either way. Since the lessons in the two books are keyed to each other in terms of vocabulary and grammar, they can either be used simultaneously, or the written material can be introduced at a later time, depending on how much of a delay the user wishes to maintain. Regardless of which method of coordination one ultimately chooses to follow, however, it must be remembered that the first three chapters of *Fundamental Written Chinese* teach about the writing system and not how to write any of the specific vocabulary in Chapters 2 and 3 of *Fundamental Spoken Chinese*. By Chapter 4, however, it is possible to coordinate the introduction of oral skills in *Fundamental Spoken Chinese* and the introduction of related written content in the parallel chapter of *Fundamental Written Chinese*.

# 前 言

## 教学宗旨

《基石汉语读写》是《基石汉语口语》的姐妹教材。在编写这两部教材的过程中，我们有三点基本的构想。第一点，口语和书面语言所代表的是两种既不同但又相互关联的体系。它们各自的要点和特点都需分别教授，同时还要确保阅读和书写技巧的教授必须是建立在学生已掌握的口语词汇和语法基础上，这样才能取得最佳的教学效果。基于这一想法，词汇和语法集中在《基石汉语口语》中教授，而《基石汉语读写》则旨在培养学生去阅读和写作他们已经学会说的东西。第二点，我们认为汉字不应与词的概念混淆。因为现代汉语中有很多词都包含一个以上的音节，因而由两个或多个汉字构成，所以现代汉语中的不少汉字并不能作为独立的词来使用，而必须与其他汉字结合才具有完整语义。譬如，"汉"的含义是"中国；中国人"，但事实上，它并不能作为一个独立的词来单独使用，而必须与其它汉字连用才具有完整语义，例如："汉语"即"中文"，"汉字"即"中国文字"，"汉人"即"汉民族的人"。第三点，我们相信教会学生掌握读写体系的最佳方法是系统地讲解汉字构成规律，如偏旁部首、语音组件、共有字形、笔划顺序及汉字书写比例分配原则；并按结构的复杂程度由简单的独立结构汉字到复杂的复合结构汉字依次讲解。讲解时最好不要在一个章节中介绍太多不同的偏旁部首及结构上互不相连的汉字来分散学生的注意力，但是要注意给出足够的例子来强化学生对新学偏旁部首的记忆。从实际情况来说，要做到这一点，只有在学习《基石汉语口语》后积累了足够数量的口语词汇，并且构成这些词汇的汉字又恰巧包含至少一个所学偏旁部首时方能实现。不过，在没有学习足够数量的这类口语词汇之前，更恰当的做法是在《基石汉语读写》的课文中用汉语拼音而不是汉字形式代表音节。

例如，"shuō"（说）首先出现于《基石汉语口语》第4章，但在《基石汉语读写》第4章中它只是以汉语拼音形式出现。在《基石汉语口语》第5章中第一次出现三个不同的音节： cí（词）、huà（话）以及yǔ（语），它们的汉字字型结构中都有言字旁，因此《基石汉语读写》第5章用这四个字一起对言字旁的用法加以说明。因为第5章中已经系统讲解了言字旁的用法，所以在以后章节中出现的言字旁的字就无须另作解释了。

除了上述几点中心思想外，对于汉字学习还有两点需要补充。一是我们强调在自然语境中练习汉字的重要性；二是教材在补充阅读练习中加入了一定数量的有关汉字组合的延伸练习。

我们始终认为，进行书写练习时要尽量避免把汉字当作孤立的符号，而应如上文所说的，将一个个独立的汉字视为构成词语和短语的组件。因此，当练习写"汉"字时，除了把它当作一个孤立的字来书写外，学生更要把它作为已经会说的真正的词语来练习书写，如"汉语"、"汉字"或"汉人"。作为词语，我们又可以将其放入更多的已学过的短语中作进一步的读写练习– 无论该短语中的字是否都已学过，例如，"xiě汉字"（写汉字），"他huì说汉语"（他会说汉语），等等。

最后我们需要指出的是，同一个汉字根据语境的不同，常常会有一系列与其核心字义相似或不同的含义。例如，"商人"一词,由两个含义已知的汉字组成："商"即"商业"，"人"即"人们"，所以不太难猜测商人即"从事商业的人"。而"书房"一词，也由两个汉字组成："书"即"书本"，"房"即"房间"，然而"书房"并不是只放书的房间（图书馆），而是看书，学习的房间。这种已知汉字因与其它汉字结合而使含义延伸从而组成新词的现象在汉语书面语中非常普遍。在补充的阅读材料中出现了部分这样的延伸词汇，当然阅读的主要目的首先在于巩固以前学过的语法和词汇，并加强对它们在自然书面语境中使用情况的理解。

## 章节结构

《基石汉语读写》的前三章旨在培养学生对读写体系的初步认识，从而为第4章的学习做好准备，了解汉字的基础知识—什么是汉字以及什么不是汉字，汉字是如何构成的，如何使用字典等。因此，前三章中，各章首先列出精选的汉字知识，并用例子说明。每章最后都要求学生动手练习并加以巩固。我们并不期望学生从第4章，即真正着手学习汉字之前就能完全掌握前三章中介绍的知识和技能，而是希望学生把它们作为学习汉语读写的一个基础。

从第4章开始，各章的结构如下：

1. 课文
2. 课文中首次出现的词汇列表并配有：
   - ⋆用汉语拼音标注的发音
   - ⋆英语含义
   - ⋆词性标识
3. 与课文配套的理解练习
4. 介绍本章独立汉字的图表（汉字自动最小化处理），每个字包括：
   - ⋆用汉语拼音标注的发音
   - ⋆在括号中给出繁体字形式[1]
   - ⋆以星号表示该汉字在现代汉语中不能独立使用[2]
   - ⋆基本含义
   - ⋆总笔划数及笔划顺序
   - ⋆偏旁部首归类
   - ⋆所有可识别的汉字组字要件
   - ⋆用方框解构汉字书写的恰当比例

1. 繁体字形仅供参考，且仅在繁体和简体字形相异时给出繁体字形式。
2. 根据《ABC综合汉英字典》编写。

5. 图表列出本章由已学的偏旁部首组成的新的复合字，每个字包括：
   ★用汉语拼音标注的发音
   ★以星号表示该汉字在现代汉语中不能独立使用
   ★基本含义
   ★总笔划数和笔划顺序
   ★偏旁部首归类
   ★综合语意线索（若存在）
   ★所有可识别的汉字组字要件
   ★用方框解构汉字书写的恰当比例
   ★综合语音线索（若存在）
6. 以图表形式列出本章新的偏旁部首及汉字示范，形式同上。
7. 用顺口溜或其它线索帮助记忆汉字组成[3]
8. 汉字书写练习，词汇练习和结构练习
9. 一至两篇补充材料[4]
10. 每个汉字旁有八个空方框供书写练习[5]

## 特点[6]

1. 系统介绍汉字
   《基石汉语读写》与其姐妹篇《基石汉语口语》有很多相似的特点。该教材的编写不仅着眼于授课内容，更注重为学生今后的学习培养良好的习惯，教材在讲解汉字时对偏旁部首及语音的强调就是很好的例子。本教材对每个汉字的构成规律都加以解释使其便于记忆，引导学生关注汉语书面语汇的组织原则。同样的，本教材对于笔划顺序的强调也是出于上述目的，比如从最初就强调查字典对于学汉字的重要性。教材还设计了一些小测试来检测学生的学习情况，比如，让学生“写出该字的第四笔划”。另外，由于很多汉字在现代汉语中不能独立使用，教材对这一类字用星号加以标注。
2. 拼音加汉字的书写方式
   如我们所认为的，语言是由词语而不是由单个汉字组成，而且往往涵盖比单个句子更大的语言范畴，同时语言的使用又关联着每个汉字的使用顺序和方式。因此，课文中必须限制性地使用拼音加汉字的书写方式，用拼音来表达尚未学过的汉字。不过，这种混合的书写表达方式只在本教材的前几章中较为常见。

---

3. 从历史学和语言学角度来说这些线索并不总是正确，但却不失为有效记忆汉字结构的好方法。

4. 给出这些补充材料的目的一方面是通过额外阅读来巩固学生已学过的词汇，语法结构及汉字，同时让学生通过阅读活生生的语句及较长文章中出现的新的合成词来增加词汇知识。

5. 除上文所说汉字的书写练习应尽量放在词语和短语的背景下进行以外，学习者还应记住学写新汉字就像学习弹奏乐器或掌握新的体育项目一样，需用大量的重复练习来开发身体自主记忆能力，从而流畅、自然的完成各种指定动作。对于汉语初学者而言，把一个新汉字练习写八遍并不能实现身体自主记忆而流畅书写。因此留出的八个方框只是书写练习的开始而非终了。

6. 该部分很大程度上采纳了一位匿名校阅者对初稿的意见。

3. 独立的课文编写
   我们有意识地使两本教材中的课文，对话内容不尽相同。这样就需要学生切实读懂《基石汉语口语》中的对话和课文内容，而不是仅仅通过汉语拼音才能搞清对话含义。
4. 满足华裔学生的汉语学习需求
   《基石汉语读写》可以独立于《基石汉语口语》而单独使用，从而满足那些父辈为华人的学生或口语较流利而不需要过多关注口语能力的学生学习汉语的需求。
5. 两本教材的互动
   在汉语教学界，存在着一个颇有争议的课题，即究竟应该是从一开始就教授汉字读写，还是和母语儿童的正常学习顺序一样，在口语已经达到一定程度之后再教学汉字。我们在编写《基石汉语读写》时兼顾同时这两种意见—由于两本教材中的词汇和语法彼此对应，因此它们既可以同时使用，也可以先学口语稍后再学汉字读写，这取决于使用者想在这两者之间保持多大的学习间距。无论最终选择哪种教学方式，都要记住一点，即《基石汉语读写》的前三章讲授的是关于书写体系的知识，而不是真正教写《基石汉语口语》第2和第3章中出现的具体词汇。从第4章开始，口语和书写技能的教授则可齐头并进，一边教授《基石汉语口语》中的口语技能，一边教授《基石汉语读写》中对应章节的相关书写内容。

# Acknowledgments

A project of this size could never be sustained to fruition without the obliging assistance and altruistic support of an enormous number of people. Without their many contributions, none of this would have been possible.

Heartfelt thanks are particularly extended to Professor Timothy Wong of Arizona State University, with whom I shared conversations about issues in Chinese language teaching literally on a daily basis over the five years we worked together at the Ohio State University. The hope and enthusiasm generated by those conversations served as the impetus for *Fundamental Spoken Chinese* and *Fundamental Written Chinese.* Thanks must also be expressed to Arizona State University's College of Liberal Arts and Sciences and Center for Asian Studies for providing an apartment and office free of charge for the nine months I was there on sabbatical leave from the University of Auckland in 1998. Professor Wong's contributions at that time together with those of Emeritus Professor Gary Tipton, Eugenia Tu, and Patricia Pang led to the first of many generations of *Fundamental Spoken Chinese* vocabulary lists, dialogues, and exercises. Additionally, Professors Hu Wenze of the United States Naval Academy and Mark Hansell of Carleton College deserve special mention for their excellent suggestions for improving the factual content and presentation of some of the more problematic grammar notes. Also deserving of special acknowledgment is the strong moral and material support we received over the past seven years from colleagues within the University of Auckland School of Asian Studies, including three different heads of school and the many teachers and students who field-tested earlier drafts of both textbooks. A very sincere expression of gratitude goes out to Atsuko Tsukamoto not only for creating all of the line drawings used to illustrate the exercise and activity portions of each chapter of *Fundamental Spoken Chinese,* but also for the mammoth task of reformatting many of our very primitive attempts at page design in each textbook into something more visually acceptable. We also wish to thank Carrie Huang for her work in producing the well-developed illustrations that accompany the *Fundamental Spoken Chinese* dialogues and *Fundamental Written Chinese* passages as well as Mr. Chan Wan Yiu, whose calligraphy adorns the cover and title page of each textbook. Beyond this, we are especially thankful to our colleague Dr. Richard Phillips for volunteering to take on the Herculean task of reading through the near-final drafts of both *Fundamental Spoken Chinese* and *Fundamental Written Chinese* to ensure that each textbook could be purged of as many remaining content, coordination, stylistic, and typographical problems as possible. Finally, a special debt of gratitude is owed to Patricia Crosby of University of Hawai'i Press for her unflinching and upbeat support, even in the most difficult and challenging of times, and to the two anonymous reviewers of the draft manuscripts, whose thoughtful comments and suggestions have improved the quality of each book immeasurably. Of course, any and all remaining errors, of which there are certain to be many, are solely the fault of the authors.

Robert Sanders
February 2008

# CHAPTER ONE
# Demystifying Chinese Writing

Welcome to the exciting world of Chinese characters, where you have the chance to learn a system of writing with a history of over 3,500 years that today is used by hundreds of millions of people. For many people embarking upon the study of Chinese, however, this writing system represents an intimidating object of fear. While it is true that you will need to put in a significant amount of "blood, sweat, and tears" before you are able to read a Chinese newspaper or write a Chinese letter to a friend, nevertheless, many misconceptions and exaggerations about the writing system do exist, not only within the minds of the general public outside of China, but even within the minds of many native speakers. These misconceptions and exaggerations include

1. Chinese characters are mostly pictures and *ideographs* (pictures of abstract concepts).
2. Chinese characters do not indicate anything about their pronunciation.
3. There is no rhyme or reason as to how Chinese characters are constructed. Because of this they are extremely difficult to memorize.
4. One needs to memorize thousands upon thousands of Chinese characters in order to become literate.
5. If you are not extremely careful while writing down a particular character, you can easily and erroneously transform the intended character into a completely different one instead.
6. People on the Chinese mainland and in Taiwan use two completely different systems of writing. Knowing only one of these systems means that it is next to impossible to understand the other system.

Let us now examine each of these statements in more detail:

1. *Chinese characters are mostly pictures and ideographs.* In fact, *pictographs* (simplification of shapes of real objects) and ideographs comprise just 3 percent of all Chinese characters.

From a logical perspective alone, the statement makes little practical sense. While it is easy to draw a picture of a mountain or a horse or to project the concept of "top; upper" or "brightness" by means of a diagram, it becomes much more difficult to imagine how to do this for absolutely everything we would ever want to write down on paper. What unambiguous picture or diagram could easily be drawn to express "democracy," "ideal," or completed action? What about the differences among "ideal," "ideals," and "idealism"? How easy would it be to write a short paragraph like this one if we were limited only to using pictures and diagrams?

Thus it is not at all surprising that pictographs and ideographs are not the only types of Chinese characters in existence. Traditionally Chinese have recognized six kinds of characters according to their construction strategy: pictographs, simple *indicatives* (graphic expressions of concepts), compound indicatives, phonetic loans, semantic-phonetic compounds, and mutual explanatories, with indicatives corresponding to ideographs. In modern times, however, this system has been reanalyzed and reduced to a total of four: pictographics, which are simplified drawings of an object's shape, such as 月 (moon) or 日 (sun); simple indicatives, signs used to suggest a certain meaning, such as the simple characters 一 (one), 二 (two), and 三 (three); compound indicatives, formed by combining simple elements or characters to provide new meanings, such as 休 (to rest), showing a person (人) leaning against a tree (木), or 明 (bright), showing the combination of the sun and the moon ; and semantic-phonetic compounds, which are characters that consist of one component providing a pronunciation clue (called the *phonetic*) and another component providing a meaning clue, such as 妈 *mā* (mother), which is composed of the meaning meaning clue "female" (女) plus the pronunciation clue 马 *(mǎ)*. While pictographs and ideographs (i.e., indicatives) comprise three of the four categories, those three categories only account in total for 3 percent of all the characters found in a dictionary. In other words, 97 percent of all Chinese characters actually belong to the semantic-phonetic compound category, whose name indicates that sound plays a role in their construction. Semantic-phonetic compounds are discussed under point 2 below.

Why, then, have Chinese characters been almost universally categorized as pictures and ideographs, completely devoid of pronunciation information? This is a direct result of their history.

The earliest examples of Chinese writing known today were carved onto cattle bones and tortoise shells more than three thousand years ago. The purpose of these inscriptions was to record events, and a large percentage were concerned with the prophecies of fortune-tellers. Later, inscriptions of worship were found on ceremonial bronze vessels. Because of the content and limited nature of what was written there, a large proportion of those characters were indeed pictographs and ideographs. However, if writing is actually intended to record anything and everything one might say, then these pictures and ideographs are not sufficient to fully meet the needs of its users. This problem was overcome by ignoring the meaning of a picture altogether and focusing instead on its pronunciation.

Imagine a picture of an eye: . If we focus only on its meaning, then it can only be used to write the meaning "eye." However, if we focus instead on its pronunciation in English, then not only can it be used to represent the words "eye" and "I," but it can also be used to indicate the *ai* sound in "ideal," "island," "ivy," and so on. In this manner, the power of a picture to record spoken language is expanded hugely. What has just been illustrated is called the *rebus principle,* and it is a key operating principle in the construction of semantic-phonetic compounds in Chinese. This principle is not unique to the history of Chinese and in fact is observed in many other so-called pictographic orthographies, including Egyptian hieroglyphics and Mayan writing.

2. *Chinese characters do not indicate anything about their pronunciation.* Approximately 97 percent of all Chinese characters contain a sound clue, although these clues are rarely as predictive of pronunciation as an alphabetic spelling.

As its name implies, the idealized semantic-phonetic compound contains two pieces of information about itself: a meaning clue and a pronunciation clue. The meaning clue is called the *radical,* and the pronunciation clue is called the *phonetic.* As with all clues, some are clearer and more helpful than others. Let us look at a few commonly used radicals in Chinese:

王 jade　　女 female
石 stone　　木 tree
虫 insect　　口 mouth

Combining each of these radicals with the phonetic clue 马, which by itself is pronounced *mǎ* and means "horse," we end up with the following results:

| Radical | Phonetic | Semantic-Phonetic Compound |
|---|---|---|
| 王 'jade' | | 玛 *mǎ* 'agate' |
| 石 'stone' | | 码 *mǎ* 'weights' |
| 虫 'insect' | | 蚂 *mǎ* 'ant' |
| 女 'female' | (马 *mǎ* 'horse') | 妈 *mā* 'mother' |
| 木 'tree' | | 杩 *mà* 'clamp' |
| 口 'mouth' | | 骂 *mà* 'scold' |
| 口 'mouth' | | 吗 *ma* 'question particle' |

Though it does not always indicate the correct tone, the phonetic clue in the above set is nevertheless highly predictive of the overall correct pronunciation for each of the compound characters in which it is used. Many similar phonetics exist in Chinese, though a fairer example of the degree of reliability of a sound clue in Chinese might be something like

| Radical | Phonetic | Semantic-Phonetic Compound |
|---|---|---|
| 亻 'person' | | 侥 *jiǎo* 'lucky' |
| 氵 'water' | | 浇 *jiāo* 'sprinkle' |
| 日 'sun' | | 晓 *xiǎo* 'dawn' |
| 马 'horse' | | 骁 *xiāo* 'fine horse' |
| 扌 'hand' | 尧 (*yáo* 'legendary emperor') | 挠 *nǎo* 'scratch' |
| 女 'female' | | 娆 *ráo* 'graceful' |
| 纟 'silk' | | 绕 *rào* 'wind around' |
| 艹 'grass' | | 荛 *ráo* 'rushes' |
| 饣 'food' | | 饶 *ráo* 'abundant' |
| 火 'fire' | | 烧 *shāo* 'burn' |

And there are many sound clues that are even less helpful than what we see illustrated above. Sound clues in Chinese characters are usually less helpful than an alphabetic spelling for three important reasons. First, most of these characters were put together well over two thousand years ago. Language, including pronunciation, changes radically over that amount of time, so it is understandable that irregularities will arise as a result. Second, pronunciation varies over time and space, and not all characters were created at one time or in one place. Third, we cannot say for sure how meticulous the creators of a particular semantic-phonetic compound were in choosing a phonetic clue that would exactly match the intended pronunciation of the new character.

3. *There is no rhyme or reason as to how Chinese characters are constructed. Because of this they are extremely difficult to memorize.* Writing by itself is not an independent language. Rather, it is based heavily on speech and in fact cannot exist without it. Therefore, a Chinese character, especially a semantic-phonetic compound, is much easier to memorize if you already know its meaning and pronunciation in spoken language. For that reason, for a longer while than you may care to contemplate, it will probably not be very easy for you to memorize new characters quickly. However, you will eventually reach a point when your spoken vocabulary is great enough and your familiarity with a range of radicals, phonetics, and repeating combinations of individual character strokes (see Chapter 2) is also great enough to allow you to see a new character and immediately be able to identify its sound, meaning, and structural properties in your mind and lodge that information away for later use. Once you reach that stage, new characters will not usually present themselves as a particularly formidable challenge. In the meantime, this textbook introduces the structure, meaning, and pronunciation of each character in a systematic, coherent fashion that will assist you in gaining an overall sense of the writing system as smoothly as possible.

4. *One needs to memorize thousands upon thousands of Chinese characters in order to become literate.* Although authoritative Chinese dictionaries can list up to more than 48,000 different characters, achieving basic, native literacy in Chinese "only" requires a knowledge of approximately 3,000 characters. Even a well-educated native speaker only has a working knowledge of between 4,000 and 5,000 characters. As you will discover, however, many words in Chinese are made up of two characters and not just one, and it is common in Chinese to take one character from one word and join it to a single character from a second word in order to form yet a third word. For example, the 中 *Zhōng* of *Zhōng.guó,* "China," and the 美 *Měi* of *Měi.guó,* "America," are used to form 中美 *Zhōng-Měi,* "Sino-American." Note as well that the basic meaning of 中 is "middle," while the basic meaning of 美 is "beautiful." For these reasons, although basic literacy "only" requires a knowledge of 3,000 *characters,* it actually requires command of a much larger quantity of vocabulary items.

5. *If you are not extremely careful while writing down a particular character, you can easily and erroneously transform the intended character into a completely different one instead.* Very few Chinese characters differ from one another by just the variation of a single stroke. Failure to write your strokes in the proper way is largely a sign of sloppy penmanship. Many native speakers consider penmanship to be a window into the personality, level of education, and makeup of the writer. Also, a lack of certainty about the proper formation of strokes and the correct sequencing of these strokes in the formation of individual characters will disadvantage you later on when you encounter and try to decode the mature handwriting of native speakers.

There do exist several examples in which the graphic difference between one character and another can be boiled down to just a slight variation in one stroke. However, this is very rare. In fact, when we examine the classic set of characters to illustrate this supposedly dangerous situation, we can see just how limited the danger really is:

田 cultivated field　　甲 first of the ten Heavenly Stems
由 from　　申 ninth of the twelve Earthly Branches

Some will point out that whether the central vertical stroke (line) stays completely within the borders of the box, extends upward above the box, extends downward below the box, or extends both upward above the box *and* downward below the box determines what the final written result will mean. But keep in mind that this only relates to one particular stroke in one particular set of characters. Should any one of the other strokes in any one of the four characters vary in any way, for example, if the box shape of the third or fourth character was as square as the box shape in characters one and two, then the end result would merely be a somewhat odd-looking character whose intended meaning would still be understood. Rather than appearing as the wrong character, the variation in a single stroke or two is much more likely to broadcast the message that you do not know or are not careful about the proper way to write the strokes.

Although bad penmanship will not likely cause confusion to others, there are two compelling reasons for why the proper way to write each stroke and why you should know the proper sequencing of those strokes ("stroke order") to form each character are important. First, for many Chinese, the visual qualities of your written characters say a lot about the quality of your personal character. The positive reaction that can be generated by good penmanship can never be underestimated. Second, in the real world most native speakers don't actually take the time to write out every stroke in painstaking detail once they have become adept at the basics of writing. Instead, they speed through the process following customary shortcuts based on conventions established over the centuries (much as many native English speakers rarely print out their words but write them in script instead). These conventions call for a fixed sequence of movements of the pen in a fixed pattern that can be traced from start to finish *only* if you (as the writer or as the reader) are well-grounded in both the basic stroke directions and the particular stroke order of each character involved. Some examples of "print forms" (the way characters are first learned by native-speaking children and the way they are taught in this book) and their script alternatives (the way they are often written by mature native writers) are shown below:

| English | Romanization | Print Form | Script Form |
|---|---|---|---|
| Beer | *píjiŭ* | 啤酒 | 啤酒 |
| Bustling | *rènào* | 热闹 | 热闹 |
| Car | *qìchē* | 汽车 | 汽车 |
| Chinese language | *Hànyŭ* | 汉语 | 汉语 |
| Pencil | *qiānbĭ* | 铅笔 | 铅笔 |
| Trousers | *kùzi* | 裤子 | 裤子 |

6. *People on the Chinese mainland and in Taiwan use two completely different systems of writing. Knowing only one of these systems means that it is next to impossible to understand the other system.* The problems involved in being able to read both simplified and traditional characters are not insurmountable. First, a large number of characters are written exactly the same way in both systems. Second, there are many regularized differences between the two systems that, once learned, allow the user of one system mechanically to convert a character into the form used in the other system. This being the case, it is still true that it requires less effort for those who only know traditional forms to be able to recognize simplified forms than it is for those who have learned only simplified forms to be able to recognize traditional forms.

As explained earlier, a gap has existed for centuries between the meticulous appearance of the official printed forms of Chinese characters and the unofficial, flowing script employed by many Chinese on an everyday basis. These script forms have always embodied conventions for systematically simplifying graphic complexity, thus saving time. What happened on the Chinese mainland in 1956 was that a government introduced new official versions of the characters that, with some glaring exceptions, better matched everyday writing habits followed for centuries in China and still employed unofficially in Taiwan today. This can be illustrated below:

| English | Romanization | Traditional Print Form* | Traditional Script Form | "Simplified" Print Form |
|---|---|---|---|---|
| Beer | *píjiŭ* | 啤酒 | 啤酒 | 啤酒 |
| Bustling | *rènào* | 熱鬧 | 热闹 | 热闹 |
| Car | *qìchē* | 汽車 | 汽车 | 汽车 |
| Chinese language | *Hànyŭ* | 漢語 | 汉语 | 汉语 |
| Pencil | *qiānbĭ* | 鉛筆 | 铅笔 | 铅笔 |
| Trousers | *kùzi* | 褲子 | 裤子 | 裤子 |

*and still officially recognized in Taiwan

For these reasons most people in Taiwan do have the ability to read simplified characters without too much prior training, and claims to the contrary likely have more to do with subjective factors than with objective ones. As for language students who only know traditional print forms but not the unofficial script ones, their ability to recognize simplified characters is dependent on the same sort of training (only in the opposite direction) required of simplified character users and discussed immediately below.

People on the Chinese mainland who may never have been formally taught the traditional forms of characters at school might seem to require considerable training to learn to read these older forms. However, many characters only differ from one another in terms of the way a radical or phonetic (both discussed in point 2 above) is written, with the remaining part of the character beyond the radical written exactly the same way in both systems. By learning the correspondences between the simplified and traditional forms of a relatively small number of radicals together with some other mechanical correspondences involving other graphic elements in the character, it is possible to account for a relatively high percentage of the characters that are written differently in each system. Examples of a few common radical correspondences are shown below:

| Traditional Radical | Simplified Radical | Examples | |
|---|---|---|---|
| | | Traditional | Simplified |
| 金 | 钅 | 銀<br>鏡<br>鉛<br>釘 | 银<br>镜<br>铅<br>钉 |
| 門 | 门 | 問<br>聞<br>間<br>闊 | 问<br>闻<br>间<br>阔 |
| 食 | 饣 | 飯<br>餃<br>館<br>餓 | 饭<br>饺<br>馆<br>饿 |
| 言 | 讠 | 話<br>語<br>課<br>謝 | 话<br>语<br>课<br>谢 |
| 車 | 车 | 軋<br>較<br>輩<br>轍 | 轧<br>较<br>辈<br>辙 |
| 鳥 | 鸟 | 島<br>鴨<br>鶩<br>鵲 | 岛<br>鸭<br>骛<br>鹊 |

To be fair, it should be noted that many more character pairs differ from one another not only in the respective ways their shared radical is written, but also in terms of the phonetic element each character uses or other systematic graphic differences between the two characters. And occasionally the simplified system uses just one graphic element to take the place of more than one graphic element in the traditional system. This can be illustrated by what is unquestionably the single most extreme example of collapsing multiple traditional graphic elements into a single simplified element:

| Traditional Element | Traditional Character | Simplified Element | Simplified Character |
|---|---|---|---|
| 又 | 反, 友, 取, 受 | | 反, 友, 取, 受 |
| 𦰩 | 漢, 艱, 灘 | | 汉, 艰, 滩 |
| 雚 | 歡, 觀 | 又 | 欢, 观 |
| 丵 | 對 | | 对 |
| 奚 | 鷄 | | 鸡 |
| | 聖 | | 圣 |
| | 雙 | | 双 |
| | 發 | | 发 |

Largely because of examples like this, it requires more training for someone who only knows the simplified system to be able to recognize characters in the the traditional system than it does for someone who only knows the traditional system to be able to recognize simplified characters. Nevertheless, even for those who are learning to recognize traditional characters from the perspective of the simplified system, enough similarities and systematic correspondences exist that the process of learning how to recognize the other system is not as difficult as is often claimed.

## EXERCISES

**1. Try to match each pictograph or ideograph in column A with an English meaning in column B:**

| A | B |
|---|---|
| 二 | mountain |
| 上 | sun |
| 月 | one |
| 雨 | top |
| 三 | sheep |
| 下 | rain |
| 日 | three |
| 一 | moon |
| 羊 | two |
| 山 | bottom |

2. Given the meanings of each of the following nine radicals and the pronunciation of each of the following two sound clues

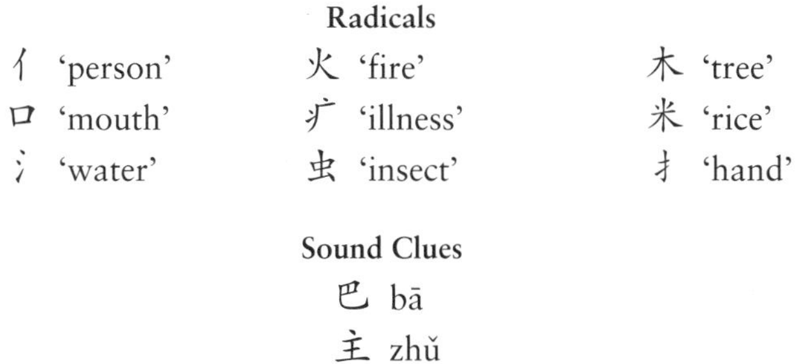

Radicals

亻 'person' 火 'fire' 木 'tree'
口 'mouth' 疒 'illness' 米 'rice'
氵 'water' 虫 'insect' 扌 'hand'

Sound Clues

巴 bā
主 zhǔ

match the character in column A with the Chinese pronunciation and English meaning in column B.

| A | B |
|---|---|
| 注 | *zhù* 'reside' |
| 粑 | *bǎ* 'grasp' |
| 炷 | *zhù* 'moth' |
| 住 | *bā* 'scar' |
| 疤 | *ba* 'interjection particle' |
| 吧 | *zhù* 'pour' |
| 柱 | *zhù* 'burn' |
| 疰 | *bā* 'cake' |
| 把 | *zhù* 'post; pillar' |
| 蛀 | *zhù* 'a type of summer disease' |

3. Using the information in the table on page 8, try to match the character in column A with the character in column B.

| A | B |
|---|---|
| 鴉 | 输 |
| 餞 | 辆 |
| 飾 | 钓 |
| 釣 | 钱 |
| 閣 | 饯 |
| 鵑 | 鸦 |
| 輸 | 饰 |
| 錢 | 鹃 |
| 悶 | 阁 |
| 輛 | 闷 |

# CHAPTER TWO
# The Design and Construction of Chinese Characters

## 1. Background

Architecture and the process of erecting buildings are two useful metaphors for understanding how Chinese characters are put together. They explain much about the process by which one starts with a handful of basic building materials that are then assembled to form larger structural units. Then, depending on the particular design pattern shown on the blueprint, some of those larger units are given additional customized add-on pieces, until the building itself is finally completed. At the same time, as these structures are being assembled, one must continually pay attention to questions of structural integrity, design aesthetics, and fitting in with the immediately surrounding environment. All but the aesthetic points will be touched on in this chapter.

## 2. Basic Strokes

All Chinese characters, regardless of how complex they are, share a common process of formation. This process begins with a closed set of eleven basic strokes that combine together to form increasingly larger and larger clusters. The direction of movement of each stroke and the type of ending it should take are crucial and will be discussed in slightly more detail later in this chapter.

| Stroke | Direction | Name | Example |
|---|---|---|---|
| ㇔ | ↘ | diǎn 点 | 小 家 觉 |
| 一 | → | héng 横 | 木 兰 同 |

| | | | |
|---|---|---|---|
| ㇑ | | shù 竖 | 半 下 做 |
| ㇒ | | piě 撇 | 公 话 具 |
| ㇏ | | nà 捺 | 八 全 两 |
| ㇀ | | tí 提 | 冰 打 我 |
| ㇖ | | hénggōu 横钩 | 写 学 安 |
| ㇚ | | shùgōu 竖钩 | 水 拉 事 |
| ㇂ | | xiégōu 斜钩 | 找 成 试 |
| ㇕ | | héngzhé 横折 | 因 星 漂 |
| ㇗ | | shùzhé 竖折 | 东 他 每 |

At each step along the way, a certain unit or combination of units may be able to stand alone as an *independent character.* An independent character possesses both a known meaning and a known pronunciation, and it cannot be further subdivided into smaller units capable of standing alone in a written text. Of the basic eleven strokes shown above, only one of them, 一, referred to as *héng* when it functions as a stroke, can function as an independent character. As an independent character it has the meaning of "one" and is pronounced *yī.*

## 3. The Construction Process

It doesn't take much effort, however, to combine two or more of these basic strokes to form other full-fledged characters. For example, we can combine two *héng* strokes to form 二 *èr,* "two." We can also combine a *piě* stroke, ㇒, and a *nà* stroke, ㇏, to form 人 *rén,* "person." Or, we can combine a *héng* stroke, 一, a *piě* stroke, ㇒, and a *nà* stroke, ㇏, to form 大 *dà,* "big."

Most full-fledged characters, however, are not composed of just two or three basic strokes in total, but are rather the end product of the joining together of two or more graphically complex subparts. For example, the character 到 *dào,* meaning "to arrive," can be broken down into the two different subparts 至 and 刂, as illustrated in the following schema: 至 | 刂.

Here is how this plays out: one starts with one piece or sector of the full character, in this case 至, assembling that piece stroke by stroke until it is finished before moving on to the next piece, in this case 刂, and if necessary the next piece (not applicable for 到), until the final mosaic, in this case 到, is complete.

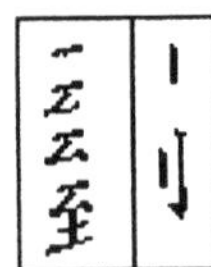

Which piece of a character one should start with, which piece one should move on to next, and the stroke order one should follow when constructing each piece are all subject to strict rules that will be discussed later in this chapter.

As your experience reading and writing Chinese increases, you will begin to recognize more and more familiar subcharacter building blocks shared across characters. Some common examples will possess little significance beyond their visual similarity. However, other common clusters of strokes will have great relevance, owing to centuries-old conventions used to arrange characters in Chinese dictionaries based on a list of over 180 (214 in the case of traditional characters) different key graphic elements that constitute only one part of a particular character in which it is embedded. That is, each entry in a Chinese dictionary is arranged either in the index or in the body of the text according to which particular key graphic cluster from that list of 180-plus items happens to be embedded in it. These 180-plus graphic classifying labels are called *radicals*. In terms of the semantic-phonetic compounds discussed in the Chapter 1, what we have called "meaning clues" generally correspond to radicals. Not every radical is a meaning clue, and not every meaning clue is in fact useful in revealing the meaning of the character in which it is contained. Nevertheless, for dictionary bookkeeping purposes, every character does have a radical.

Radicals fall into two major types—those that are able to stand alone as full-fledged characters and those that cannot. Of those radicals that are unable to stand alone as characters, most have meaning but lack a pronunciation. Some are graphic abbreviations of full-fledged characters and continue to convey the same meaning contained in their original, fuller forms. Common examples include

| Radical Form | Character Form | Meaning | Examples |
|---|---|---|---|
| 讠 | 言 | 'language' | 话 'words', 说 'say', 语 'language', 谚 'proverb' |
| 氵 | 水 | 'water' | 汗 'sweat', 江 'river', 沙 'sand', 泳 'swim' |
| 扌 | 手 | 'hand' | 打 'hit', 扔 'throw', 扯 'pull', 摸 'stroke' |
| 钅 | 金 | 'metal' | 钉 'nail', 铅 'lead (Pb)', 铜 'copper', 锁 'lock' |

Other meaning-containing radicals cannot stand alone as full-fledged characters and are not themselves derived from full-fledged characters. Some common examples of these include

| | Meaning | Examples |
|---|---|---|
| 宀 | 'roof' | 安 'peace', 室 'room', 家 'family', 宿 'lodge for the night' |
| 辶 | 'road; walking' | 达 'arrive', 过 'pass over', 返 'return', 退 'retreat' |
| 艹 | 'grass; plant' | 花 'flower', 芽 'bud; sprout', 菜 'vegetable', 茶 'tea' |
| 疒 | 'illness, disease' | 疼 'ache', 病 'illness', 痴 'idiotic', 癌 'cancer' |

Common examples of the radicals that can also stand alone as full-fledged characters without any change to their appearance include

| Radical | Meaning | Example |
|---|---|---|
| 女 | 'female' | 妈 'mother', 妹 'younger sister', 姑 'father's sister', 妻 'wife' |
| 马 | 'horse' | 驴 'donkey', 驾 'harness', 骑 'ride', 骠 'fast (of horses)' |
| 木 | 'tree' | 杖 'cane; stick', 杏 'apricot', 板 'board', 松 'pine tree' |
| 石 | 'stone' | 岩 'cliff', 矿 'ore', 砚 'inkstone', 碗 'bowl' |

## 4. Construction Principles

The assembling of a Chinese character is not a random or arbitrary process but is subject to very strict rules. The type of rule you should be most concerned about is proper stroke order, because one must possess command of the specific stroke order for a large number of individual characters before being able to read the everyday handwriting of most native speakers or to look up a character in a dictionary. In this regard, there is a widely quoted pair of principles that account for the proper stroke order of most characters in a simple way: top-to-bottom and left-to-right. That is, when writing a character, you should start from the top and work your way down, step by step. And likewise, you should take care of the left part before the right part.

However, the situation is not quite so simple. Besides the potential for contradiction between these two principles, another problem with the simple way that these two ideas are ordinarily conveyed is that "top-to-bottom" and "left-to-right" do not usually apply to the character as an integral whole (unless that character is an independent character), but rather to its subcomponents. That is, because most Chinese characters are *compound characters,* that is, characters that are made up of an independent character plus at least one extra stroke, and not independent characters, "top-to-bottom" and "left-to-right" work first to prioritize the sequence in which each individual building block within the character undergoes construction and then determine the order in which each of the strokes is written within each of the individual building blocks.

Let us examine a few representative examples to see how this plays out in practice:

| Type | Block Sequencing | Example | Stroke Cluster Distribution | Block-Internal Stroke Order |
|---|---|---|---|---|
| | 1<br>2 | 怎 | 乍<br>心 | 丿 𠂉 午 乍 乍<br>丶 心 心 心 |
| | | 条 | 夂<br>朩 | 丿 ク 夂<br>一 十 才 木 |
| | 1 2 | 到 | 至 刂 | 一 云 云 至 \| 丨 刂 |
| | | 休 | 亻 木 | 丿 亻 \| 一 十 才 木 |
| | 1<br>2<br>3 | 常 | 𫩏<br>口<br>巾 | 丨 ⺌ 𫩏<br>口<br>丨 冂 巾 |
| | | 桌 | ⺊<br>曰<br>木 | 丨 ⺊<br>丨 冂 日 日<br>一 十 才 木 |

| | | | | |
|---|---|---|---|---|
| 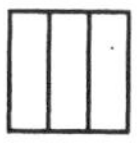 | 1 2 3 | 搬 | 扌 舟 殳 | 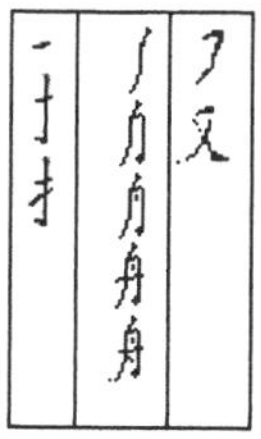 |
| | | 谢 | 讠 身 寸 | 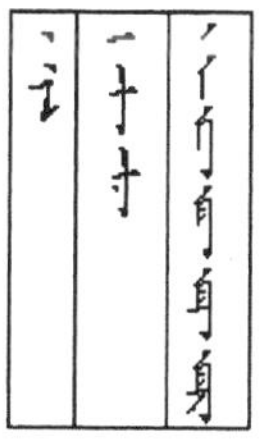 |
| 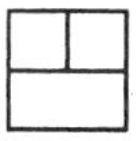 | 1 2<br>3 | 坐 | 人 人<br>土 | 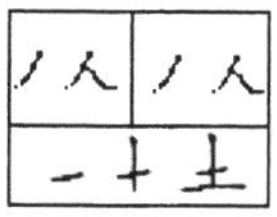 |
| | | 然 | 夕 犬<br>灬 | 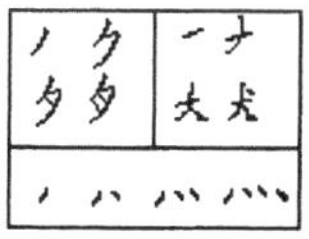 |
| 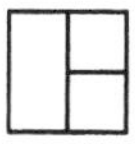 | 1 2<br>3 | 骑 | 马 大<br>可 | 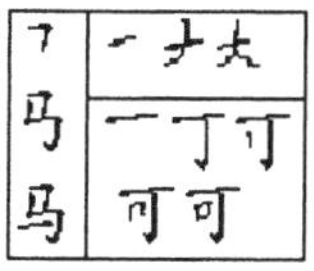 |
| | | 楼 | 木 米<br>女 | 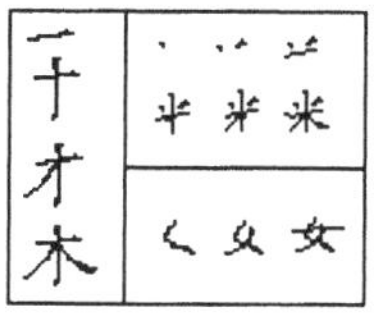 |
| 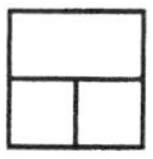 | 1<br>2 3 | 前 | 䒑<br>月 刂 | 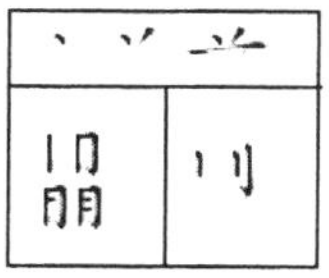 |
| | | 最 | 曰<br>耳 又 | 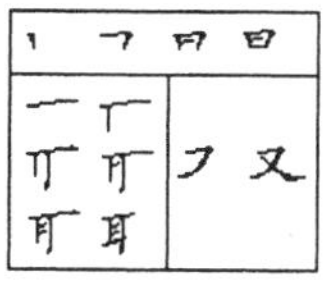 |

| | | | | |
|---|---|---|---|---|
| 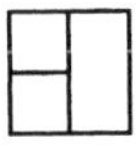 | 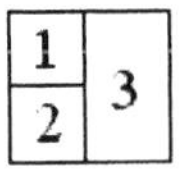 | 数 | 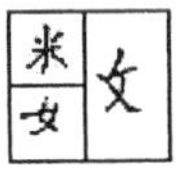 | 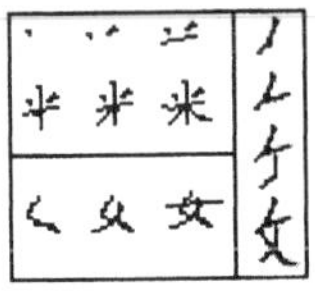 |
| | | 影 | 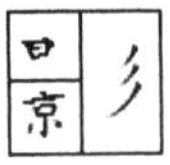 | 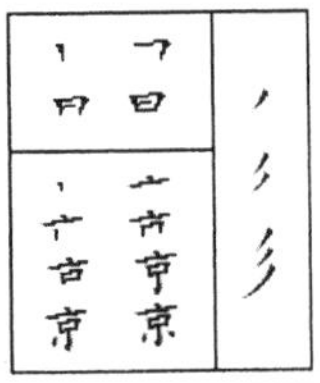 |
| 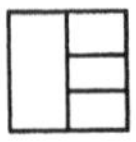 | 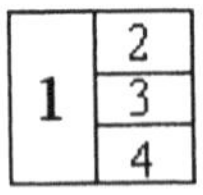 | 慢 | 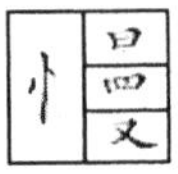 | 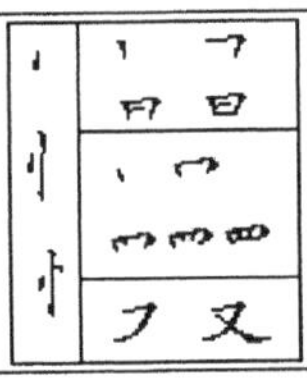 |
| | | 镜 | 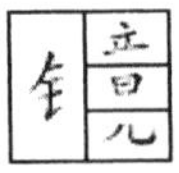 | 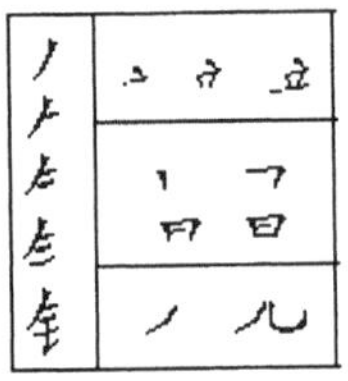 |
| 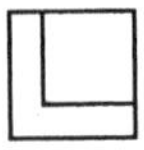 | 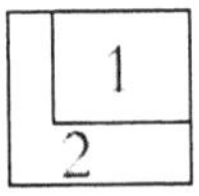 | 还 | 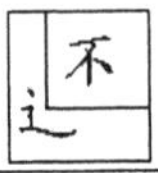 | 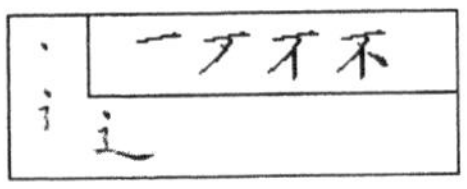 |
| | | 建 | 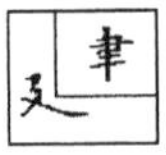 | 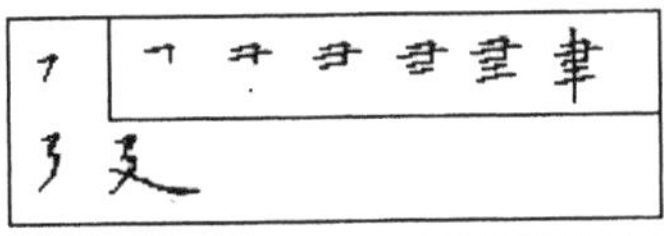 |
| 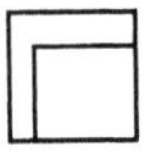 | 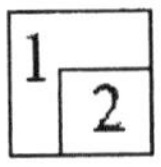 | 有 | 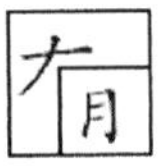 | 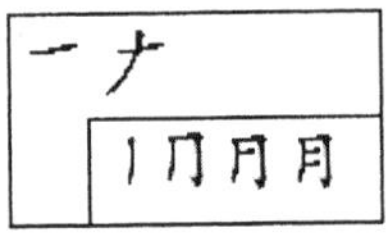 |
| | | 病 | 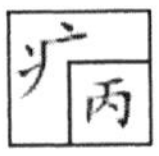 | 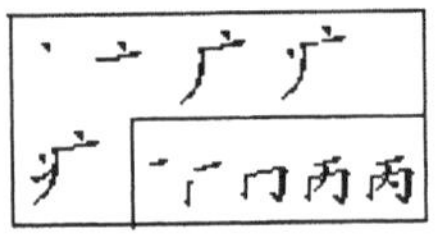 |

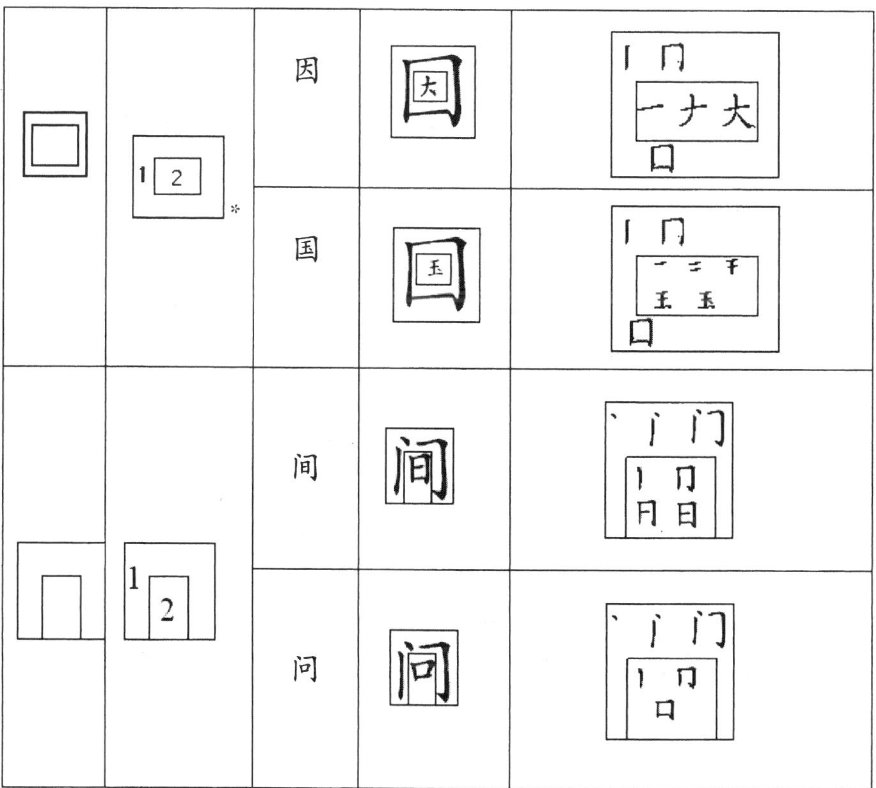


*Please note that for characters that include graphic material inside a box, only after everything inside the box is first inserted within its three borders is the bottom of the box finally sealed.

As one can see, the ordering of the subcomponents is determined by the internal structure of the character. As a rule, one usually starts with the component that occupies the upper-left corner, though there are exceptions to this (see the "walking person last" and "X" principles below for two such counterexamples). Generally speaking, there is a tendency to take care of every component on the left of the character before proceeding to the component(s) on the right. The only exception to this tendency involves cases where the very bottom component of a character serves as its base or foundation and extends fully across from the bottom left to the bottom right: 1 2 3 and 1 2 .

Beyond the general top-to-bottom and left-to-right principles illustrated above, there exist other stroke order principles specific to particular stroke order clusters.

## The Kebab Principle (Open at Bottom)

When skewering one or more horizontal strokes with a single vertical stroke that protrudes through the bottommost horizontal stroke, first write every horizontal stroke *including* the very bottom one 三, then finish with the vertical stroke 丰 , as in 十, 用, 丰, 干.

## The Kebab Principle (Closed at Bottom)

When skewering two or more horizontal strokes with a single vertical stroke that finishes immediately upon reaching the bottommost horizontal stroke, first write every horizontal stroke *except* the very bottom one 二 , followed by the vertical stroke that temporarily protrudes at the bottom 干 , and then finish up with the bottommost horizontal stroke that seals the skewer 王 , as in 土, 王, 难, 住.

### The Box Principle

When forming a box that contains additional strokes inside of it, first write the left side of the box 丨 , followed by a single stroke that takes care of both the top and the right sides 冂 , then insert inside the box all of the contents that are fully contained within it 因 , and finally seal the box at the bottom 因, as in 国, 因, 田.

### The X Principle

When forming an X-like shape using two diagonal strokes, first write the stroke that starts toward the upper right and finishes around the lower left before writing the stroke that starts toward the upper left corner and finishes around the lower right, as in 义, 更, 人.

### The Walking-Person-Last Principle

Any time that the radical 辶 is used, it should be written last 文 , 这 , as in 边, 这, 道.

Look again at the eleven basic strokes:

| Stroke | Direction | Name | Example |
|---|---|---|---|
| ㇔ | ↘ | diǎn | 小 家 觉 |
| ㇐ | → | héng | 木 兰 同 |
| ㇑ | ↓ | shù | 半 下 做 |
| ㇓ | ↙ | piě | 公 话 具 |
| ㇏ | ↘ | nà | 八 全 两 |
| ㇀ | ↗ | tí | 冰 打 我 |
| ㇖ | → ↙ | hénggōu | 写 学 安 |
| ㇚ | ↓ ↖ | shùgōu | 水 拉 事 |
| ㇂ | ↘ ↑ | xiégōu | 找 成 试 |
| ㇕ | → ↓ | héngzhé | 因 星 漂 |
| ㇗ | ↓ → | shùzhé | 东 他 每 |

You will need to master these eleven strokes in order to write characters correctly, decode the mature handwriting of native speakers, and be able to look up characters in a Chinese dictionary. In order to master each stroke, you will need to pay special attention to several features:

1. In which direction does the stroke flow—horizontally, vertically, or diagonally?
2. Is the movement to the left or to the right?
3. Does it move up or down?
4. Is the stroke a straight line, or is there some degree of curve?
5. Is there a single direction to the stroke, or is there an abrupt change of direction?
6. Does the stroke end without ceremony, or does it end with a hook?

Paying attention to each of these questions will help you to master the eleven basic strokes as quickly as possible. Then you will want to put everything together in as aesthetically appealing a manner as possible.

## 5. Aesthetics: Coherence and Balance

It is not enough simply to know how to write each individual stroke separately. Ultimately one must know how to assemble these many individual strokes into a single, holistic, and well-proportioned structure. The frame of reference for what is meant by "well-proportioned" is a square box, usually imaginary but often, especially at the beginning stages of learning how to write properly, laid out boldly on paper.

Generally speaking, a character, especially one with many strokes, should spread out equally in all directions within that real or imaginary square and should not look as if it has been squashed, squeezed, pinched, or tilted. Nor should it look too top-heavy or as if half of the character dwarfs the other half. Let us examine some examples of common beginning student problems.

| **Problem** | **Ill-Proportioned Example** | **Well-Proportioned Example** |
|---|---|---|
| Top-heavy | 黑 | 黑 |
| Tilted | 多 | 多 |
| Squashed | 街 | 街 |
| Squeezed | 学 | 学 |

| Problem | Ill-Proportioned Example | Well-Proportioned Example |
|---|---|---|
| Pulled Apart | 彳 亍 | 行 |
| Deflated-Inflated | 走戉 | 越 |
| Inflated-Deflated | 京尤 | 就 |

Let us now convert each of the poorly proportioned forms shown above into its corresponding well-proportioned form.

Key:

| | |
|---|---|
| → | move in this direction |
| ↔ | reduce in size |
| \| \| | involving portion of character on this side of the square within these lines |

| Problem | Ill-Proportioned Example | Well-Proportioned Example |
|---|---|---|
| Top-heavy | 黑 | 黑 |
| Tilted | 夕夕 | 多 |
| Squashed | 街 | 街 |

| Squeezed | 学 | 学 |
|---|---|---|
| Pulled Apart | 行 | 行 |
| Deflated-Inflated | 越 | 越 |
| Inflated-Deflated | 就 | 就 |

EXERCISES

1. Indicate the direction of each of the following strokes in grey using a line with an arrow at the end:

大 汉 形 语

解 书 升 里

口 家 笔 空

2. For each character below, identify as many different stroke types as you can that have been used to make the character:

a. 休 b. 小 c. 我 d. 她 e. 把 f. 买

**3. Write the number of the character in the column on the right next to its corresponding structural box:**

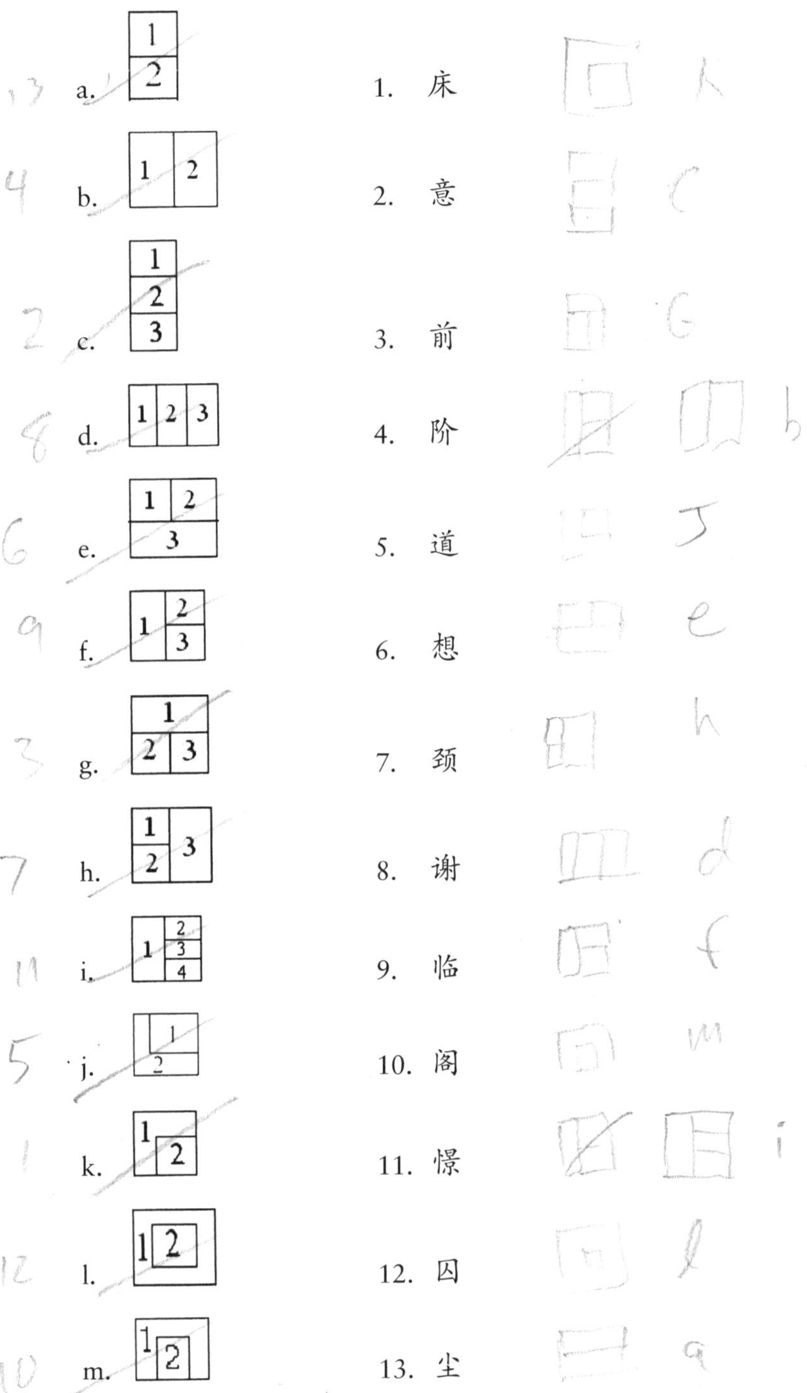

4. **Draw a suitable box for each of the following characters.**

**Example:** 好 ⿰

| | | | |
|---|---|---|---|
| a. 楼 | b. 新 | c. 热 | d. 最 |
| e. 茶 | f. 边 | g. 右 | h. 做 |
| i. 因 | j. 人 | k. 闸 | l. 晚 |

# CHAPTER THREE
# How to Use Reference Books

## 1. Toward Independence

To become a proficient reader and writer of Chinese requires a considerable investment of time and effort, most of which must take place outside of the classroom on your own time. To set the foundation for your own effort, you will need to know how to make full use of the content of the chapters that follow this one. And once you have acquired a sufficient quantity of written characters and words to embark upon new texts with less-controlled content, you will also need to know how to look up unknown characters, words, and phrases in a dictionary.

## 2. Looking Up an Unknown Character in a Dictionary

What happens when someone encounters an unknown character and wants to look it up in a dictionary? Where does one begin? The knowledge of radicals, stroke shapes, and fundamental stroke order principles is important here. You first identify the character's radical and then count the total number of *remaining* strokes beyond—that is, not including—that radical. With that information you are in a position to locate that character in a dictionary. Once you have done this, you will be able to learn its pronunciation and meaning if you are looking it up in a *zìdiǎn* (character dictionary). If you are looking it up in a *cídiǎn* (word dictionary), its pronunciation, meaning, and the meaning of compounds in which it serves as the first character. Let us demonstrate this using the following examples: 他, 做, 话, 说, 国, 图. To be able to look each of these characters up in a dictionary, one should follow the following steps:

1. Identify the character's radical.
2. Count the number of strokes within that radical.
3. Locate the radical within the dictionary's radical index and use that index to identify the page number on which all characters of that shared radical are listed.
4. Count the number of remaining strokes in the character outside of the radical.
5. Go to the correct radical page number and then locate the desired character under its radical header according to the number of its remaining strokes.
6. Go to the character's indicated page number to learn its pronunciation and meaning(s).

**Step 1: Identify the character's radical.**

| Character | Radical |
|---|---|
| 他 | 亻 |
| 做 | 亻 |
| 话 | 讠 |
| 说 | 讠 |
| 英 | 艹 |
| 草 | 艹 |
| 国 | 囗 |
| 图 | 囗 |

**Step 2: Count the number of strokes within that radical.**

| Radical | Stroke Order | Number of Strokes |
|---|---|---|
| 亻 | 丿 亻 | 2 |
| 讠 | 丶 讠 | 2 |
| 艹 | 一 十 艹 | 3 |
| 囗 | 丨 冂 囗 | 3 |

**Step 3: Going to the dictionary's radical index, which lists every radical sequentially by stroke number, locate the desired radical. Indicated next to each radical is the page number on which all characters sharing that same radical are listed.**

| One Stroke | | 亠 | 18 | 彳 | 30 | 木 | 39 |
|---|---|---|---|---|---|---|---|
| 一 | 14 | 冫 | 19 | 饣 | 31 | 车 | 41 |
| 丨 | 15 | **讠** | **19** | 广 | 31 | 戈 | 41 |
| 丿 | 15 | 阝 | 20 | 门 | 31 | 日 | 42 |
| 丶 | 15 | 刀 | 21 | 氵 | 32 | 水 | 42 |
| 乙 | 15 | 厶 | 21 | 忄 | 34 | 见 | 43 |
| Two Strokes | | 又 | 21 | 宀 | 34 | 牛 | 43 |
| 二 | 15 | Three Strokes | | 辶 | 35 | 手 | 43 |
| 十 | 15 | 土 | 21 | 女 | 36 | 毛 | 43 |
| 厂 | 16 | **艹** | **22** | 子 | 37 | 气 | 43 |
| **亻** | **16** | 大 | 24 | 纟 | 37 | 攵 | 43 |
| 八 | 18 | 扌 | 25 | 马 | 38 | 父 | 44 |
| 人 | 18 | 小 | 26 | 幺 | 38 | 月 | 44 |
| 儿 | 18 | 口 | 27 | Four Strokes | | 文 | 45 |
| 几 | 18 | **囗** | **29** | 王 | 38 | 方 | 45 |

From the above radical index we know the following:

| Character | Radical | Radical Page Number |
|---|---|---|
| 他 | 亻 | 16 |
| 做 | 亻 | 16 |
| 话 | 讠 | 19 |
| 说 | 讠 | 19 |
| 英 | 艹 | 22 |
| 草 | 艹 | 22 |
| 国 | 囗 | 29 |
| 图 | 囗 | 29 |

**Step 4: Count the number of remaining strokes in the character outside of the radical.**

| Character | Remainder | Remaining Stroke Breakdown | Remaining Stroke Count |
|---|---|---|---|
| 他 | 也 | 𠃌 乜 也 | 3 |
| 做 | 故 | 一 十 十 古 古 古丿 古𠂉 古攵 故 | 9 |
| 话 | 舌 | 丿 二 千 千 舌 舌 | 6 |
| 说 | 兑 | 丶 丷 丷 丷口 丷口 兄 兑 | 7 |
| 英 | 央 | 丨 冂 口 央 央 | 5 |
| 草 | 早 | 丨 冂 日 日 旦 早 | 6 |
| 国 | 玉 | 一 二 王 王 玉 | 5 |
| 图 | 冬 | 丿 夕 夂 冬 冬 | 5 |

We now have the following necessary information about these unknown characters:

| Character | Radical | Radical Page Number | Remaining Stroke Count |
|---|---|---|---|
| 他 | 亻 | 16 | 3 |
| 做 | 亻 | 16 | 9 |
| 话 | 讠 | 19 | 6 |
| 说 | 讠 | 19 | 7 |
| 英 | 艹 | 22 | 5 |
| 草 | 艹 | 22 | 6 |
| 国 | 囗 | 29 | 5 |
| 图 | 囗 | 29 | 5 |

**Step 5: Going to the appropriate radical page number, locate the desired character under its radical header according to the number of its remaining strokes.**

Page 16 (for 他 and 做):

| The Radical 厂 | | 仍 | 1068 | 使 | 1149 |
|---|---|---|---|---|---|
| 厂 | 6<br>143 | 化 | 536<br>534 | 供 | 439<br>442 |
| 2 to 6 strokes | | **3 strokes** | | 7 to 8 strokes | |
| 厅 | 1257 | 仗 | 1587 | 俩 | 780 |
| 历 | 776 | 代 | 240 | 修 | 1416 |
| 厕 | 126 | 仙 | 1360 | 保 | 44 |
| 7 to 8 strokes | | **他** | **1215** | 借 | 651 |
| 厚 | 528 | 4 to 6 strokes | | 候 | 529 |
| 原 | 1547 | 休 | 1415 | **9 strokes** | |
| 9 to 10 strokes | | 伤 | 1103 | 债 | 373 |
| 厢 | 1374 | 伙 | 576 | **做** | **1688** |
| 厨 | 188 | 伪 | 1311 | 偷 | 1269 |
| **The Radical 亻** | | 何 | 509 | The Radical 八 | |
| 1 stroke | | 但 | 247 | 2 to 4 strokes | |
| 亿 | 1490 | 你 | 924 | 公 | 434 |
| 2 strokes | | 佳 | 604 | 半 | 35 |
| 仁 | 1065 | 侨 | 1020 | 共 | 441 |

From the information above we now know which pages to turn to in order to find the meaning and pronunciation of both 他 and 做.

| Character | Character Page Number |
|---|---|
| 他<br>做 | 1215<br>1688 |

**Step 6: Go to the character's indicated page number to learn its pronunciation and meaning(s).**

Page 1215 (for 他):

| 它 | tā | it |
|---|---|---|
| **他** | **tā** | **①he, ②s/he, ③other; another; some other** |
| 她 | tā | she |
| 塔 | tǎ | ①(Buddhist) pagoda, ②tower, ③column <chem.> |

Page 1688 (for 做):

| | | |
|---|---|---|
| 柞 | zuò | oak tree *(quercus)* |
| 胙 | zuò | sacrificial meat (in ancient times) |
| 座 | zuò | ①se at; place, ②stand; pedestal; base, ③constellation <astr.>, ④classifier for large buildings and mountains |
| **做** | **zuò** | **①make; produce; manufacture, ②cook; prepare, ③do; act; engage in, ④be; become, ⑤write; compose, ⑥hold a family celebration, ⑦be used as, ⑧form or contract a relationship** |

## 3. Looking Up an Unknown Word or Phrase in a Dictionary

A word in Chinese is usually made up of more than one character. Looking up an unknown word or phrase in a dictionary involves focusing on the first character in the word and following the procedures outlined above to look up that first character in a dictionary.

Returning to the character 做 directly above, then, imagine needing to look up the following four words or phrases in a dictionary: 做伴, 做法, 做事, 做贼心虚.

Going through the procedures for finding 做, we come to page 1688. On that page we find 做 and immediately below it a list of words and phrases beginning with 做 arranged in semi-alphabetical order based on the romanized spelling of the character following 做. If you do not know the pronunciation of that second character, you simply need to start from the beginning of the word/phrase entry list and scan it until you find the desired entry.

Page 1688 (for 做):

| | | |
|---|---|---|
| 做 | zuò | ①make; produce; manufacture, ②cook; prepare, ③do; act; engage in, ④be; become, ⑤write; compose, ⑥hold a family celebration, ⑦be used as, ⑧form or contract a relationship |
| **[做伴]** | **zuòbàn** | **keep sb. company** |
| [做东] | zuò dōng | play the host; host sb.; act as host to sb. |
| **[做法]** | **zuòfǎ** | **way of doing or making sth.; method of work; practice** |
| [做客] | zuò kè | be a guest |
| [做媒] | zuò méi | be a matchmaker |
| [做梦] | zuò mèng | ①have a dream; dream, ②have a pipe dream; daydream |
| **[做事]** | **zuò shì** | **①handle affairs; do a deed; act, ②work; have a job** |
| [做寿] | zuò shòu | celebrate the birthday (usu. of elderly people); hold a birthday party |
| **[做贼心虚]** | **zuòzéixīnxū** | **have a guilty conscience** |
| [做作] | zuòzuo | affected; artificial |

## 4. Final Bits of Information about How to Use This Textbook

So far you have learned some important things about the nature of the Chinese writing system, including the prominent role that sound and meaning clues play in knowing what a character means and how to pronounce it. You have also been introduced to the use of radicals as a bookkeeping device to classify characters and the central role they play in the process of looking up characters in a dictionary.

You have also learned about the eleven basic stroke types and the principles used to put them together to form larger and larger building blocks in a stable, well-balanced manner within an imaginary square. Additionally, you have seen how to reverse the construction process, that is, how to go about decomposing independent and complex characters into smaller and smaller units, eventually boiling them down to individual, countable strokes of the pen or pencil.

In the following chapters each new character will be systematically introduced together with the specific factual details of how it is constructed and classified. Since not every character can stand alone as a full-fledged word in modern Chinese, each character that is unable to do so will be marked with an asterisk (*).

Also, from time to time, a brief mnemonic clue will be offered. These mnemonic clues are not always etymologically correct; their utility lies primarily in helping you quickly remember how to write a character and not in providing you with an accurate picture of how a particular character came to be written the way it is.

Finally, next to each new character are eight blank squares. Use these to practice how to properly write each character. Please bear in mind that, like learning to play a musical instrument or mastering a sport, learning how to write Chinese characters requires constant repetition in order to develop muscle memory. In other words, you will need to practice writing each new character many, many more times than just eight.

You are about to embark on an exciting journey. Good luck!

### EXERCISES

**1. Identify the radicals of each of the following characters; then count the number of the strokes of the radical for each.**

a. 作　　b. 楼　　c. 汤

d. 谢　　e. 筷　　f. 花

**2. Write down the number of remaining strokes beyond the radical for the following characters:**

a. 吵　　b. 除　　c. 妈

d. 位　　e. 双　　f. 忙

3. **Using the radical table shown under Step 1 above, identify the radical of each of the following characters; you may want to find each radical in the radical index of your own dictionary as well.**

a. 快　　b. 肚　　c. 昨

d. 奶　　e. 架　　f. 咱

4. **Look up the following characters in any dictionary of your choice. Then write down the pronunciation of the character you find.**

a. 超　　b. 和　　c. 志

d. 所　　e. 笔　　f. 钟

5. **Try to find the following words in your dictionary; then write down their English definitions.**

a. 希望　　b. 杂志　　c. 小说

d. 外衣　　e. 办公楼

# CHAPTER FOUR
# 第　四　课

## Text 1

我kàn书，我也mǎi书。[1] 我yǒu<u>中文</u>书，一、[2] 二、三、四、五。我也yǒu<u>日文</u>书，liù、七、八、九、十。我de书不大，我de书也不小。Nǐ yǒu<u>中文</u>书hái.shì<u>日文</u>书？

### 生词 New Words

| | | |
|---|---|---|
| 我 | wǒ | (Pr) I, me |
| 书 | shū | (N) book |
| 也 | yě | (Adv) also |
| <u>中文</u> | <u>Zhōngwén</u> | (N) Chinese (language) |
| 一 | yī, yì, yí | (Nu) one |
| 二 | èr | (Nu) two |

1. The Chinese period/full stop is written as a small circle rather than as a dot.
2. Chinese has two kinds of commas. One looks like the English comma, while the other—“ 、”—is used exclusively between parallel items (things, actions, and so on) in a list. The “English” comma is used everywhere else that a comma would be used in English.

| | | |
|---|---|---|
| 三 | sān | (Nu) three |
| 四 | sì | (Nu) four |
| 五 | wǔ | (Nu) five |
| 日文 | Rìwén | (N) Japanese (language) |
| 七 | qī | (Nu) seven |
| 八 | bā | (Nu) eight |
| 九 | jiǔ | (Nu) nine |
| 十 | shí | (Nu) ten |
| 不 | bù-, bú-, bu- | (Adv) not |
| 大 | dà | (SV) be big, be large |
| 小 | xiǎo | (SV) be small, be minor |

## Text 2

Tā shì 中.guó[3]人，Tā jiào 王中书。Nǐ不shì 中.guó人，我也不shì 中.guó人。Nǐ shì Xīn西lán人，我shì 日本人。我xìng 中本，jiào 一也。Tā shuō 中文，Nǐ shuō Yīng文，我shuō 日文，Nǐ xué 中文，我也xué 中文。再见。

### 生词 New Words

| | | |
|---|---|---|
| 中.guó | Zhōng.guó | (N) China |
| 人 | rén | (N) person, human being |
| 王 | Wáng | (N) a Chinese surname |
| 王中书 | Wáng Zhōngshū | (N) a personal name |
| Xīn西lán | Xīnxīlán | (N) New Zealand |
| 日本 | Rìběn | (N) Japan |
| 中本 一也 | Zhōngběn Yīyě | (N) a Japanese personal name |
| Yīng文 | Yīngwén | (N) English (language) |
| 再见 | zàijiàn! | (Ex) good-bye, au revoir! |

3. Proper nouns are underlined in Chinese.

## COMPREHENSION QUESTIONS

**Answer the following questions, using Chinese characters wherever possible.**

TEXT 1

1. Nǐ kàn 书 ma?

______________________________

2. Nǐ mǎi shénme?

______________________________

3. Nǐ yǒu 中文书 hái.shì 日文书?

______________________________

4. Nǐ de 书大不大?

______________________________

TEXT 2

1. 王中书 shì 中.guó人, hái.shì 日本人?

______________________________

2. Nàge 日本人 jiào shénme míng.zì?

______________________________

3. Shéi xué 中文?

______________________________

4. Shéi shuō 中文?

______________________________

## Writing Help

As noted previously, every Chinese character can be divided into a radical plus a remainder, unless the character itself is a radical. Most characters embody more complexity than a radical and contain one or more substructures beyond the radical itself. Characters that Chinese have historically considered to be of a single structure are called *independent characters* and are written mentally in a simple, undivided square; they are presented in this textbook with an empty square for you to work with. Characters that contain substructures beyond the radical are called *compound characters* and fill out that same mental square, which can then be divided further according to the compound structure. In this book characters are introduced using these two categories.

| Character | Basic Meaning | No. of Strokes | Stroke Order | Radical | Components | Structure |
|---|---|---|---|---|---|---|
| 一 yī, yì, yí | one | (1) | 一 | 一 | 一 | □ |
| 七 qī | seven | (2) | 一 七 | 一 | 七 | □ |
| 八 bā | eight | (2) | ノ 八 | 八 | 八 | □ |
| 九 jiù | nine | (2) | 丿 九 | 丿 | 九 | □ |
| 十 shí | ten | (2) | 一 十 | 十 | 十 | □ |
| 人 rén | person | (2) | 丿 人 | 人 | 人 | □ |
| 大 dà | big | (3) | 一 ナ 大 | 大 | 大 | □ |
| 小 xiǎo | small, little | (3) | 亅 小 小 | 小 | 小 | □ |
| 也 yě | also | (3) | ㇆ 𠃌 也 | 乙 | 也 | □ |
| 五 wǔ | five | (4) | 一 丅 五 五 | 一 | 五 | □ |

| | | | | | | |
|---|---|---|---|---|---|---|
| *中 zhōng[4] | middle | (4) | 丨 冂 口 中 | 丨 | 口 丨 | □ |
| *文 wén | language | (4) | 丶 亠 亣 文 | 文 | 文 | □ |
| 不 bù-, bú-, bu- | not | (4) | 一 丆 不 不 | 一 | 不 | □ |
| *日 rì | sun | (4) | 丨 冂 日 日 | 日 | 日 | □ |
| 王 wáng | king; surname | (4) | 一 二 干 王 | 王 | 王 | □ |
| 书(書)[5] shū | book | (4) | ㇆ 𠃌 书 书 | 乙 | 书 | □ |
| 见(見) jiàn | see | (4) | 丨 冂 贝 见 | 见 | 冂 儿 | □ |
| 四 sì | four | (5) | 丨 冂 冂 四 四 | 口 | 四 | □ |
| *本 běn | origin | (5) | 一 十 才 木 本 | 木 | 木 一 | □ |
| 西 xī | west | (6) | 一 丆 丙 丙 西 西 | 西 | 西 | □ |
| 我 wǒ | I, me | (7) | 丿 二 于 手 我 我 我 | 戈 | 我 | □ |

## Independent Characters

Compound characters are formed by combining a radical with one or more independent characters and/or symbols. The radical usually relates to the meaning in the compound character.

4. An asterisk next to a character indicates that the character can never stand alone as an independent word in modern standard Chinese.

5. When the traditional form of the Chinese character differs from its simplified form, then the traditional form of the character is placed in parentheses for reference purposes.

## Radical

This chapter focuses on the radical 一, which appears in the characters 二, 三, and 再, introduced in this chapter.

| Character | Basic Meaning | No. of Strokes | Stroke Order | Radical | Compo-nents | Structure |
|---|---|---|---|---|---|---|
| 二 èr | two | 2 | 一 二 | 一 | 一 一 | ⊟ |
| 三 sān | three | 3 | 一 二 三 | 一 | 一 一 一 | ☰ |
| 再 zài | again | 6 | 一 丆 冂 币 再 再 | 一 | 一 冉 | ⊟ |

## EXERCISES

### I. Character Exercises

1. Add one or two strokes to each of the following characters to form a new character:

   一 ______ 十 ______ 口 ______ 人 ______

2. Delete one or two strokes from each of the following characters to form a new character:

   七 ______ 三 ______ 大 ______ 王 ______

3. Write the third stroke for each of the following characters:

   书 ______ 西 ______ 再 ______ 我 ______

4. Write the characters for the following:

   Zhōngwén yī, qī, shí, sān, wǔ, jiǔ, èr, bā, sì ______________________

   Shū bú dà, yě bù xiǎo. Zàijiàn. ______________________

## II. Written Exercises

**1. Complete the following phrases/sentences in Chinese characters.**

a. 我 kàn书，我 ________ mǎi书。

b. 你de书 ________ 大，我de ________ 也不 ________ 。

c. 我 shì 日本 ________，我shuō ____________。

**2. 中本一也 is a Japanese boy. He speaks Japanese and is learning Chinese. His telephone number is 439-1872. Fill in the following form for him in Chinese characters.**

| Surname | |
|---|---|
| First Name | |
| Native Language | |
| Learning Language | |
| Phone Number | |

**3. Translate the following sentences into Chinese, using Chinese characters for learned words:**

a. Can you write 1, 2, 3, 4, 5, 6, 7, 8, 9, 10 (numbers in Chinese)?

______________________________________________

b. He is Japanese. He can speak Japanese.

______________________________________________

c. Hello, my name is Wáng Dàlán. I am Chinese. My friend is also Chinese. Bye.

______________________________________________

d. My book is big, but Xiǎoxī's book is small.

______________________________________________

## Supplementary Reading

王小文: Zǎo!

中本一也: Zǎo!

王小文: Nǐ shì 中.guó 人 hái.shì 日本人?

中本一也: 我 shì 日本人。Nǐ shì 中.guó 人 ma?

王小文: 我 shì 中.guó 人。我 jiào 王小文。Nǐ jiào shénme míng.zì?

中本一也: 我 jiào 中本一也。

### COMPREHENSION QUESTIONS

1. 王小文 shì 中.guó 人 ma?

_______________________________________________

2. 中本一也 shì 中.guó 人 hái.shì 日本人?

_______________________________________________

## Character Practice

| 一 | 一 | | | | | | | | |
|---|---|---|---|---|---|---|---|---|---|
| 七 | 七 | | | | | | | | |
| 八 | 八 | | | | | | | | |

| 九 | 九 | | | | | | | | |
|---|---|---|---|---|---|---|---|---|---|
| 十 | 十 | | | | | | | | |
| 人 | 人 | | | | | | | | |
| 大 | 大 | | | | | | | | |
| 小 | 小 | | | | | | | | |
| 也 | 也 | | | | | | | | |
| 五 | 五 | | | | | | | | |
| 中 | 中 | | | | | | | | |
| 文 | 文 | | | | | | | | |
| 不 | 不 | | | | | | | | |
| 日 | 日 | | | | | | | | |
| 王 | 王 | | | | | | | | |
| 书 | 书 | | | | | | | | |

| 见 | 见 | | | | | | | | |
|---|---|---|---|---|---|---|---|---|---|
| 四 | 四 | | | | | | | | |
| 本 | 本 | | | | | | | | |
| 西 | 西 | | | | | | | | |
| 我 | 我 | | | | | | | | |
| 二 | 二 | | | | | | | | |
| 三 | 三 | | | | | | | | |
| 再 | 再 | | | | | | | | |

# CHAPTER FIVE
# 第　五　课

**Text 1**

王先生yǒu一千二百五十四本书，他yǒu中文书、Yīng文书，háiyǒu日文书。他问文文yǒu什么书，yǒu几本书。文文只yǒu几本Yīng文小说。王先生说文文可以kàn他de中文书。可shì文文不dǒng中文，文文不会说中.guó话，也不会kàn中文书。文文只会说："你hǎo！　再见。"王先生sòng文文一本中Yīng词diǎn，他说他可以jiāo文文中文。文文yào xué中文！

## 生词 New Words

| | | |
|---|---|---|
| 先生 | xiān.shēng | (N) teacher, sir, Mr., husband |
| 王先生 | Wáng Xiān.shēng | (N) Mr. Wang |
| 千 | qiān | (Nu) thousand |
| 百 | bǎi | (Nu) hundred |
| 本 | -běn | (Cl) volume (for books) |
| 他 | tā | (Pr) he, him |
| 问 | wèn | (V) ask (a question) |
| 文文 | Wénwen | (N) a personal name |
| 什么 | shénme | (QW) what |
| 几? | jǐ? | (Q) How many? (classifier required) |
| 只 | zhǐ | (Adv) only, just |
| 几 | jǐ- | (Q) a few, several (classifier required) |
| 小说 | xiǎoshūō | (N) fictional work (Cl -本) |
| 说 | shūō | (V) say, speak |
| 可以 | kě.yǐ | (Aux) allowed to, can |
| 可shì | kě.shì | (Conj) but, however |
| 会 | huì | (Aux) may, can |
| 话 | huà | (N) spoken language |
| 你 | nǐ | (Pr) you (singular) |
| 词diǎn | cídiǎn | (N) dictionary (Cl -本) |

## Text 2

我shì Xīn西lán人。我会说Yīng语、[1] 日语。我也会xiě几个中文zì。我jiāo王太太de儿子、女儿说日语。王太太sòng我三支毛bǐ。我问tā:"你可以jiāo我xiě毛bǐ zì吗?" Tā说:"可以。" Tā真hǎo。你们呢? 你们yào xué xiě毛bǐ zì吗? 我可以sòng你们两支毛bǐ。

1. In lists of items, objects, or things, Chinese uses a special comma which written as "、". In all other instances where a comma is used, the ordinary "," is employed.

## 生词 New Words

| | | |
|---|---|---|
| Yīng语 | Yīngyǔ | (N) English (language) |
| 日语 | Rìyǔ | (N) Japanese (language) |
| 个 | -gè | (Cl) (general classifier) |
| 太太 | tàitai | (N) Mrs., wife |
| 王太太 | Wáng Tàitai | (N) Mrs. Wang |
| 儿子 | érzi | (N) son |
| 女儿 | nǚ'ér | (N) daughter |
| 支 | -zhī | (Cl) (for pens, pencils) |
| 毛bǐ | máobǐ | (N) writing brush (Cl - 支) |
| 吗 | ma | (P) (indicates a question) |
| 真 | zhēn | (Adv) really, truly |
| 你们 | nǐmen | (Pr) you (plural) |
| 呢 | ne | (P) (forms a reverse question) |
| 两 | liǎng | (Q) two (classifier required) |

## COMPREHENSION QUESTIONS

**1. Answer the following questions based on Text 1.**

a. 王先生yǒu duōshǎo本书?

______________________________

b. 王先生yǒu什么书?

______________________________

c. 文文yǒu几本书?

______________________________

d. 文文yǒu什么书?

______________________________

e. 文文会说中.guó话ma?

______________________________

f. 王先生sòng文文什么?

---

g. Shéi可以jiāo文文中文?

---

h. 文文yào bu yào xué中文?

---

2. Complete each of the following sentences according to Text 2:

a. 我shì ________

b. 我会 ________

c. 我jiāo ________

d. 王太太sòng我 ________

## Writing Help

### Independent Characters

| Character | Basic Meaning | No. of Strokes | Stroke Order | Radical | Compo-nents | Structure |
|---|---|---|---|---|---|---|
| 儿(兒) ér | son | 2 | 丿 儿 | 儿 | 儿 | ☐ |
| *几(幾) jǐ | several | 2 | 丿 几 | 几 | 几 | ☐ |
| 千 qiān | thousand | 3 | 丿 二 千 | 十 | 丿 十 | ☐ |
| *么(麼) me | | 3 | 丿 么 么 | 丿 | 丿 厶 | ☐ |

| | | | | | | |
|---|---|---|---|---|---|---|
| *子 zǐ | son, little boy, child | 3 | ㇇ 了 子 | 子 | 子 | □ |
| *女 nǚ | daughter | 3 | ㄑ 女 女 | 女 | 女 | □ |
| 毛 máo | hair; surname | 4 | 丿 二 三 毛 | 毛 | 毛 | □ |
| 太 tài | overly | 4 | 大 太 | 大 | 大 丶 | □ |
| *可 kě | can | 5 | 一 叵 可 | 口 | 口 丁 | □ |
| 生 shēng | student | 5 | 丿 𠂉 𠂒 牛 生 | 生 | 生 | □ |
| *两(兩) liǎng | two | 7 | 一 丆 冂 丙 两 | 一 | 一 冂 人 人 | □ |

## Compound Characters

The new compound character with learned radical 一 in this chapter is 百.

| Character | Basic Meaning | No. of Str. | Stroke Order | Radical | Mean. Clue | Phon. Clue | Compo- nents | Structure |
|---|---|---|---|---|---|---|---|---|
| 百 bǎi | hundred | 6 | 一 丆 丆 丙 百 百 | 一 | 一 | 白 | 一, 白 | ⊟ |

## Radicals

The radicals of focus in this chapter are 儿, 亻, 讠, 人, 十, and 口.

### 1. 儿

This can be a character as well as a radical.

| Character | Basic Meaning | No. of Str. | Stroke Order | Mean. Clue | Phon. Clue | Compo- nents | Structure |
|---|---|---|---|---|---|---|---|
| 先 xiān | first | 6 | 丿 𠂉 𠂒 生 先 | | | 生 儿 | ⊟ |

2. 亻

As a character this radical means "human" and is written as 人. As a radical it is often used as the left part in a compound character to form characters related to humans or to things related to human activities. In such characters it is written as 亻. The compound characters in this chapter that contain this radical are 什, 们, 他, and 你.

| Character | Basic Meaning | No. of Str. | Stroke Order | Mean. Clue | Phon. Clue | Components | Structure |
|---|---|---|---|---|---|---|---|
| *什(甚) shén | what (什么) | 4 | 丿 亻 仁 什 | | 十 | 亻 十 | ◫ |
| *们(們) men | (plural for personal pronouns) | 4 | 亻 亻 亻 们 | 亻 | 门 mén | 亻 门 | ◫ |
| 他 tā | he/him | 5 | 亻 他 | 亻 | | 亻 也 | ◫ |
| 你 nǐ | you | 7 | 亻 亻 亻 你 | 亻 尔 (ěr, *you*) | | 亻 尔 (𠂊 小) | ◫ |

他: 他 is also (也) human!

3. 讠

As a character, it means "spoken words or speech" and is written as 言 yán. As a radical it is used as the left part in a compound character and is written as 讠 to form characters related to words, speech, and the action of speaking. The compound characters in this chapter that contain this radical are 词, 说, 话, and 语.

| Character | Basic Meaning | No. of Str. | Stroke Order | Mean. Clue | Phon. Clue | Components | Structure |
|---|---|---|---|---|---|---|---|
| 词(詞) cí | word | 7 | 丶 讠 订 订 词 | 讠 | 司 sī | 讠 司 (𠃌 一 口) | ◫ |
| 话(話) huà | talk | 8 | 讠 讦 话 | 讠 舌(shé, *tongue*) | | 讠 舌 (千 口) | ◫ |

| 说(說) shuō | speak | 9 | 讠 讠丶 讠丷 讠⿱丷口 说 | 讠 | | 讠 兑(丷 口 儿) | 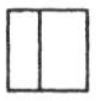 ⿰ |
|---|---|---|---|---|---|---|---|
| *语(語) yǔ | language | 9 | 讠 讠五 语 | 口 (kǒu, *mouth)* | | 讠 五 口 | 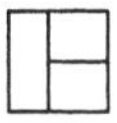 ⿰ |

语: Think of it as being composed of speaking with five mouths, thus "language."

## 4. 人

This form of 人 is used as a radical mostly in compound characters of top-bottom structure and sometimes in characters of left-right structure. In this chapter, the characters that contain this radical are 以, 会, and 个.

| **Character** | **Basic Meaning** | **No. of Str.** | **Stroke Order** | **Mean. Clue** | **Phon. Clue** | **Compo-nents** | **Structure** |
|---|---|---|---|---|---|---|---|
| *个(個) gè | ( a classifier) | 3 | 丿 人 个 | 人, 丨 (一个人) | | 人, 丨 |  ⿱ |
| 以 yǐ | according to | 4 | 𠄌 𠄌丶 以 | | | 𠄌丶, 人 |  ⿰ |
| 会(會) huì | may, can | 6 | 人 亼 会 会 | 人 | | 人 云 (二 厶) |  ⿱ |

## 5. 十

This can be both a character and a radical. Usually, as a radical, it appears on the top part of a character. The compound characters in this chapter that contain this radical are 支 and 真.

| **Character** | **Basic Meaning** | **No. of Str.** | **Stroke Order** | **Mean. Clue** | **Phon. Clue** | **Compo-nents** | **Structure** |
|---|---|---|---|---|---|---|---|
| 支 zhī | branch | 4 | 十 ⿱十フ 支 | | 十 | 十 又 |  ⿱ |
| 真 zhēn | true, truth | 10 | 十 冇 有 直 真 | | | 直 八 |  ⿱ |

6. 口

口 can be both a character and a radical. 口 *kǒu* means "mouth" as an independent character (see Chapter 6). As a radical it is often used to form characters related to the mouth or action of the mouth. The compound characters in this chapter that contain this radical are 只, 问, 吗, and 呢.

| Character | Basic Meaning | No. of Str. | Stroke Order | Mean. Clue | Phon. Clue | Compo- nents | Structure |
|---|---|---|---|---|---|---|---|
| 只 zhǐ | only | 5 | 口 只 | | | 口 八 | ⊟ |
| 问(問) wèn | ask | 6 | 门 问 | 口 | 门 mén | 门 口 | ⊡ |
| 吗(嗎) ma | (question word) | 6 | 口 叮 吗 吗 | 口 | 马 mǎ | 口 马 | ◫ |
| 呢 ne | (forms a reverse question) | 8 | 口 叮 叮 呎 呢 呢 | 口 | 尼 ní | 口 尼 (尸 匕) | ◫ |

EXERCISES

I. Character Exercises

1. **Find the independent characters you have learned hidden in the following characters:**

语 ______ 你 ______ 太 ______ 什 ______

说 ______ 以 ______ 个 ______ 生 ______

2. **Add more strokes to each of the following to form new characters:**

四 ______ 门 ______ 儿 ______ 也 ______

口 ______ 千 ______ 尸 ______ 又 ______

3. Write the fourth stroke for each of the following characters:

真 ________ 两 ________ 会 ________ 吗 ________

4. Fill in the blanks with characters that have the radical shown:

亻: ________ ________ ________

讠: ________ ________ ________

5. Write the characters for the following:

xiǎoshuō xiān.shēng Nǐmen shuō Rìyǔ. Wǒ ké.yǐ wèn.

________________________________________________

## II. Vocabulary Exercises

1. Fill in each of the following squares with a single character to form two-character words with the character already shown.

a.

| | 儿 |
|---|---|
| | |

b.

| | 们 |
|---|---|
| | |

## III. Structure Exercises

1. Write the correct classifier character to complete each of the following phrases.

十 ________ 词diǎn 五 ________ 儿子

七 ________ 小说 九 ________ 毛bǐ

2. Complete each of the sentences below with appropriate adverbs.

a. 他yǒu hěn duō书，我 ______ yǒu三本书。

b. 小王hěn gāo，小文 ______ hěn gāo，他们 ______ hěn gāo。

3. Rearrange the elements of each of the entries to make a grammatical sentence.

a. 会 中文 王太太 说

b. shì 他们 人 日本

c. 他 yǒu 个 儿子 两

4. Write four sentences about "我" in Chinese using Chinese characters you have already learned. You may include vocabulary you have learned how to say but don't yet know how to write in characters. In such cases you may use Hànyǔ Pīnyīn.

______________________________

______________________________

______________________________

______________________________

5. Translate the following sentences into Chinese, using Chinese characters for learned words:

a. What kind of books do you have? ______________________________

b. Zhōnglán has ten Japanese dictionaries. ______________________________

c. That gentleman can speak Japanese. ______________________________

d. Mrs. Wang has three daughters and two sons. ______________________________

e. This lady has four children. ______________________________

f. These two dictionaries are really big. ______________________________

g. This school has 2,001 students. ______________________________

## Supplementary Reading

中本一也:　你hǎo!　Qǐng问，你会说日语吗?

王文:　我只会说一、二、三、四、五、liù, 七、八、九、十。你shì日本人吗?

中本一也:　我shì日本人。可shì，我太太shì中.guó人。

王文:　你会说中文。你太太会说日语吗?

中本一也:　我太太会说日语。

王文:　他shì你de儿子吗?

中本一也:　Shì。

王文:　你de儿子会说中文hái.shì日文?

中本一也:　他会说中文，也会说日文。

### COMPREHENSION QUESTIONS

1. 王文会说日语吗? ______________________________

2. 中本一也de太太shì中.guó人 hái.shì日本人? ______________________________

3. 中本一也de儿子会说中文吗? ______________________________

## Character Practice

| | | | | | | | | | |
|---|---|---|---|---|---|---|---|---|---|
| 儿 | 儿 | | | | | | | | |
| 几 | 几 | | | | | | | | |
| 千 | 千 | | | | | | | | |
| 么 | 么 | | | | | | | | |
| 子 | 么 | | | | | | | | |
| 女 | 女 | | | | | | | | |
| 毛 | 毛 | | | | | | | | |
| 太 | 太 | | | | | | | | |
| 可 | 可 | | | | | | | | |
| 生 | 生 | | | | | | | | |
| 两 | 两 | | | | | | | | |
| 百 | 百 | | | | | | | | |

| 先 | 先 | | | | | | | | |
|---|---|---|---|---|---|---|---|---|---|
| 什 | 先 | | | | | | | | |
| 们 | 先 | | | | | | | | |
| 他 | 他 | | | | | | | | |
| 你 | 你 | | | | | | | | |
| 词 | 词 | | | | | | | | |
| 话 | 话 | | | | | | | | |
| 说 | 说 | | | | | | | | |
| 语 | 语 | | | | | | | | |
| 个 | 个 | | | | | | | | |
| 以 | 以 | | | | | | | | |
| 会 | 会 | | | | | | | | |

| 支 | 支 | | | | | | | | |
|---|---|---|---|---|---|---|---|---|---|
| 真 | 真 | | | | | | | | |
| 只 | 只 | | | | | | | | |
| 问 | 问 | | | | | | | | |
| 吗 | 吗 | | | | | | | | |
| 呢 | 呢 | | | | | | | | |

# CHAPTER SIX
# 第　六　课

**Text 1**

我 de 好 péng.yǒu 文生姓万，他家一共 yǒu 八口人，bàba，妈妈、一个姐姐、两个妹妹、一个哥哥、一个弟弟 hé 文生。兄弟姐妹一半 shì nánde，一半 shì 女 de。他姐姐 yǒu 四本日文词典、两份中.guó 画 bào、三本 Xīn 西兰小说。他 de 两个妹妹 dōu shì 小 xué 生，她们不 xǐ.huān kàn 小说，她们要 kàn 小人书。她们说小人书很好 kàn，字也很 shǎo。他弟弟 hé 文生 dōu 不要 kàn 书，他们要 kàn 电 shì。他们说电 shì 很好 kàn。

## 生词 New Words

| | | |
|---|---|---|
| 好 | hǎo | (SV) be well, be good |
| 姓 | xìng | (V) be surnamed |
| 万 | wàn | (N) a Chinese surname |
| | | (Q) ten thousand |
| <u>万文生</u> | <u>Wàn Wénshēng</u> | (N) a personal name |
| 家 | jiā | (N) family, home |
| 一共 | yígòng | (Adv) altogether |
| 口 | -kǒu | (Cl) (classifier for persons) |
| 妈妈 | māma | (N) mother |
| 姐姐 | jiějie | (N) older sister |
| 妹妹 | mèimei | (N) younger sister |
| 哥哥 | gēge | (N) older brother |
| 弟弟 | dìdi | (N) younger brother |
| 兄弟姐妹 | xiōngdì-jiěmèi | (N) brothers and sisters; siblings |
| 一半 | yíbàn | (Q) half |
| 女de | nǚde | (N) woman, female |
| 词典 | cídiǎn | (N) dictionary (Cl -本) |
| 份 | -fèn | (Cl) (issues of newspapers, magazines, and so on) |
| 画bào | huàbào | (N) illustrated periodical; picture magazine (Cl -份) |
| <u>Xīn西兰</u> | <u>Xīnxīlán</u> | (PW) New Zealand |
| 小xué.生 | xiǎo xué.shēng | (N) elementary school pupil |
| 他/她们 | tāmen | (Pr) they, them |
| 要 | yào | (V) want, want to |
| 小人书 | xiǎorénshū | (N) children's picture book (Cl -本) |
| 很 | hěn | (Adv) quite, very |
| 好kàn | hǎokàn | (SV) good-looking; have an interesting story |
| 字 | zì | (N) (Chinese) character(s) (Cl -个) |
| 电shì | diànshì | (N) television |

## Text 2

我hé姐姐dōu méi.yǒu自行车。我得买一liàng自行车。自行车七百四十kuài九毛五分一liàng，不guì也不便宜。我姐姐也要买一liàng。两liàng车一共duōshǎo qián？ 你告诉我，好吗？ 哎呀！

一共要一千四百八十一kuài九毛。不行，我们只yǒu一千kuài qián，只néng买一liàng。我父母yǒu很duō qián，他们yǒu几万kuài qián。他们说他们可以sòng我们两liàng自行车。我父母真好!

**生词 New Words**

| | | |
|---|---|---|
| 自行车 | zìxíngchē | (N) bicycle (Cl -*liàng* 辆) |
| 得 | děi | (Aux) must |
| 买 | mǎi | (V) buy |
| 毛 | -máo | (Cl) dimes |
| 分 | -fēn | (Cl) pennies |
| 便宜 | pián.yí | (SV) be cheap |
| 告诉 | gàosu | (V) tell, inform |
| 哎呀 | āiya! | (Ex) Oh! Oh my! |
| 不行 | bùxíng | (Ex) Can't be done. |
| 我们 | wǒmen | (Pr) we, us |
| 父母 | fùmǔ | (N) parents |

## COMPREHENSION QUESTIONS

**Answer the following questions.**

TEXT 1

1. 你 de péng.yǒu jiào 什么 míng.zì?

___

2. 他家yǒu 几口人?

___

3. 他 yǒu 几个兄弟姐妹?

___

4. 他姐姐yǒu 什么书?

___

5. 他妹妹 ài kàn 什么书?

______________________________

6. 他 hé弟弟ài kàn什么?

______________________________

TEXT 2

1. 我hé姐姐要买什么?

______________________________

2. 两liàng自行车一共duōshǎo qián?

______________________________

3. 他们néng买几liàng自行车?

______________________________

4. Shéi sòng他们自行车? 为什么(Why)?

______________________________

## Writing Help

### Independent Characters

| Character | Basic Meaning | No. of Str. | Stroke Order | Radical | Components | Structure |
|---|---|---|---|---|---|---|
| 万(萬) wàn | ten thousand; surname | 3 | 一 丆 万 | 一 | 万 | ☐ |
| 口 kǒu | mouth | 3 | 口 | 口 | 口 | ☐ |
| 车(車) chē | vehicle | 4 | 一 ㄊ 斗 车 | 车 | 车 | ☐ |
| *父 fù | father | 4 | 八 父 | 父 | 父 | ☐ |
| *半 bàn | half | 5 | 丷 兰 半 | 八 | 半 | ☐ |

| | | | | | | |
|---|---|---|---|---|---|---|
| *母 mǔ | mother | 5 | 𠃊 𠃌 毋 母 母 | 母 | 母 | |
| 电(電) diàn | electrical | 5 | 曰 电 | 曰 | 曰 乚 | |
| *自 zì | self | 6 | ′ 白 自 自 | 自 | 自 | |
| 买(買) mǎi | to buy | 6 | 乛 乛 乛 买 | 乙 | 乛 头 | |
| 画(畫) huà | to draw | 8 | 一 丆 丙 丙 而 画 画 画 | 凵 | 一 田 凵 | |

## Compound Characters

The new compound characters in this chapter with radicals you have learned are 兄, 份, 便, 兄, 告, 呀, 哎, 哥, and 诉.

| Character | Basic Meaning | No. of Str. | Stroke Order | Radical | Mean. Clue | Phon. Clue | Compo-nents | Struct-ure |
|---|---|---|---|---|---|---|---|---|
| *兄 xiōng | elder brother | 5 | 口 兄 | 口 | 儿 | | 口 儿 | |
| *份 fèn | portion | 6 | 亻 八 分 分 | 亻 | | 分 fēn | 亻 八 刀 | |
| 告 gào | to inform | 6 | 生 告 | 口 | 口 | | 生 口 | |
| 呀 ya | Oh! | 7 | 口 吓 呀 呀 | 口 | 口 | 牙 yá | 口 牙 | |
| *诉(訴) sù | to inform | 7 | 讠 讠 订 诉 诉 诉 | 讠 | 讠<br>斥(chì, *to scold*) | | 讠<br>斥 (斤 丶) | |
| 哎 āi | Oh! | 8 | 口 吖 吖 哎 哎 | 口 | 口 | 艾 ài | 口 艹 乂 | |
| *便 pián | conve-nient | 9 | 亻 亻 佰 便 便 | 亻 | | | 亻 一 曰 乂 | |
| 哥 gē | elder brother | 10 | 可 哥 | 口 | 口 | 可+可 | 可 可 | |

## Radicals

The radicals of focus in this chapter are 八, 女, 宀, and 彳.

### 1. 八

The 八 radical is sometimes written as 丷 and is used as the top or bottom part of a character. The compound characters in this chapter that contain this radical are 分, 兰, 共, 弟, and 典.

| Character | Basic Meaning | No. of Str. | Stroke Order | Mean. Clue | Phon. Clue | Compo-nents | Struct-ure |
|---|---|---|---|---|---|---|---|
| 分 fēn | to divide | 4 | 分 | 刀 (dāo, *knife*) | | 八 刀 | ⊟ |
| *兰(蘭) lán | orchid | 5 | 丶 丷 亠 兰 兰 | | | 丷 三 | ⊟ |
| *共 gòng | altogether | 6 | 一 十 廾 龷 共 | | | 龷 八 | ⊟ |
| 弟 dì | younger brother | 7 | 丷 䒑 当 肖 弟 弟 | | | 丷 弔 | ⊟ |
| *典 diǎn | standard word | 7 | 丨 冂 冂 巾 曲 曲 典 | | | 曲 八 | ⊟ |

### 2. 女

女 can be both a character and a radical. It means "female" as an independent character. As a radical it can be put on the left or underneath a character to indicate what are considered to be femalelike things. The compound characters in this chapter that contain this radical are 她, 妈, 好, 姓, 姐, 妹, and 要.

| Character | Basic Meaning | No. of Str. | Stroke Order | Mean. Clue | Phon. Clue | Compo-nents | Struct-ure |
|---|---|---|---|---|---|---|---|
| 她 tā | she/her | 6 | 女 她 | 女 | | 女 也 | ⊞ |
| 妈(媽) mā | mother | 6 | 女 妈 | 女 | 马 mǎ | 女 马 | ⊞ |
| 好 hǎo | good | 6 | 女 好 | 女,子 | | 女 子 | ⊞ |
| 姓 xìng | surname | 8 | 女 姓 | 女, 生 *birth* | 生 shēng | 女 生 | ⊞ |

| Character | Basic Meaning | No. of Str. | Stroke Order | Mean. Clue | Phon. Clue | Compo-nents | Struct-ure |
|---|---|---|---|---|---|---|---|
| 姐 jiě | elder sister | 8 | 女 如 如 姐 姐 | 女 | 且 qiě | 女 且 | |
| *妹 mèi | younger sister | 8 | 妒 妹 妹 妹 | 女 | 未 wèi | 女 未 | |
| 要 yào | to want | 9 | 西 要 | | | 西 女 | |

好: 女*woman/mother/daughter* + 子 *son* = good.
姓: 女*woman* + 生 *birth* = surname; 生 is also a phonetic clue.

3. 宀

The 宀 radical is used at the top position of a character to indicate a roof or something under cover. The compound characters in this chapter that contain this radical are 字, 宜, and 家.

| Character | Basic Meaning | No. of Str. | Stroke Order | Mean. Clue | Phon. Clue | Compo-nents | Struct-ure |
|---|---|---|---|---|---|---|---|
| 字 zì | character | 6 | 丶 丷 宀 字 | | 子 | 宀 子 | |
| *宜 yí | suitable | 8 | 宀 宜 | | | 宀 且 | |
| 家 jiā | family, home | 10 | 宀 宀 宀 宇 宇 家 家 家 | 宀, 豕(shǐ, *pig*) | | 宀 豕 | |

家: A pig lives under a roof: family. A pig was a must in traditional Chinese households, as pork is the most common meat for Chinese.

4. 彳

彳 is called the double human radical. It is used as the left part in a compound character of a left-right structure. The compound characters in this chapter that contain this radical are 行, 很, and 得.

| Character | Basic Meaning | No. of Str. | Stroke Order | Mean. Clue | Phon. Clue | Compo-nents | Struct-ure |
|---|---|---|---|---|---|---|---|
| 行 xíng | all right | 6 | 丿 彡 彳 行 行 | | | 彳 亍 | |
| 很 hěn | very | 9 | 彳 很 很 很 很 很 很 | | 艮 gěn | 彳 艮 | |
| 得 děi | must | 11 | 彳 得 得 得 得 | | | 彳 日 寸 | |

## EXERCISES

### I. Character Exercises

1. **Add one or more strokes to the following characters to form a new character:**

十 ________ 女 ________ 也 ________ 人 ________

2. **Write the fourth stroke for each of the following characters:**

她 ________ 要 ________ 兄 ________ 份 ________

姓 ________ 字 ________ 画 ________ 哥 ________

3. **Write the third stroke for each of the following characters:**

电 ________ 半 ________ 弟 ________ 母 ________ 共 ________

4. **Write the Pinyin for the following characters, and then put the phonetic element of that character in the parentheses.**

字: ______________ (　　　)　　什: ______________ (　　　)

5. **Add the same radical to each character in the set to make different characters:**

? + 马, 且, 未 → (　　　), (　　　), (　　　)

? + 马, 牙, 尼, 艾 → (　　　), (　　　), (　　　), (　　　)

6. **Solve the character riddles:**

a. Take half of "you" and half of "she." Who is it? ________________.

b. One plus one is not two but ________________.

c. One minus one is not zero but ________________.

7. **Write the characters for the following:**

fùmǔ zìxíngchē jiěmèi yígòng āiya

______________________________________________

## II. Vocabulary Exercises

1. **Add one or more characters to the following to form a word or phrase, then make a sentence with each of the new words/phrases:**

吗: ______________________________________________

妈: ______________________________________________

分: ______________________________________________

份: ______________________________________________

## III. Structure Exercises

1. **Rearrange the elements of each of the following entries to make a grammatical sentence.**

a. 自行车 得 我们 买

b. de 我 真 小人书 好kàn 妹妹

c. 一共 人 家 八 yǒu 他 口

2. **Introduce your family briefly, then write one or two sentences in Chinese characters about each of your family members.**

______________________________________________

______________________________________________

______________________________________________

______________________________________________

3. **Make a sentence with each of the following words:**

告诉: ______________________________

兄弟姐妹: ______________________________

父母: ______________________________

4. **Complete the passage using appropriate characters, one character per blank.**

我 ____ 王，jiào 兰兰。我家 yǒu四 ____ ____，bàba，____ ____、哥哥 hé 我。____ méi.yǒu ____ ____，____ ____，____ méi.yǒu弟弟。我哥哥shì大xué.生。他 ____ gāo，zuì ài kàn 书，hái ài xiě ____。我shì中xué.生，我 ____ ài kàn书，可.shì 我 ài kàn ____ shì。

5. **Translate the following sentences into Chinese, using Chinese characters for learned words:**

a. The magazine is $5.50, and the children's book is $12.00. Altogether it's $17.50.

______________________________

b. There are a lot of people, more than two hundred sixty thousand.

______________________________

c. My little brother has three and a half dollars.

______________________________

d. Chinese bicycles are quite good.

______________________________

e. How many are there in your family?

______________________________

f. He told me that he would buy that work of fiction.

______________________________

g. There are six people (who) want to buy that dictionary.

______________________________________________

h. I have altogether four older sisters.

______________________________________________

## Supplementary Reading

### Reading 1

大西：文生，你家yǒu什么人？

文生：Bàba、妈妈、一个姐姐、两个妹妹、一个哥哥、一个弟弟hé我。

大西：你家人dōu会说中文吗？

文生：他们dōu会说中文。你yǒu几个兄弟姐妹？

大西：我只yǒu一个弟弟。

文生：你弟弟会说中文吗？

大西：他只说Yīng文。

#### COMPREHENSION QUESTIONS

1. 文生yǒu几个兄弟姐妹？

______________________________________________

2. 文生de兄弟姐妹会说中文吗？

______________________________________________

3. 大西yǒu几个兄弟姐妹？

______________________________________________

## Reading 2

中本一也买de nèi liàng日本车不便宜，可.shì他说不guì。他说好de日本车一liàng要三、四万kuài qián。他de只要一万kuài qián。他买de车真不guì。

### COMPREHENSION QUESTIONS

1. 中本一也de nèi liàng车duōshǎo qián?

______________________________

2. 中本一也说他de车guì不guì?

______________________________

## Character Practice

| 万 | 万 | | | | | | | | |
|---|---|---|---|---|---|---|---|---|---|
| 口 | 口 | | | | | | | | |
| 车 | 车 | | | | | | | | |
| 父 | 父 | | | | | | | | |
| 半 | 半 | | | | | | | | |
| 母 | 母 | | | | | | | | |

电 电

自 自

买 买

画 画

兄 兄

份 份

告 告

呀 呀

诉 诉

哎 哎

便 便

哥 哥

分 分

| 兰 | 兰 | | | | | | | | |
|---|---|---|---|---|---|---|---|---|---|
| 共 | 共 | | | | | | | | |
| 弟 | 弟 | | | | | | | | |
| 典 | 典 | | | | | | | | |
| 她 | 她 | | | | | | | | |
| 妈 | 妈 | | | | | | | | |
| 好 | 好 | | | | | | | | |
| 姓 | 姓 | | | | | | | | |
| 姐 | 姐 | | | | | | | | |
| 妹 | 妹 | | | | | | | | |
| 要 | 要 | | | | | | | | |
| 字 | 字 | | | | | | | | |

| 宜 | 宜 | | | | | | | | |
|---|---|---|---|---|---|---|---|---|---|
| 家 | 家 | | | | | | | | |
| 行 | 行 | | | | | | | | |
| 很 | 很 | | | | | | | | |
| 得 | 得 | | | | | | | | |

# CHAPTER SEVEN

# 第　七　课

**Text**

快要吃午饭了，我真饿，可.shì 不想做饭。我想qù 中.guó 饭馆儿吃小吃，再喝一diǎn儿酒。中.guó 小吃很好吃，可.shì 不好做。兰兰说她也很饿，她也要qù 吃午饭，可.shì 她想吃日本cài，喝冰水，喝可口可乐。兰兰de伯伯hé伯母shì一家日本饭馆儿de lǎobǎn，生意很忙，客人也不shǎo。他们饭馆儿de cài很好吃，可.shì 他们de咖啡不好喝。他们以前也卖酒，xiànzài不卖了。兰兰还说她知道伯伯不会要我们de qián，他很xǐ.huān请客。我们不必客气，也不必送他东西，没关xi，他shì兰兰de伯伯。可.shì伯伯xǐ.huān说汉语，我们qù他de饭馆儿吃饭得说汉语。太好了！ 我会说一diǎn儿汉语，我也xǐ.huān说汉语，我还会xiě几个汉字。

## 生词 New Words

| | | |
|---|---|---|
| 快(要)……了 | kuài (yào)...le | (Pat) about to... |
| 吃 | chī | (V) eat, consume |
| 午饭 | wǔfàn | (N) lunch |
| 饿 | è | (SV) be hungry |
| 想 | xiǎng | (V) think; want to |
| 做 | zuò | (V) do, take the role of |
| 饭馆儿 | fànguǎnr | (PW) restaurant (Cl -家) |
| 小吃 | xiǎochī | (N) snack, refreshment, simple dish |
| 再 | zài | (Adv) again; additionally |
| 喝 | hē | (V) drink |
| 一diǎn儿 | yìdiǎnr | (Q) a bit, a little |
| 酒 | jiǔ | (N) liquor |
| 好吃 | hǎochī | (SV) be delicious |
| 好做 | hǎozuò | (SV) be easy to do |
| <u>兰兰</u> | <u>Lánlan</u> | (N) a personal name |
| 她 | tā | (Pr) she, her |
| 要 | yào | (Aux) going to; will, must, should |
| 冰水 | bīngshuǐ | (N) ice water |
| 可乐 | kělè | cola; Coke (Cl -*guàn* 罐, -*píng* 瓶) |
| <u>可口可乐</u> | <u>Kěkǒu Kělè</u> | (N) Coca-Cola (Cl -*guàn* 罐, -*píng* 瓶) |
| 伯伯 | bóbo | (N) uncle (father's elder brother) |
| 伯母 | bómǔ | (N) aunt (wife of father's elder brother) |
| 家 | -jiā | (Cl) (for businesses) |
| 生意 | shēng.yì | (N) (commercial) business |
| 忙 | máng | (SV) be busy |
| 客人 | kèrén | (N) guest; shop/restaurant customer |
| 卖 | mài | (V) sell |
| 咖啡 | kāfēi | (N) coffee |
| 好喝 | hǎohē | (SV) be delicious to drink |
| 以前 | yǐqián | (TW) formerly, before |
| 了 | le | (P) (indicates a new situation) |
| 还 | hái | (Adv) also, additionally |
| 知道 | zhī.dào | (V) know, know of, know that |
| 请客 | qǐng kè | (VO) to treat someone to food or entertainment |
| 不必 | búbì | (Aux) need not, not have to |
| 客气 | kèqi | (SV) be polite |

| | | |
|---|---|---|
| 送 | sòng | (V) escort, deliver; present, give |
| 东西 | dōngxi | (N) thing (physical) |
| 没关xi | méi guānxi | (Ex) Never mind. It doesn't matter. |
| 汉语 | Hànyǔ | (N) Chinese (language) |
| 太 | tài | (SV) overly, too |
| 汉字 | hànzì | (N) Chinese character(s) |

COMPREHENSION QUESTIONS

**Read the text of this chapter and answer the following questions.**

1. 兰兰de bàba shì一家饭馆儿de lǎobǎn, duì吗?

_______________

2. Zhè家饭馆儿卖什么?

_______________

3. 兰兰de伯伯只说日本话，shì吗?

_______________

4. 饭馆儿de生意不忙，客人也不少，duì吗?

_______________

## Writing Help

### Independent Characters

| Character | Basic Meaning | No. of Str. | Stroke Order | Radical | Compo-nents | Struct-ure |
|---|---|---|---|---|---|---|
| 了 le | (particle) | 2 | 了 | 乙 | 了 | □ |
| *午 wǔ | noon | 4 | 丿 𠂉 午 | 丿 | 丿 干 | □ |
| 水 shuǐ | water | 4 | 亅 才 水 | 水 | 水 | □ |
| 气(氣) qì | air | 4 | 𠂉 ⺈ 气 | 气 | 气(⺈ 乁) | □ |
| *必 bì | surely | 5 | 丶 心 心 必 必 | 心 | 心 丿 | □ |

| | | | | | | |
|---|---|---|---|---|---|---|
| 乐(樂) lè | happy | 5 | 𠂊 𠂉 乐 | 丿 | 𠂊 ⺊ 小 | |
| 东(東) dōng | east | 5 | 一 左 东 | 一 | 东 | |

## Compound Characters

The new compound characters in this chapter with radicals already learned are 吃, 关, 伯, 知, 咖, 卖, 前, 客, 请, 做, 啡, and 喝.

| Character | Basic Meaning | No. of Str. | Stroke Order | Radical | Mean. Clue | Phon. Clue | Compo-nents | Struct-ure |
|---|---|---|---|---|---|---|---|---|
| 吃 chī | to eat | 6 | 口 吖 吃 | 口 | 口 | 乞 qǐ | 口 乞(𠂉 乙) | |
| 关(關) guān | to close | 6 | 丷 兰 关 | 八 | | | 丷 天 | |
| *伯 bó | father's elder brother | 7 | 亻 伯 | 亻 | 亻 | 白 bái | 亻 白 | |
| 知 zhī | to know | 8 | 𠂉 矢 知 | 口 | 口 | 矢 shǐ | 矢 口 | |
| *咖 kā | Coffee (咖啡) | 8 | 口 叻 叻 咖 | 口 | 口 | 加 jiā | 口 力 口 | |
| 卖(賣) mài | to sell | 8 | 十 卖 | 十 | 十 | 买 mǎi | 十 买(乛 头) | |
| *前 qián | front | 9 | 䒑 䒑 前 前 前 前 | 八 | | | 丷 一 月 刂 | |
| 客 kè | guest | 9 | 宀 穸 夕 安 客 | 宀 | 宀 | 各 gè | 宀 各(夂 口) | |
| 请(請) qǐng | to invite | 10 | 讠 讠 讠 讠 讠 请 | 讠 | 讠 | 青 qīng | 讠 ⺻ 月 | |
| 做 zuò | to do/ make | 11 | 亻 什 估 做 做 | 亻 | 亻 | | 亻 十 口 攵 | |
| *啡 fēi | coffee (咖啡) | 11 | 口 미 叫 叫 叫 唰 唰 啡 啡 | 口 | 口 | 非 fēi | 口 非 | |
| 喝 hē | to drink | 12 | 口 吅 吅 喝 喝 喝 | 口 | 口 | 曷 hé | 口 曰 勾 | |

## Radicals

The radicals of focus in this chapter are 冫, 忄/心, 饣, 氵, and 辶.

### 1. 冫

This radical is used as the left part in a compound character. It is used to indicate coldness or ice.

| Character | Basic Meaning | No. of Str. | Stroke Order | Mean. Clue | Phon. Clue | Compo-nents | Struct-ure |
|---|---|---|---|---|---|---|---|
| 冰 bīng | ice | 6 | 冫 冰 | 冫 水 | | 冫 水 | |

### 2. 忄/心

心 is the image of the heart in ancient Chinese. 心 *xīn* can be used as an independent character or as a radical to be put underneath a character. *Xīn* takes the form of 忄 when it used as the left part in a compound character. This radical involves things or activities that are connected with a person's mind. The compound characters in this chapter that contain this radical are 忙, 快, 想, and 意.

| Character | Basic Meaning | No. of Str. | Stroke Order | Mean. Clue | Phon. Clue | Compo-nents | Struct-ure |
|---|---|---|---|---|---|---|---|
| 忙 máng | busy | 6 | 丶 丷 忄 忄丶 忙 忙 | 忄, 亡(wáng, *death*) | 亡 wáng | 忄 亡 | |
| 快 kuài | quick | 7 | 忄 忄フ 快 | 忄 | 夬 guài | 忄 夬 | |
| 想 xiǎng | to think, want | 13 | 木 相 相 想 想 想 | 心 | 相 xiāng | 木 目 心 | |
| *意 yì | idea, wish, meaning | 13 | 亠 立 立 音 意 | 心 | | 立 日 心 | |

忙: When you are busy, your heart is dead.

### 3. 饣

As an independent character, it means "food" and is written as 食 *shí*. As a radical, it is used as the left part in a compound character and is written as 饣. It means food or things related to cuisine. The compound characters in this chapter that contain this radical are 饭, 馆, and 饿.

| Character | Basic Meaning | No. of Str. | Stroke Order | Mean. Clue | Phon. Clue | Components | Struct-ure |
|---|---|---|---|---|---|---|---|
| 饭(飯) fàn | cooked rice, meal | 7 | ノ ⺈ 饣 饣 饣 饭 | 饣 | 反 fǎn | 饣 反 | |

| | | | | | | | |
|---|---|---|---|---|---|---|---|
| *馆(館) guǎn | place for public use | 11 | 饣 饣宀饣宀饣宀 馆馆馆 | 饣 | 官 guān | 饣 官(宀㠯) | ⿰ |
| 饿(餓) è | hungry | 10 | 饣 饿 | 饣 | 我 (usually indicates the sound 'è' when used as a phonetic) | 饣我 | ⿰ |

4. 氵

This radical is used as the left part in a compound character, and it means water or things related to water. The compound characters in this chapter that contain this radical are 汉, 没, and 酒.

| Character | Basic Meaning | No. of Str. | Stroke Order | Mean. Clue | Phon. Clue | Compo-nents | Struct-ure |
|---|---|---|---|---|---|---|---|
| *汉(漢) hàn | Chinese nationality; name of a river | 5 | 丶 汈 汉 | 氵 | | 氵又 | ⿰ |
| 没 méi | not | 7 | 氵 氵⺇ 氵几 没 | | | 氵几 又 | ⿰(⿱) |
| 酒 jiǔ | wine, alcohol | 10 | 氵 洒洒酒 | 氵 | 酉 yǒu | 氵酉 | ⿰ |

*Note the difference between the right top part of 没 (几) and 几 in writing.

5. 辶

辶 is used in compound characters to indicate things related to a road or walking. The compound characters in this chapter that contain this radical are 还, 送, and 道.

| Character | Basic Meaning | No. of Str. | Stroke Order | Mean. Clue | Phon. Clue | Components | Struct-ure |
|---|---|---|---|---|---|---|---|
| 还(還) hái | also, additionally | 7 | 不 丶不 还 还 | | | 辶 不 | ⿺ |
| 送 sòng | to give as a gift, to see someone off | 9 | 关 送 | 关(guān, *close (gate)*) | | 辶 关(丷 天) | ⿺ |
| 道 dào | principle, way | 12 | 丷 䒑 首 道 道 | 辶, 首 (shǒu, *head*) | | 辶 首(丷一自) | ⿺ |

## EXERCISES

### I. Character Exercises

1. Add one or more strokes to the following characters to form a new character:

了 ________ 水 ________ 关 ________ 小 ________

2. Find independent characters you have learned hidden in each of the following characters:

客 ________ 午 ________ 关 ________ 要 ________

3. In the parentheses below write the component common to all three given characters:

汉, 饭, 支, (      )

4. Write the Pinyin for the following characters, and put the phonetic element of that character in the parentheses.

卖: ______________ (      ) 字: ______________ (      )

5. Add a radical to each of the following to make different characters:

(    ) + 不, 关 → (      ), (      )

(    ) + 反, 我, 官 → (      ), (      ), (      )

6. Write as many characters you can think of that you have learned and that use the 口 radical:

______________________________________________

7. Correct the errors in the following characters:

泳 䜣 怏

8. Correct the wrong characters used in the following:

送他乐西 → ________

饭关儿不太。→ ________

9. **Write the characters for the following Pinyin:**

   a. Qǐng kè, chī fàn bù kě.yǐ méi jiǔ.

   ______________________________

   b. Wǒ gēge hěn máng.

   ______________________________

## II. Vocabulary Exercises

1. **Form as many words or phrases as possible by using the characters given below:**

   a. 吃 → ______________________________

   b. 喝 → ______________________________

   c. 饭 → ______________________________

   d. 好 → ______________________________

   e. 很 → ______________________________

   f. 汽 → ______________________________

   g. 客 → ______________________________

   h. 可 → ______________________________

   i. 知 → ______________________________

   j. 汉 → ______________________________

   k. 以 → ______________________________

## III. Structure Exercises

1. **Rearrange the elements in each of the items below to make a grammatical sentence.**

a. 酒， 不， 王， 了， 喝， 先生

→ ______________________________

b. 生意， 以前， 不， 他， 做

→ ______________________________

c. 汉语， 我， 说， 弟弟， 了， 会

→ ______________________________

d. 好吃， 卖， 小吃， 饭馆儿， 很， de

→ ______________________________

e. 酒， 不， 只， 喝， 咖啡， 我， 喝， 日本

→ ______________________________

2. **Fill in the blanks with the most appropriate characters, using one character for each blank.**

王关乐家 ______ ______ yǒu十个人：bàba，妈妈，一个哥哥，______ 个姐姐，三个弟弟，一个妹妹 hé他。兄弟姐妹一半 shì nánde，一 ______ shì女 de。王关乐de妈妈 ______ de日本小吃真好 ______。大姐姐做 de冰咖啡 ______ 很好 ______。他们一家人dōu很客气，很xǐ.huān请客。王关乐______我 qù他们家吃午饭。我送他妈妈______ ______东西______?

## Supplementary Reading

### Reading 1

文汉：小兰，zhè xiē 中.guó小吃shì你做de吗?

小兰：Shì。

文汉：真好吃。

小兰：好吃jiù duō吃一diǎnr。

文汉：真de? Nà，我jiù不客气了。

小兰：没问tí。Néng吃duōshǎo jiù 吃duōshǎo。Bié 客气。

TRUE OR FALSE QUESTIONS

1. 小兰做de中.guó小吃不好吃。(    )

2. 文汉很xǐ.huān吃小兰做de中.guó小吃。(    )

### Reading 2

我很xǐ.huān喝冰水。可shì中.guó人说喝冰水不好。中.guó de 饭馆儿不卖冰水，也不gěi客人冰水。他们gěi客人中.guó chá。中.guó人说喝中.guó chá好。我de Měi.guó péngyǒu 说喝可乐好。你说呢?

COMPREHENSION QUESTIONS

1. 我很xǐ.huān喝什么?

_______________________________________________

2. 中.guó 饭馆儿gěi客人喝什么?

_______________________________________________

## Character Practice

| | | | | | | | | | |
|---|---|---|---|---|---|---|---|---|---|
| 了 | 了 | | | | | | | | |
| 午 | 午 | | | | | | | | |
| 水 | 水 | | | | | | | | |
| 气 | 气 | | | | | | | | |
| 必 | 必 | | | | | | | | |
| 乐 | 乐 | | | | | | | | |
| 东 | 东 | | | | | | | | |
| 吃 | 吃 | | | | | | | | |
| 关 | 关 | | | | | | | | |
| 伯 | 伯 | | | | | | | | |
| 知 | 知 | | | | | | | | |
| 咖 | 咖 | | | | | | | | |
| 卖 | 卖 | | | | | | | | |

| | | | | | | | | | |
|---|---|---|---|---|---|---|---|---|---|
| 前 | 前 | | | | | | | | |
| 客 | 客 | | | | | | | | |
| 请 | 请 | | | | | | | | |
| 做 | 做 | | | | | | | | |
| 啡 | 啡 | | | | | | | | |
| 喝 | 喝 | | | | | | | | |
| 冰 | 冰 | | | | | | | | |
| 忙 | 忙 | | | | | | | | |
| 快 | 快 | | | | | | | | |
| 想 | 想 | | | | | | | | |
| 意 | 意 | | | | | | | | |
| 饭 | 饭 | | | | | | | | |
| 馆 | 馆 | | | | | | | | |

| 饿 | 饿 | | | | | | | | |
|---|---|---|---|---|---|---|---|---|---|
| 汉 | 汉 | | | | | | | | |
| 没 | 没 | | | | | | | | |
| 酒 | 酒 | | | | | | | | |
| 还 | 还 | | | | | | | | |
| 送 | 送 | | | | | | | | |
| 道 | 道 | | | | | | | | |

# CHAPTER EIGHT
# 第 八 课

**Text**

这是我de好朋友，他de名字叫毛乐生。小毛是法国人。他很有意思，xǐ欢买地道de法国东西。他chuān de那双法国皮xié很guì，四百duō块qián一双。我只买便宜de皮xié，我de旧皮xié都只有八十块qián一双。有人说小毛很cōng明，可是我说他真笨。你kàn，他chuān很guì de法国皮xié，可是没有qián买吃de东西了。他xiàn在不吃早饭了，只喝牛奶，午饭也不吃了，只喝一diǎn儿汤。不吃饭真不容yì。我问他饿不饿，他说没问tí。我真不明白，他不néng不吃东西吧。我想请他吃晚饭。他很xǐ欢地道de法国东西，可是不xǐ欢吃法国cài。对了，他xǐ欢吃中国cài，我请小毛去我叔叔de中国饭馆儿吃晚饭。小毛太饿了。他没有吃早饭，没有吃午饭，只吃晚饭。他说那家饭馆儿做de cài太好吃了。他xiàn在不饿了，吃饱了。我叔叔还送小毛一支中国毛笔，一本中国地图呢。

## 生词 New Words

| | | |
|---|---|---|
| 这 | zhè | (Pr) this |
| 是 | shì | (V) be, is, am, are |
| 朋友 | péng.yǒu | (N) friend |
| 名字 | míng.zì | (N) name |
| 叫 | jiào | (V) be called, call |
| 毛乐生 | Máo Lèshēng | (N) a personal name |
| 法国 | Fǎ.guó | (PW) France |
| 有意思 | yǒuyìsi | (SV) be interesting |
| xǐ欢 | xǐ.huān | (V) like, prefer, enjoy, like to |
| 地道 | dì.dào | (SV) be authentic |
| 那 | nà | (Pr) that |
| 双 | -shuāng | (Cl) a pair of |
| 皮xié | píxié | (N) leather shoes (Cl -双) |
| 块 | -kuài | (Cl) dollars |
| 都 | dōu | (Adv) in all cases |
| 旧 | jiù | (SV) be old (of objects, *not* living things) |
| 有 | yǒu | (V) have, has |
| 有人 | yǒu rén | (Ph) somebody |
| cōng明 | cōng.míng | (SV) be intelligent, be smart |
| 可是 | kě.shì | (Conj) but, however |
| 笨 | bèn | (SV) be stupid |
| 没(有) | méi(.yǒu) | (V) not have, has not |
| xiàn在 | xiànzài | (TW) presently, now |
| 早饭 | zǎofàn | (N) breakfast |
| 牛奶 | niúnǎi | (N) milk |

| | | |
|---|---|---|
| 汤 | tāng | (N) soup |
| 容yì | róng.yì | (SV) be easy |
| 没问tí | méi wèntí | (Ex) not a problem |
| 明白 | míngbai | (V) understand |
| 吧 | ba | (P) (indicates an assumption) |
| 请 | qǐng | (V) please; treat; hire; invite |
| 晚饭 | wǎnfàn | (N) supper |
| 对 | duì | (SV) be correct |
| 去 | qù | (V) go to (a place) |
| 叔叔 | shūshu | (N) uncle (father's younger brother) |
| 吃饱了 | chībǎole | (Ex) to be full (from eating) |
| 毛笔 | máobǐ | (N) writing brush (see Chapter 5) |
| 地图 | dìtú | (N) map (Cl -*zhāng* 张); atlas (Cl -本) |
| 呢 | ne | (P) (used at the end of a sentence for emphasis) |

## COMPREHENSION QUESTIONS

**Read the text of this chapter and answer the following questions.**

1. Shéi是我de好朋友?

___

2. 他是nǎ国人?

___

3. 他xǐ欢什么?

___

4. 他chuān什么皮xié?

___

5. 小毛很有qián，是吗？

________________________________________

6. 我wèishénme (why) 请小毛吃晚饭？

________________________________________

7. 我们去nǎ儿吃晚饭？

________________________________________

8. 小毛 xǐ欢吃什么？

________________________________________

9. 我叔叔送小毛什么？

________________________________________

## Writing Help

### Independent Characters

| Character | Basic Meaning | No. of Str. | Stroke Order | Radical | Components | Structure |
|---|---|---|---|---|---|---|
| 牛 niú | ox | 4 | ノ 𠂉 牛 | 牛 | 牛 | ☐ |
| 白 bái | white; surname | 5 | 白 | 白 | 白 | ☐ |
| 皮 pí | leather, skin | 5 | 一 厂 广 皮 | 皮 | 皮 | ☐ |

## Compound Characters

The new compound characters in this chapter with radicals you have learned are 叫, 奶, 名, 汤, 吧, 这, 法, 饱, 思, and 容.

| Character | Basic Meaning | No. of Str. | Stroke Order | Radical | Mean. Clue | Phon. Clue | Compo-nents | Struct-ure |
|---|---|---|---|---|---|---|---|---|
| 叫 jiào | to call | 5 | 口 口ㄴ 叫 | 口 | 口 | Pinyin 'j' is written as '丩' in earlier version | 口 丩 | |
| 奶 nǎi | milk, grandma* | 5 | 女 奶 奶 | 女 | 女 | 乃 nǎi | 女 乃 | |
| *名 míng | name | 6 | ノ 夕 夕 名 | 口 | 口 | | 夕 口 | |
| 汤(湯) tāng | soup | 6 | 氵 汤 汤 汤 | 氵 | 氵 | 𠃓 (indicating sound of -ang) | 氵 𠃓 | |
| 吧 ba | (partical) | 7 | 口 口 口 口 吧 | 口 | 口 | 巴 bā | 口 巴 | |
| 这(這) zhè | this | 7 | 文 这 | 辶 | | | 辶 文 | |
| *法 fǎ | method, law | 8 | 氵 汢 法 | 氵 | | | 氵 去 | |
| 饱(飽) bǎo | to have eaten one's fill | 8 | 饣 饣 饣 饱 | 饣 | 饣 | 包 bāo | 饣 包 | |
| *思 sī | to think | 9 | 田 思 | 心 | 心 | | 田 心 | |
| *容 róng | face; appearance | 10 | 宀 穴 容 容 | 宀 | 宀, 口 | | 宀 八 八 口 | |

容: To remember this character, think of it as the facial features of a person: with a hat on top, two eyebrows below it, then two sides of a very bushy moustache, and finally a mouth at the bottom.

## Radicals

The radicals of focus in this chapter are 又, 阝, 口, 土, 日, 月, and 竹.

### 1. 又

As an independent character, 又 *yòu* means "again." As a radical, it indicates a hand. It is used in characters related to "hand." The compound characters in this chapter that contain this radical are 双, 友, 对, 欢, and 叔.

| Character | Basic Meaning | No. of Str. | Stroke Order | Mean. Clue | Phon. Clue | Components | Structure |
|---|---|---|---|---|---|---|---|
| *双(雙) shuāng | pair | 4 | 又 双 | 又(yòu, *again*), 又 | | 又 又 | |
| *友 yǒu | friend, friendly | 4 | 一 ナ 友 | ナ | 又 yòu | ナ 又 | |
| 对(對) duì | correct | 5 | 又 又一 对 对 | | | 又 寸 | |
| *欢(歡) huān | happy | 6 | 又 又ケ 欢 | | | 又 欠(⺈人) | |
| 叔 shū | father's younger brother | 8 | ⺊ 未 叔 | | | 上 小 又 | |

### 2. 阝

阝, as an image of an ear, can be used as either a right or a left part of a character. In this chapter 阝 is only used as a right-hand radical. The compound characters in this chapter that contain this radical are 那 and 都.

| Character | Basic Meaning | No. of Str. | Stroke Order | Mean. Clue | Phon. Clue | Components | Structure |
|---|---|---|---|---|---|---|---|
| 那 nà | that | 6 | ㇆ ヨ ヨ 月 那 那 | | | 冄 阝 | |
| 都 dōu | all | 10 | 土 耂 者 都 | | | 者(土 丿 日)阝 | |

## 3. 囗

The radical 囗 is found on the outside of a character to indicate enclosure, as in the border of a nation, a picture frame, and so on. The compound characters in this chapter that contain this radical are 图 and 国.

| Character | Basic Meaning | No. of Str. | Stroke Order | Mean. Clue | Phon. Clue | Components | Structure |
|---|---|---|---|---|---|---|---|
| 图(圖) tú | picture | 8 | 冂 冈 图 图 图 | 囗, 冬(dōng, *winter*) | | 囗 夂 ⺀ | ⿴ |
| 国(國) guó | country | 8 | 冂 国 国 国 | 囗, 玉 (yù, *jade*), indicating the emperor's jade seal | | 囗 玉 | ⿴ |

图: A winter scene in a frame.

## 4. 土

土 (*tǔ*) can be both an independent character and a radical. It means "earth" or "soil" as an independent character. As a radical it is usually used to form characters related to the earth or soil. The compound characters in this chapter that contain this radical are 去, 地, 块, and 在.

| Character | Basic Meaning | No. of Str. | Stroke Order | Mean. Clue | Phon. Clue | Components | Structure |
|---|---|---|---|---|---|---|---|
| 去 qù | to go (to a place) | 5 | 土 去 | | | 土 厶 | ⿱ |
| 地 dì | ground, land | 6 | 一 十 土 地 | 土, 也 | | 土 也 | ⿰ |
| *块(塊) kuài | lump of earth | 7 | 土 圴 圵 坱 块 | 土 | 夬 guài | 土 夬(⺈ 大) | ⿰ |
| 在 zài | be present | 6 | 一 ナ 才 才 在 在 | | | 才 土 | ⿸ |

地: In classical Chinese "地, 土也" means "Earth is soil."

5. 日

日 can be both an independent character and a radical. The character 日 (*rì*) is the image of the sun. As a radical it is used in characters related to the sun and time. The compound characters in this chapter that contain this radical are 旧, 早, 明, 是, and 晚.

| Character | Basic Meaning | No. of Str. | Stroke Order | Mean. Clue | Phon. Clue | Components | Struct-ure |
|---|---|---|---|---|---|---|---|
| 旧(舊) jiù | old | 5 | 丨 旧 | 日 | | 丨 日 | |
| 早 zǎo | early, morning | 6 | 日 早 | 日, 十 | | 日 十 | |
| *明 míng | bright, tomorrow | 8 | 日 明 | 日, 月( yuè, *moon*) | | 日 月 | |
| 是 shì | to be | 9 | 日 旦 早 早 昇 是 | 日, 正(zhèng, *correct*) | | 日 𤴓 | |
| 晚 wǎn | later, evening | 12 | 日 日′ 日ク 日ク 日ク 日免 晚 | 日 | 免 miǎn | 日 免 (ク 口 儿) | |

早: It looks like the sun (日) just above the trees: early morning.
是: Anything under the sun (日) is certain, correct (正). Now it means "to be."

6. 月

月 *yuè* means "moon" or "month" when it is an independent character. As a radical 月 is used to form characters related to flesh, meat, or the moon. The compound characters in this chapter that contain this radical are 有 and 朋.

| Character | Basic Meaning | No. of Str. | Stroke Order | Mean. Clue | Phon. Clue | Compo-nents | Struct-ure |
|---|---|---|---|---|---|---|---|
| 有 yǒu | to have | 6 | ナ 有 | ナ( *hand*) | | ナ 月 | |
| *朋 péng | friend | 8 | 月 朋 | 月, 月(two side by side) | | 月 月 | |

有: To have meat in hand is 有, "to have."

## 7. ⺮

⺮ can be both an independent character and a radical. As an independent character, 竹 (*zhú*) means "bamboo." As a radical, it is usually put on the top of the character to indicate a relationship to bamboo. The compound characters in this chapter that contain this radical are 笔 and 笨.

| Character | Basic Meaning | No. of Str. | Stroke Order | Mean. Clue | Phon. Clue | Compo-nents | Struct-ure |
|---|---|---|---|---|---|---|---|
| 笔(筆) bǐ | pen | 10 | 丿 𠂉 𠂉 𠂉丿 𥫗 ⺮ 笔 | 竹, 毛 | | ⺮ 毛 | ⿱ |
| 笨 bèn | stupid | 11 | ⺮ 笨 | 竹 | 本 | ⺮ 木 一 | ⿱ |

笔: The writing brush, an Chinese ancient writing tool, is made of a bamboo tube on the top with animal hair at the bottom.

笨: The bamboo radical indicates a blocked brain (stupidity), like the structure inside of bamboo.

## EXERCISES

### I. Character Exercises

1. **Add more stroke(s) to the character on the left side to form a new character that has at least one fewer stroke than the character to its right:**

一 (　　) 土 (　　) 玉 (　　)

一 (　　) 日 (　　)

2. **Find independent characters you have learned hidden in the following characters:**

笔 ________ 容 ________ 早 ________

3. **Add a radical to make different characters, then form a word or a sentence with the new character:**

也 → a. ______________________________

b. ______________________________

c. ______________________________

4. **Write in the parentheses the component that is common to all of the following characters:**

白, 晚, 明, 意, 都 → (        )

5. **Write as many characters you have learned as you can think of that are vertically symmetrical that is, they can be turned left to right without changing the meaning.**

**Example:** 本

______________________________

6. **Solve the character riddles:**

a. 一半朋一半友: __________

b. 一口 bites off the tail of 牛: __________

c. Although it has many mouths, it has only one heart. If you want to guess what it is, you need to think it over: __________

7. **Write all the characters you have learned that you can think of using the 氵 radical:**

______________________________

## II. Vocabulary Exercises

1. **Complete the following sentences in Chinese characters:**

a. Bàba de哥哥是我de __________。

b. Bàba哥哥de太太是我de __________。

c. Bàba de弟弟是我de __________。

d. 我是个女hái子，我是我父母de __________。

e. 我哥哥hé弟弟是我父母de __________。

III. Structure Exercises

**Rearrange the elements in each of the entries to make a grammatical sentence.**

1. 一，地图，de，送，我，大，他，中国，本，很

→ ______________________________

2. 法国，de，地道，太，了，不，便宜，东西

→ ______________________________

3. 书，好kàn，书，有de，很，有意思，有de，不

→ ______________________________

4. 你，这，de，朋友，吧，是，名字

→ ______________________________

## Supplementary Reading

### Reading 1

Lǎobǎn: 买自行车吗?

万文生: 这liàng自行车 duōshǎo qián?

Lǎobǎn: 八百块qián.

万文生: 六百，行吗?

Lǎobǎn: 不行。七百吧!

万文生: 太guì了。两liàng一千二zěnme yàng?

Lǎobǎn: 一千三吧!

万文生: 太guì了。不买了。

Lǎobǎn： 好吧！Jiù卖你一千二。

万文生： 好，gěi 你一千五。

Lǎobǎn： Zhǎo 你三百。

COMPREHENSION QUESTIONS

1. 万文生买几liàng自行车?

______________________________

2. 万文生买de自行车duōshǎo qián一liàng?

______________________________

## Reading 2

### 买东西

我买píngguǒ。我问lǎobǎn píngguǒ一jīn duōshǎo qián。他说："一块八毛五。"他问我要几jīn。我说太guì了。我问他一块五毛一jīn卖不卖。他说我得买五jīn。我说："好吧！"我gěi他七块五。你说对不对?

TRUE OR FALSE QUESTIONS

1. 一jīn píngguǒ 卖一块八毛五。(　　　)

2. 七jīn píngguǒ 卖七块五。(　　　)

## Character Practice

| 牛 | 牛 | | | | | | | | |
|---|---|---|---|---|---|---|---|---|---|
| 白 | 白 | | | | | | | | |
| 皮 | 皮 | | | | | | | | |
| 叫 | 叫 | | | | | | | | |
| 奶 | 奶 | | | | | | | | |
| 名 | 名 | | | | | | | | |
| 汤 | 汤 | | | | | | | | |
| 吧 | 吧 | | | | | | | | |
| 这 | 这 | | | | | | | | |
| 法 | 法 | | | | | | | | |
| 饱 | 饱 | | | | | | | | |
| 思 | 思 | | | | | | | | |

容 容

双 双

友 友

对 对

欢 欢

叔 叔

那 那

都 都

图 图

国 国

去 去

地 地

块 块

| | | | | | | | | | |
|---|---|---|---|---|---|---|---|---|---|
| 在 | 在 | | | | | | | | |
| 旧 | 旧 | | | | | | | | |
| 早 | 早 | | | | | | | | |
| 明 | 明 | | | | | | | | |
| 是 | 是 | | | | | | | | |
| 晚 | 晚 | | | | | | | | |
| 有 | 有 | | | | | | | | |
| 朋 | 朋 | | | | | | | | |
| 笔 | 笔 | | | | | | | | |
| 笨 | 笨 | | | | | | | | |

# CHAPTER NINE
# 第　九　课

**Text**

城lǐ有家有名的大商diàn。那家diàn卖很duō东西，lóu上卖衣fu hé皮xié。那儿有衬衫、汗衫、wài衣、内衣、毛衣、hé牛仔kù，东西都很便宜。你看，我chuān的这件毛衣好看吗？就四十块qián，不guì吧。那儿卖的袜子hé皮xié也很好看。Lóu下大门东边儿卖手biǎo hé眼jìng。那儿的手biǎo不便宜，一千duō块qián一块；眼jìng也不便宜，六百duō块qián一fù。那家商diàn没有便宜的手biǎo hé眼jìng。不要在那儿买手biǎo，也不要买眼jìng。大门西边儿卖书、报、杂志、笔、画报hé地图，都是中国的。大门前边儿卖吃的，喝的东西。你想不想去那儿买东西？你想喝冰牛奶还是喝可乐？ 哎呀！ 我忘了告诉你商diàn在什么地方。商diàn在北京jiē，不nán找。商diàn的老板姓方，叫方宜思。他很高，我认识他。他住我家的右边儿，他的fáng子很大，上边儿有四个fángjiān，下边儿有两个fángjiān。方老板hé他的家人都很忙，他们很shǎo在家。我很xǐ欢去他的商diàn买东西。为什么？ 因为他卖的东西很好呀。你知道我xiàn在要去哪儿吗？ 我要去方老板的商diàn。你要gēn我一块儿去吗？

### 生词 New Words

| | | |
|---|---|---|
| 城 | chéng | (N) city, town |
| 有 | yǒu | (V) there is, there are |
| 有名 | yǒumíng | (SV) be famous |
| 的 | de | (P) (indicates possession, used to join a modifying clause with the noun it modifies) |
| 商diàn | shāngdiàn | (PW) shop; store (Cl -家) |
| lóu上 | lóu.shàng | (PS/PW) upstairs |
| 衣fu | yīfu | (N) clothing (Cl -件) |
| 那儿 | nàr | (PW) there, that place |
| 衬衫 | chènshān | (N) shirt (Cl -件) |
| 汗衫 | hànshān | (N) T-shirt (Cl -件) |
| wài衣 | wàiyī | (N) jacket (Cl -件) |
| 内衣 | nèiyī | (N) underwear (Cl -件) |
| 毛衣 | máoyī | (N) sweater (Cl -件) |
| 牛仔kù | niúzǎikù | (N) denim jeans (Cl -*tiáo* 条) |
| 看 | kàn | (V) look; read |
| 件 | -jiàn | (Cl) (for clothing covering the upper half of the body) |
| 就 | jiù | (Adv) only, just |
| 袜子 | wàzi | (N) socks (Cl -双, "pair"; -*zhī* 只, "single") |
| lóu下 | lóu.xià | (PS/PW) downstairs |
| 大门 | dàmén | (N) main entrance |

| | | |
|---|---|---|
| 东边儿 | dōng.biānr | (PS/PW) the east |
| 手biǎo | shǒubiǎo | (N) watch (Cl -块) |
| 块 | -kuài | (Cl) a piece of (also used for 表) |
| 眼jìng | yǎnjìng | (N) eyeglasses (Cl -副) |
| 六 | liù | (Nu) six |
| 没有 | méi.yǒu | (V) there isn't, there aren't |
| 在 | zài | (CV) at, in |
| 西边儿 | xī.biānr | (PS/PW) the west |
| 报 | bào | (N) newspaper |
| 杂志 | zázhì | (N) magazine (Cl -本 or -份) |
| 笔 | bǐ | (N) pen, writing instrument |
| 画报 | huàbào | (N) illustrated periodical; picture magazine |
| 中国 | Zhōng.guó | (PW) China |
| 前边儿 | qián.biānr | (PS/PW) in front |
| 还是 | hái.shì | (Conj) or |
| 忘了 | wàngle | (V) forget |
| 在 | zài | (V) be located at, be present |
| 地方 | dì.fāng | (PW) place, location |
| 北京 | Běijīng | (PW) capital city of the People's Republic of China |
| 北京jiē | Běijīng jiē | (PW) name of a street |
| 找 | zhǎo | (V) to give change; to look for (something) |
| 老板 | lǎobǎn | (N) boss, owner |
| 方宜思 | Fāng Yísī | (N) a personal name |
| 高 | gāo | (SV) be tall or high |
| 认识 | rènshi | (V) be acquainted with |
| 住 | zhù | (V) reside |
| 右边儿 | yòu.biānr | (PS/PW) the right |
| fáng子 | fángzi | (N) house |
| 上边儿 | shàng.biānr | (PS) above |
| 下边儿 | xià.biānr | (PS/PW) below |
| 家人 | jiārén | (N) family members |
| 为什么? | wèishénme? | (Adv) why? |
| 因为…… | yīn.wèi… | (Pat) because… |
| 呀 | ya | (P) (tells listener he or she really should have known that) |
| 哪儿 | nǎr | (PW) where? |
| 一块儿 | yíkuàir | (Adv) together |

## COMPREHENSION QUESTIONS

**Read the text above and answer the following questions.**

1. 那家有名的商diàn在什么地方?

______________________________

2. 商diàn的lóu上卖什么?

______________________________

3. Lóu下大门东边儿卖的手biǎo便宜吗?

______________________________

4. 商diàn的老板叫什么名字?

______________________________

5. 他住在哪儿?

______________________________

6. 什么地方卖书，报hé 杂志?

______________________________

7. 大门的前边儿卖什么?

______________________________

8. 说说方老板的家。

______________________________

## Writing Help

### Independent Characters

| Character | Basic Meaning | No. of Str. | Stroke Order | Radical | Compo-nents | Struct-ure |
|---|---|---|---|---|---|---|
| 上 shàng | top | 3 | 上 | 一 | 上 | |
| 下 xià | bottom | 3 | 一 丁 下 | 一 | 下 | |
| 门(門) mén | door | 3 | 门 | 门 | 门 | |
| 为(為) wèi | for | 4 | 丶 丿 为 为 | 丶 | 为 | |
| 手 shǒu | hand | 4 | 一 二 三 手 | 手 | 手 | |
| 方 fāng | square; surname | 4 | 亠 亠 方 | 方 | 丶 万 | |
| 内 nèi | inside | 4 | 丨 冂 内 | 冂 | 冂 人 | |
| *衣 yī | clothes | 6 | 亠 衣 衣 | 衣 | 衣 | |
| 老 lǎo | old | 6 | 土 耂 老 老 | 耂 | 土 丿 匕 | |

### Compound Characters

The new compound characters in this chapter with radicals you have learned are 认, 仔, 边, 右, 汗, 因, 件, 住, 识, 志, 忘, 城, and 哪.

| Character | Basic Meaning | No. of Str. | Stroke Order | Radical | Mean. Clue | Phon. Clue | Compo-nents | Struct-ure |
|---|---|---|---|---|---|---|---|---|
| 认(認) rèn | to recognize | 4 | 讠 认 | 讠 | 讠 | 人 | 讠 人 | |
| *仔 zǎi | little boy, son | 5 | 亻 仔 | 亻 | 亻 | 子 | 亻 子 | |
| 边(邊) biān | side | 5 | 力 边 | 辶 | | | 辶 力 | |

| | | | | | | | | |
|---|---|---|---|---|---|---|---|---|
| *右 yòu | right | 5 | 𠂇 右 | 口 | 𠂇 | | 𠂇 口 | |
| 汗 hàn | sweat | 6 | 氵 氵一 汗 | 氵 | 氵 | 干 gàn | 氵 干 | |
| 因 yīn | because | 6 | 口 因 | 口 | | | 口 大 | |
| *件 jiàn | (a classifier) | 6 | 亻 牛 | 亻 | | | 亻 牛 | |
| 住 zhù | to live | 7 | 亻 亻' 亻二 亻干 住 | 亻 | 亻 | 主 zhǔ | 亻 主 | |
| 识(識) shì | to know; to recognize | 7 | 讠 识 | 讠 | 讠 | 只 | 讠 口 八 | |
| *志 zhì | will, determination | 7 | 士 志 | 心 | 心 | 士 shì | 士 心 | |
| 忘 wàng | to forget | 7 | 亡 忘 | 心 | 心 | 亡 wáng | 亡 心 | |
| 城 chéng | city, town | 9 | 扌 圹 圹 坜 城 城 城 | 土 | 土 | 成 chéng | 土 成 | |
| 哪 nǎ | where?; which? | 9 | 口 哪 | 口 | 口 | 那 | 口 𠮷 阝 | |

右: To better remember 右, think of it as showing 𠂇, the image of a hand, taking food to mouth.
件: As a classifier 件 is never used for 人 or 牛.

## Radicals

The new radicals of focus in this chapter are 丨, 亠, 扌, 木, 白, 衤, and 目.

### 1. 丨

What character have you learned using this radical?

| Character | Basic Meaning | No. of Str. | Stroke Order | Mean. Clue | Phon. Clue | Components | Structure |
|---|---|---|---|---|---|---|---|
| 北 běi | north | 5 | 丨 丬 丬 丬' 北 | | | 丬 匕 | |

## 2. 亠

This radical is put on top of a character to indicate coverage. The compound characters in this chapter that contain this radical are 六, 京, 高, 商, and 就.

| Character | Basic Meaning | No. of Str. | Stroke Order | Mean. Clue | Phon. Clue | Components | Structure |
|---|---|---|---|---|---|---|---|
| 六 liù | six | 4 | 亠 八 | | | 亠 八 | |
| *京 jīng | capital | 8 | 亠 古 京 | 亠 | | 亠 口 小 | |
| 高 gāo | tall, high; surname | 10 | 亠 古 高 高 | 亠 | | 亠 口 冂 口 | |
| *商 shāng | commerce; surname | 11 | 亠 亠 产 产 商 | 亠 | | 亠 丷 冂 八 口 | |
| 就 jiù | only, just | 12 | 京 京 就 就 就 | | 尤 yóu | 亠 口 小 尤 | |

高: 高 is an image of a high tower or building.

## 3. 扌

As an independent character, 扌 means "hand" and is written as 手. As a radical, it is used as the left part in a compound character and is written as 扌 to form characters for hand-related activities. The compound characters in this chapter that contain this radical are 报 and 找.

| Character | Basic Meaning | No. of Str. | Stroke Order | Mean. Clue | Phon. Clue | Components | Structure |
|---|---|---|---|---|---|---|---|
| 报(報) bào | newspaper | 7 | 扌 报 | 扌 | | 扌 艮 | |
| 找 zhǎo | to look for | 7 | 扌 扌 找 找 找 | 扌 | | 扌 戈 | |

报: 又 indicates a hand (see Chapter 8). To help you better remember this character, think of it as showing the opening of a newspaper with both hands.

找: Note the difference between the way 我 and 找 are written.

4. 木

木 *mù* is the image of a tree in ancient Chinese. As an independent character, it means "wood." As a radical it can be put on the left, bottom, or right part of a character, indicating things associated with trees or wood. The compound characters in this chapter that contain this radical are 杂 and 板.

| Character | Basic Meaning | No. of Str. | Stroke Order | Mean. Clue | Phon. Clue | Compo- nents | Struct- ure |
|---|---|---|---|---|---|---|---|
| 杂(雜) zá | multi kinds, chaotic | 6 | 九 杂 | 九, 木 (all kinds of wood) | | 九 木 | ⊟ |
| 板 bǎn | board; plank | 8 | 木 板 | 木 | 反 fǎn | 木 反 | ◫ |

5. 白

白 can be both a radical and an independent character. With one additional stroke above the sun, this character, *bái* (white), and radical implies the white light of the sun.

| Character | Basic Meaning | No. of Str. | Stroke Order | Mean. Clue | Phon. Clue | Components | Struct- ure |
|---|---|---|---|---|---|---|---|
| 的 de | (particle) | 8 | 白 白丿 的 的 | | | 白 勺(勹 丶) | ◫ |

6. 衤

As an independent character this is written as 衣. As a radical it is used as the left-hand part in compound characters related to clothing. The compound characters in this chapter that contain this radical are 衬, 衫, and 袜.

| Character | Basic Meaning | No. of Str. | Stroke Order | Mean. Clue | Phon. Clue | Compo- nents | Struct- ure |
|---|---|---|---|---|---|---|---|
| *衬(襯) chèn | shirt | 8 | 丶 ㇇ 衤 衤 衤 衬 | 衤 | 寸 cùn | 衤 寸 | ◫ |
| *衫 shān | 上衣 | 8 | 衤 衫 | 衤 | 三 | 衤 彡 | ◫ |
| *袜(襪) wà | socks | 10 | 衤 袜 | 衤, 末 (mò, *end*) | | 衤 末 | ◫ |

7. 目

目 *mù* is the image of eyes in ancient Chinese. As an independent character it means "eye." When it is used as a radical, it is put at a character's left, right, or bottom, indicating a meaning related to eyes. The compound characters in this chapter that contain this radical are 看 and 眼.

| Character | Basic Meaning | No. of Str. | Stroke Order | Mean. Clue | Phon. Clue | Compo-nents | Struct-ure |
|---|---|---|---|---|---|---|---|
| 看 kàn | to look | 9 | 三 手 看 | 手, 目 | | 手 目 | ⊟ |
| 眼 yǎn | eye | 11 | 目 眼 | 目 | | 目 艮 | ◫ |

## EXERCISES

### I. Character Exercises

1. **Find the independent characters you have learned hidden in the following characters:**

   京____________ 件____________ 杂____________

2. **Add something inside of 口 to form as many characters as you can:**

   ________________________________________

3. **Write five characters you have learned that are of a top-bottom structure:**
   **Example:** 兄

   ______ ______ ______ ______ ______

4. **Solve the character riddle below:**

   上字的下边儿，下字的上边儿：__________.

5. **Write as many characters as you can think of that use the 心 radical:**

   ________________________________________

6. Rearrange the following characters in the order of their numbers of strokes:

商，吧，必，真，车，说，字

→ ______________________________________________

II. Vocabulary Exercises

1. Write two characters in each set of homonyms, then form a word with each character:

a. shū: __________ b. zài: __________

shū: __________ zài: __________

2. Use the following characters to form as many words as possible:

a. 做 → ______________________________________________

b. 有 → ______________________________________________

c. 老 → ______________________________________________

d. 客 → ______________________________________________

e. 好 → ______________________________________________

f. 地 → ______________________________________________

3. Write the antonym of each of the following:

a. 西 → ( ) b. 上 → ( )

c. 大 → ( )

4. **Form a few words/phrases with each of the following characters, paying attention to their pronunciations, meanings, and slight differences in form between members of the same pair.**

a. 我 → ______

找 → ______

b. 板 → ______

饭 → ______

c. 高 → ______

商 → ______

d. 京 → ______

就 → ______

## III. Structure Exercises

1. **Rearrange the words below to form sentences. You may need to add some extra words in order to form a complete sentence:**

a. 他说， 去， xiàn在， 就

→ ______

b. 商diàn， 有名的， 一家， 有

→ ______

c. 不容yì， 找， 地图， 没有

→ ______

d. 小王， 手biǎo， 想， 买

→ ______

e. 知道， 他， 哪儿， 在， 吗

→ ______

2. Connect the above sentences into a short passage according to their meanings. Add some extra words if necessary.

______________________________________________

______________________________________________

______________________________________________

______________________________________________

______________________________________________

______________________________________________

3. Write the characters for the person indicated by the numbers below according to the following information:

王家兰在右边儿。

王家兰的前边儿是王太太。

王明志在王家兰的páng边儿。

王先生在王明志的前边儿，王太太gēn王明汉的中jiān。

王先生gēn王国京的中jiān是王太太。

王小弟在bàba gēn妈妈的前边儿。

1: ______________ 2: ______________ 3: ______________

4: ______________ 5: ______________ 6: ______________

7: ______________

## Supplementary Reading

### Reading 1

Lǎobǎn：  早！你要什么？

高意兰：  我看看。这毛衣duōshǎo qián?

Lǎobǎn：  四百八十块。

高意兰：  太guì了。

Lǎobǎn：  不guì。

高意兰：  三百八十，行吗？

Lǎobǎn：  不行。四百五十！

高意兰：  四百二十！

Lǎobǎn：  好吧，好吧，四百二十！还要别的吗？

高意兰：  就要这个。谢谢。

#### COMPREHENSION QUESTIONS

1. 高意兰要什么？

______________________________

2. 高意兰买了什么？

______________________________

## Reading 2

### 没门儿

你们都知道门是什么意思。你们的家有qián门、hòu门。可是，你们知道“没门儿”是什么意思吗？ 要是[1]你们都想去看电yǐng，可是你们要我在家看门。你们说：“我们去看电yǐng，你一个人在家看门。”我说：“要我一个人在家看门，没门儿。”这儿的“看门”是什么意思？“没门儿”呢？ 是fáng子没有门的意思还是“不行，不可néng[2]”的意思？

1. 要是：if
2. 不可néng：impossible

## COMPREHENSION QUESTIONS

1. “我们去看电yǐng, 你一个人在家看门。”这儿的“门”是什么意思？

______________________________

2. “要我一个人在家看门，没门儿。”这儿的“没门儿”是什么意思？

______________________________

## Character Practice

| | | | | | | | | | |
|---|---|---|---|---|---|---|---|---|---|
| 上 | 上 | | | | | | | | |
| 下 | 下 | | | | | | | | |
| 门 | 门 | | | | | | | | |
| 为 | 为 | | | | | | | | |
| 手 | 手 | | | | | | | | |
| 方 | 方 | | | | | | | | |
| 内 | 内 | | | | | | | | |
| 衣 | 衣 | | | | | | | | |
| 老 | 老 | | | | | | | | |
| 认 | 认 | | | | | | | | |
| 仔 | 仔 | | | | | | | | |
| 边 | 边 | | | | | | | | |
| 右 | 右 | | | | | | | | |

| 汗 | 汗 | | | | | | | | |
|---|---|---|---|---|---|---|---|---|---|
| 因 | 因 | | | | | | | | |
| 件 | 件 | | | | | | | | |
| 住 | 住 | | | | | | | | |
| 识 | 识 | | | | | | | | |
| 志 | 志 | | | | | | | | |
| 忘 | 忘 | | | | | | | | |
| 城 | 城 | | | | | | | | |
| 哪 | 哪 | | | | | | | | |
| 北 | 北 | | | | | | | | |
| 六 | 六 | | | | | | | | |
| 京 | 京 | | | | | | | | |
| 高 | 高 | | | | | | | | |

| 商 | 商 | | | | | | | | |
|---|---|---|---|---|---|---|---|---|---|
| 就 | 就 | | | | | | | | |
| 报 | 报 | | | | | | | | |
| 找 | 找 | | | | | | | | |
| 杂 | 杂 | | | | | | | | |
| 板 | 板 | | | | | | | | |
| 的 | 的 | | | | | | | | |
| 衬 | 衬 | | | | | | | | |
| 衫 | 衫 | | | | | | | | |
| 袜 | 袜 | | | | | | | | |
| 看 | 看 | | | | | | | | |
| 眼 | 眼 | | | | | | | | |

# CHAPTER TEN
# 第 十 课

**Text**

高小美是美国人，她住在上海lù，在书diàn hé咖啡diàn的中jiān。以前她孩子小，她得在家看孩子，suǒ以没有机会学中文，只会说英文，xiàn在四个孩子都大了，她néng去念书了。高太太以前连一个汉字都不会xiě，xiàn在她是大学生了，她学中文hé法文。中文不容易，老shī上课都用汉语教，中文书都是用中文xiě的。快要考试了，高太太真忙。她要考两门课，中文gēn法文。她连饭也不做了。大人，孩子都去她家后边儿的饭馆儿吃晚饭。她说要考试了，要看十几本书，有的书是中文书，有的书是法文书。

高太太有一个朋友叫王欢兰，是女的。高太太的朋友dāng中，就王欢兰是中国人。王小姐住在高太太家的北边儿，高太太可以用汉语gēn王欢兰打电话，用汉语gēn欢兰说话。王欢兰也用汉语gēn高太太说话，给她说中文故事。王欢兰会用毛笔xiě汉字，她替高太太用毛笔给中文老shī xiě中文信。高太太对欢兰也很好，请她去中国饭馆儿吃饭。王欢兰教高太太用筷子吃米饭，还给高太太介绍中国茶。高太太给王欢兰做英国菜，教王欢兰用刀子hé叉子吃牛肉。她们一块儿笑着吃饭，喝茶。高太太想，有一位中国朋友真好。她考试一dìng没问tí。真得谢谢王欢兰。

## 生词 New Words

| | | |
|---|---|---|
| 高小美 | Gāo Xiǎoměi | (N) a personal name |
| 美国 | Měi.guó | (PW) America |
| 上海 | Shànghǎi | (PW) a city in Eastern China |
| 书diàn | shūdiàn | (PW) bookshop |
| 中jiān | zhōng.jiān | (PS/PW) the middle (concrete) |
| 孩子 | háizi | (N) child, youngster |
| suǒ以…… | suǒ.yǐ… | (Pat) therefore… |
| 机会 | jī.huì | (N) opportunity |
| 英文 | Yīngwén | (N) English (language) |
| 念书 | niàn shū | (VO) study (academically) |
| 连……都/也…… | lián…dōu/yě… | (Pat) even… |
| 大学生 | dàxué.shēng | (N) university student |
| 学 | xué | (V) study, learn |
| 法文 | Fǎwén | (N) French (language) |
| 老shī | lǎoshī | (N) teacher |

| | | |
|---|---|---|
| 上课 | shàng kè | (VO) have class, attend class |
| 用 | yòng | (CV) using, by means of |
| 教 | jiāo | (V) teach |
| 考试 | kǎo shì | (VO) take a test or examination |
| 门 | -mén | (Cl) (for a course taken at school) |
| 课 | kè | (N) lesson, class, course |
| 大人 | dàrén | (N) adult |
| 后边儿 | hòu.biānr | (PS/PW) in back |
| 有的……有的…… | yǒude...yǒude... | (Pat) some...others... |
| <u>王欢兰</u> | <u>Wáng Huānlán</u> | (N) a personal name |
| 女的 | nǚde | (N) woman, female |
| dāng中 | dāngzhōng | (PS/PW) the middle (abstract) |
| 小姐 | xiǎo.jiě | (N) young lady, Miss |
| 北边儿 | běi.biānr | (PS/PW) the north |
| 打电话 | dǎ diànhuà | (VO) make a phone call |
| 给 | gěi | (CV) for, to |
| 故事 | gùshi | N) story, narrative account |
| 替 | tì | (CV) in place of |
| 信 | xìn | (N) letter (Cl *-fēng* 封) |
| 对 | duì | (CV) to, toward |
| 筷子 | kuàizi | (N) chopsticks (Cl -双) |
| 米饭 | mǐfàn | (N) cooked rice |
| 介绍 | jiè.shào | (V) introduce |
| 茶 | chá | (N) tea |
| <u>英国</u> | <u>Yīng.guó</u> | (PW) England |
| 菜 | cài | (N) food; dishes |
| 刀子 | dāozi | (N) knife (Cl *-bǎ* 把 ) |
| 叉子 | chāzi | (N) fork (Cl *-bǎ* 把) |
| 牛肉 | niúròu | (N) beef |
| 笑 | xiào | (V) laugh, smile, laugh at |
| 着 | -zhe | (P) (attached to verbs to indicate action in progress) |
| 位 | wèi | (Cl) (polite, for persons) |
| 考试 | kǎoshì | (N) test or examination |
| 一dìng | yídìng | (Adv) definitely |
| 问tí | wèntí | (N) question |
| 谢谢 | xièxie | (Ex) thank you |

## COMPREHENSION QUESTIONS

**Read the text above and answer the following questions.**

1. 高太太叫什么名字？她是哪国人？

2. 他们家住哪儿？

3. 她以前做什么？Xiàn在呢？

4. 她会说什么话？

5. 高太太要考几门课？ 考什么？

6. Xiàn在他们家人为什么都去饭馆儿吃晚饭？

7. Shéi是王欢兰？ 她住哪儿？

8. 说说王欢兰 hé 高太太一块儿的故事。

9. 为什么高太太想她考试一dìng没问tí？ 你说呢？

# Writing Help

## Independent Characters

| Character | Basic Meaning | No. of Str. | Stroke Order | Radical | Compo-nents | Struct-ure |
|---|---|---|---|---|---|---|
| 刀 dāo | knife | 2 | 𠃌 刀 | 刀 | 刀 | □ |
| *叉 chā | fork | 3 | 又 叉 | 又 | 又 、 | □ |
| 米 mǐ | rice | 6 | 米 | 米 | 米 | □ |

## Compound Characters

The new compound characters in this chapter with radicals you have learned are 介, 打, 机, 考, 后, 连, 位, 念, 事, 试, 信, 笑, 海, 课, 替, 谢, and 筷.

| Character | Basic Meaning | No. of Str. | Stroke Order | Radical | Mean. Clue | Phon. Clue | Compo-nents | Struct-ure |
|---|---|---|---|---|---|---|---|---|
| *介 jiè | to introduce | 4 | 人 亼 介 | 人 | | | 人 丿 | ⿱ |
| 打 dǎ | to hit | 5 | 扌 打 | 扌 | 扌, 丁(dīng, *nail*) | | 扌 丁 | ⿰ |
| *机(機) jī | machine | 5 | 木 机 | 木 | 木 | 几 | 木 几 | ⿰ |
| 考 kǎo | to check | 6 | 土 耂 耂 考 | 十 | | | 耂 丂 | ⿱ |
| *后(後) hòu | later, after | 6 | 一 厂 斤 后 | 口 | | | 斤 口 | ⿸ |
| 连(連) lián | to connect | 7 | 车 连 | 辶 | | | 辶 车 | ⿺ |
| *位 wèi | seat | 7 | 亻 亻 住 位 | 亻 | 亻 | | 亻 立 | ⿰ |

| | | | | | | | | |
|---|---|---|---|---|---|---|---|---|
| 念 niàn | to read aloud, to study | 8 | 人 人 今 念 | 心 | 心 | | 今 心 | ⿱ |
| 事 shì | matter, affair | 8 | 一 〒 写 写 写 事 | 一 | 口 | | 一 口 彐 亅 | □ |
| 试(試) shì | to try | 8 | 讠 讠 讠 试 试 | 讠 | 讠 | 式 shì | 讠 式 | ⿰ |
| 信 xìn | letter | 9 | 亻 亻 亻 亻 信 | 亻 | 亻, 言 (yán, *speech*) | | 亻 言 | ⿰ |
| 笑 xiào | to laugh | 10 | ⺮ 竺 笋 笑 | 竹 | 竹( shape of smiling eyes) | 夭 yāo | ⺮[1] 夭 | ⿱ |
| 海 hǎi | sea | 10 | 氵 氵 海 | 氵 | 氵 | | 氵 母 | ⿰ |
| 课(課) kè | lesson | 10 | 讠 讠 讠 讠 课 | 讠 | 讠 | | 讠 木 田 | ⿰ |
| 替 tì | for | 12 | 二 夫 扶 替 | 日 | | | 夫 夫[1] 日 | ⿱ |
| 谢(謝) xiè | to thank; surname | 12 | 讠 讠 讠 讠 讠 讠 讠 谢 | 讠 | 讠, 身 (shēn, *body*), 寸 (cùn, *inch*) | | | ⿲ |
| *筷 kuài | chopsticks | 13 | ⺮ 筷 | 竹 | 竹 | 快 | ⺮ 忄 夬 | ⿱ |

打: Think of this as showing a hand striking a nail; hit—the action of hitting with a hand.
谢: It reminds you that one needs to bow (make your body shorter) to say thanks.
1. Note the differences in the way 夭, 夭, and 夫 are written.

## Radicals

The radicals of focus in this chapter are 冂, 子, 艹, 纟, 攵, and 羊.

### 1. 冂

This radical means "border." The compound characters in this chapter that contain this radical are 用 and 肉.

| Character | Basic Meaning | No. of Str. | Stroke Order | Mean. Clue | Phon. Clue | Compo-nents | Struct-ure |
|---|---|---|---|---|---|---|---|
| 用 yòng | to use | 5 | 冂 月 月 用 | | | 冂 ‡ | □ |
| 肉 ròu | meat, flesh | 6 | 冂 内 肉 | 人, 人 | | 冂 人 人 | □ |

2. 子

This character, meaning "child," can function both as a character and as a radical. The compound characters in this chapter that contain this radical are 学 and 孩.

| Character | Basic Meaning | No. of Str. | Stroke Order | Mean. Clue | Phon. Clue | Compo-nents | Struct-ure |
|---|---|---|---|---|---|---|---|
| 学(學) xué | to study | 8 | ` `` ``` 𰀁 学 | ⺍, 冖, 子 | | 𰀁 子 | ⊟ |
| *孩 hái | child | 9 | 子 孑 孓 孩 孩 | 子 | 亥 hài | 子 亥 | ◫ |

学: A child holds a book with two hands, studying under a cover.

3. 艹

艹 is the image of the shape of two shoots, meaning "grass." As a radical it is usually put at the top of a character to form characters related to plants. The compound characters in this chapter that contain this radical are 英, 茶, and 菜.

| Character | Basic Meaning | No. of Str. | Stroke Order | Mean. Clue | Phon. Clue | Compo-nents | Struct-ure |
|---|---|---|---|---|---|---|---|
| *英 yīng | flower | 8 | 一 十 艹 芇 英 | 艹 | 央 yāng | 艹 央 | ⊟ |
| 茶 chá | tea | 9 | 艹 艾 茶 | 艹, 人, 木 | | 艹 人 木 | ⊟ |
| 菜 cài | vegetable, dish (of food) | 11 | 艹 艹 艹 艹 苃 菜 | 艹 | 采 cǎi | 艹 采 | ⊟ |

茶: To help you remember this character, think of it as indicating people picking tea leaves among tea bushes.

4. 纟

This radical means "silk." The compound characters in this chapter that contain this radical are 绍 and 给.

| Character | Basic Meaning | No. of Str. | Stroke Order | Mean. Clue | Phon. Clue | Components | Structure |
|---|---|---|---|---|---|---|---|
| *绍(紹) shào | to introduce (介绍) | 8 | 𠃋 纟 纟 纫 绍 | | 召 zhāo | 纟 刀 口 | ◫ |
| 给(給) gěi | to give | 9 | 纟 纵 纵 给 | 纟, 合(hé, *together*) | | 纟 合 (人 一 口) | ◫ |

给: Think of this as indicating people putting their hands together to present a gift of silk.

5. 攵

This character can function both as a character, 文, meaning "culture" or "language," and as a radical with a similar meaning. It is usually found on the right-hand side of a compound character. The compound characters in this chapter that contain this radical are 故 and 教.

| Character | Basic Meaning | No. of Str. | Stroke Order | Mean. Clue | Phon. Clue | Components | Structure |
|---|---|---|---|---|---|---|---|
| *故 gù | story | 9 | 十 古 故 | 古(gǔ, *old, ancient*), 攵 | 古 gǔ | 古 攵 | ◫ |
| 教 jiāo | to teach | 11 | 耂 孝 教 | 攵 | 孝 xiào | 耂 子 攵 | ◫ |

6. 羊

羊 can be both a character and a radical. As an independent character (羊 *yáng*), it is an image of a goat. The compound characters in this chapter that contain this radical are 美 and 着.

| Character | Basic Meaning | No. of Str. | Stroke Order | Mean. Clue | Phon. Clue | Components | Structure |
|---|---|---|---|---|---|---|---|
| 美 měi | beauty, beautiful | 9 | 丷 䒑 兰 羊 美 | 羊, 大 | | 𦍌 大 | ⊟ |
| *着(著) zhe | (particle) | 11 | 丷 𦍌 着 | | | 羊 目 | ⊟ |

美: To help you remember this character, think of "beauty" in terms of a big sheep.

## EXERCISES

### I. Character Exercises

1. Correct the wrong characters in the following sentences:

   a. 她友三本好看的画报。 __________

   b. 我姐姐zuì xǐ欢喝牛内汤。 __________

   c. 你gēn我一快儿去吧。 __________

2. Solve the character riddle below:

   A person is among the grass and bushes: __________

3. Write as many of the characters you have learned as you can using the 木 radical:

   ______________________________________________________________

4. Write the common part of the following characters in the parentheses:

   课，笨 → (      )

5. Decompose each of the characters below into its respective components. Then combine these parts to form different characters:

   Example: 木 (from 校) + 反 (from 饭) → 板

| 思，汉，好，吗，考，有，忙，块，呢 |
|---|

______ (from ______ ) + ______ (from ______ ) → ______

______ (from ______ ) + ______ (from ______ ) → ______

______ (from ______ ) + ______ (from ______ ) → ______

______ (from ______ ) + ______ (from ______ ) → ______

______ (from ______ ) + ______ (from ______ ) → ______

## II. Vocabulary Exercises

1. **How many words/phrases can you form using the following characters?**

先， 子， 中， 女， 生， 国， 衣， 文， 学， 儿， 日

______________________________

2. **Compare the following pairs of characters. Make words or phrases with each character.**

a. 看 → ______________ b. 有 → ______________

着 → ______________ 友 → ______________

c. 快 → ______________ d. 考 → ______________

块 → ______________ 老 → ______________

e. 只 → ______________ f. 万 → ______________

兄 → ______________ 方 → ______________

g. 门 → ______________ h. 午 → ______________

们 → ______________ 牛 → ______________

3. **Give the antonyms to the following words:**

a. 后 → (　　　) b. 晚 → (　　　)

c. 买 → (　　　) d. 饱 → (　　　)

4. 我是什么？

你们用我吃中国饭，不用我吃英国饭。可以用我吃菜，不可以用我喝茶。我是 ______________。

## III. Structure Exercises

1. Rearrange the elements of each of the entries to make a grammatical sentence.

   a. 吃，是，东西，的，都，牛肉，我，米饭，ài，菜

   →________________________________________

   b. 上，都，他，课，没，连，去

   →________________________________________

   c. 叉子，不，小文，用，chǎo饭，会，吃

   →________________________________________

   d. 你，电话，shéi，打，给

   →________________________________________

2. Correct the following wrong characters, then make a sentence with the corrected ones.

| Incorrect | Correct | Make a sentence |
|---|---|---|
| 会 | | |
| 家 | | |

3. Complete the dialogue in Chinese characters:

老板：Nín好！ Nín要吃什么？

客人：________________________________________

老板：我们这儿中国chǎo菜，日本小吃，法国汤都有。我们的Xīn西兰牛肉zuì有名了。你xǐ欢什么？

客人：________________________________________

老板：好。你用筷子还是用刀，叉？

客人：________________________________________

4. Fill in the blanks with the words provided in the box. There are more choices than there are blanks. Each word can only be used once.

| 得，的，会，néng，在，也，中jiān，dāng中，gēn，都，右边儿 |
|---|

小明是我 ________ 朋友。他家在我家 ________ 小美家的 ________。在我的朋友 ________，就小明 ________ 说汉语。他 ________ 会说日语。

## Supplementary Reading

### Reading 1

志高：小欢，我给你们介绍一下：这是我的朋友方汉。

小欢：方汉，你好！ 我叫小欢。

方汉：小欢，你好！

志高：小欢是我的línjū。她是北京大学的学生。方汉也是大学生。

方汉：我是大学生。可是我只学两门课。你呢？

小欢：我学五门。你学哪两门？

方汉：中文gēn法文。

小欢：你学中文！ 你会用毛笔xiě汉字吗？

方汉：我不会，志高会。可是我很想学。

小欢：那，志高，你教我们行吗？

志高：没问tí。

## COMPREHENSION QUESTIONS

1. 小欢学几门课?

______________________________

2. 方汉学几门课?

______________________________

3. 志高教不教小欢hé方汉写汉字?

______________________________

## Reading 2

### 没问tí

中国人xǐ欢说"没问tí"。你买的衣fu太大了。你gēn商diàn的老板说:"这件衣fu太大了。给我小的行吗?"老板说:"没问tí。"在饭馆儿吃饭,我gēn饭馆儿的老板说:"老板,我不会用筷子,给我刀子hé叉子行吗? 老板说:"没问tí。"吃饭前,我gēn我的中国朋友小王说:"小王,对不qǐ。我不吃饭了。"小王问:"为什么?"我说:"我没qián。"小王说:"没qián? 没问tí。我这儿有。"吃饭后,小王对我说:"哎呀! 有问tí。"我问:"什么问tí?"他说:"我也没qián。"你也没qián。我想这真是个问tí。

## COMPREHENSION QUESTIONS

1. 吃饭前，我gēn小王说："我没qián。"小王说什么？

______________________________

2. 要是你的朋友gēn你说："我没qián。"你会对他说什么？

______________________________

## Character Practice

| | | | | | | | | | |
|---|---|---|---|---|---|---|---|---|---|
| 刀 | 刀 | | | | | | | | |
| 叉 | 叉 | | | | | | | | |
| 米 | 米 | | | | | | | | |
| 介 | 介 | | | | | | | | |
| 打 | 打 | | | | | | | | |
| 机 | 机 | | | | | | | | |
| 考 | 考 | | | | | | | | |
| 后 | 后 | | | | | | | | |
| 连 | 连 | | | | | | | | |

| 位 | 位 | | | | | | | | |
|---|---|---|---|---|---|---|---|---|---|
| 念 | 念 | | | | | | | | |
| 事 | 事 | | | | | | | | |
| 试 | 试 | | | | | | | | |
| 信 | 信 | | | | | | | | |
| 笑 | 笑 | | | | | | | | |
| 海 | 海 | | | | | | | | |
| 课 | 课 | | | | | | | | |
| 替 | 替 | | | | | | | | |
| 谢 | 谢 | | | | | | | | |
| 筷 | 筷 | | | | | | | | |
| 用 | 用 | | | | | | | | |
| 肉 | 肉 | | | | | | | | |

| 孩 | 孩 | | | | | | | | |
|---|---|---|---|---|---|---|---|---|---|
| 英 | 英 | | | | | | | | |
| 茶 | 茶 | | | | | | | | |
| 菜 | 菜 | | | | | | | | |
| 绍 | 绍 | | | | | | | | |
| 给 | 给 | | | | | | | | |
| 故 | 故 | | | | | | | | |
| 教 | 教 | | | | | | | | |
| 美 | 美 | | | | | | | | |
| 着 | 着 | | | | | | | | |
| 学 | 学 | | | | | | | | |

# CHAPTER ELEVEN
# 第 十 一 课

**Text**

白京以是我中学的同学，xiàn在是美思大学的学生。他很cōng明，功课很好。可是他不会开车，他去哪儿都qí自行车。他说坐公共汽车很便宜，可是车上人太多，太不舒服了；打的很方便，也很舒服，可是不便宜。Suǒ以他去哪儿都qí车。

白京以晚上给我打电话，我正在看书呢。我说，我有kòng，你dào我家来liáoliao天,喝喝酒吧。他说太好了。可是他不知道怎么来我家。我告诉他我家在同心街，同心街左边儿有个火车zhàn。从火车zhàn往前一直走，就是我家。我家右边儿有个小学，左边儿有个图书馆，图书馆的外边儿开着灯，不nán找。白京以qí着车从这条街dào那条街问lù，没有人知道同心街在哪儿。白京以就不qí自行车了，他坐chū租汽车来我家。我问他为什么不买一本地图，拿着地图找lù就容yì了。他真笨，一diǎn儿也不cōng明。

晚上，我和白京以喝着中国酒liáo天。我太太给我们做很多上海小吃，南京炒菜。白京以说因为有这么好吃的菜，那么好喝的酒，suǒ以他很xǐ欢来找我喝酒liáo天。

**生词 New Words**

| | | |
|---|---|---|
| 白京以 | Bái Jīngyǐ | (N) a personal name |
| 中学 | zhōngxué | (PW) high school |
| 同学 | tóngxué | (N) fellow student, classmate |
| 大学 | dàxué | (N) university |
| 美思大学 | Měisī Dàxué | (PW) name of a university |
| 学生 | xué.shēng | (N) student |
| 功课 | gōngkè | (N) schoolwork, homework |
| 开 | kāi | (V) open; operate; drive (a car) |
| 车 | chē | (N) vehicle (Cl *-liàng* 辆) |
| 坐 | zuò | (V) sit; ride; take (a means of transportation) |
| 公共汽车 | gōnggòng qìchē | (N) public bus |
| 公车 | gōngchē | (N) same as 公共汽车 |
| 多 | duō | (SV) many, be abundant |
| 舒服 | shūfu | (SV) be comfortable |
| 打的 | dǎ dī | (VO) take a taxi (slang) |

| | | |
|---|---|---|
| 方便 | fāngbiàn | (SV) be convenient |
| 晚上 | wǎnshang | (TW) in the evening |
| 正(在)……(着)(呢) | zhèng(zài)…(zhe)(ne) | (Adv) right in the middle of… |
| 有kòng | yǒu kòng | (VO) have free time |
| 来 | lái | (V) come |
| liáo天 | liáo tiān | (VO) chat |
| 怎么 | zěnme | (Adv) how? why? |
| 同心街 | Tóngxīn Jiē | (PW) a street name |
| 左边儿 | zuǒ.biānr | (PS/PW) the left |
| 火车zhàn | huǒchēzhàn | (PW) train station |
| 从 | cóng | (CV) from |
| 往 | wàng | (CV) toward |
| 前 | qián | (PS/PW) in front |
| 拐 | guǎi | (V) turn |
| 一直 | yìzhí | (Adv) straight |
| 走 | zǒu | (V) walk, go, move along, leave |
| 就 | jiù | (Conj) then |
| 小学 | xiǎoxué | (PW) elementary school |
| 图书馆 | túshūguǎn | (PW) library |
| 外边儿 | wài.biānr | (PS/) outside |
| ……着(呢) | …-zhe (ne) | description of a state |
| 灯 | dēng | (N) lamp, lights |
| 从……dào…… | cóng…dào… | (Pat) from…to… |
| 条 | -tiáo | (Cl) (for things that are seen as long, narrow, and flexible) |
| 街 | jiē | (N) street (Cl *-tiáo* 条) |
| 问lù | wèn lù | (VO) ask the way |
| chū租汽车 | chūzū qìchē | (N) taxi |
| 拿 | ná | (V) take, bring; pick up |
| 和 | hé | (Conj) and, with |
| 南京 | Nánjīng | (PW) a city in China |
| 炒 | chǎo | (V) stir fry |
| 这么 | zhème | (Adv) in this way, this |
| 那么 | nèime (nàme) | (Adv) in that way, that |

## COMPREHENSION QUESTIONS

**1. Read the text above and answer the following questions.**

a. Shéi 是白京以? ______

b. 为什么白京以不xǐ欢坐公车? ______

c. 他xǐ欢打的吗? 为什么? ______

**d.** 晚上‘我’在家做什么? ______

e. 白京以 知道‘我’家在哪儿吗? ______

f. 请告诉他怎么来‘我’家。______

g. 白京以说‘我’家容yì不容yì找? ______

h. 为什么白京以坐chū租汽车来‘我’家? ______

i. 你说白京以cōng明还是笨? ______

j. 晚上,‘我’和白京以一块儿做什么? ______

k. 为什么白京以xǐ欢来‘我’家? ______

2. Draw a map of the neighborhood according to the passage.

同心街

## Writing Help

### Independent Characters

| Character | Basic Meaning | No. of Str. | Stroke Order | Radical | Compo-nents | Struct-ure |
|---|---|---|---|---|---|---|
| 心 xīn | heart | 4 | 心 | 心 | 心 | ☐ |
| 开(開) kāi | to open | 4 | 二 于 开 | 一 | 开 | ☐ |
| 天 tiān | sky, day | 4 | 二 天 | 大 | 一 大 | ☐ |
| 火 huǒ | fire | 4 | 丶 丷 少 火 | 火 | 火 | ☐ |
| 正 zhèng | upright | 5 | 一 丅 下 正 正 | 一 | 一 止 | ☐ |
| 来(來) lái | to come | 7 | 一 丆 丷 亚 平 来 来 | 一 | 一 米 | ☐ |
| 走 zǒu | to walk, to go | 7 | 土 走 | 走 | 土 龰 | ☐ |

## Compound Characters

The following are the new compound characters in this chapter with radicals you have learned: 公, 从, 同, 坐, 汽, 条, 服, 往, 拐, 直, 怎, 南, 拿, 街, and 舒.

| Character | Basic Meaning | No. of Str. | Stroke Order | Radical | Mean. Clue | Phon. Clue | Compo-nents | Struct-ure |
|---|---|---|---|---|---|---|---|---|
| *公 gōng | public | 4 | 八 公 | 八 | | | 八 厶 | |
| 从(從) cóng | follow | 4 | 人 从 | 人 | 人, 人 | | 人 人 | |
| *同 tóng | together | 6 | 冂 冂 同 | 冂 | 一, 口 | | 冂 一 口 | |
| 坐 zuò | sit | 7 | 人 人人 坐 | 土 | 人, 人, 土 (tǔ, *soil*) | | 人 人土 | |
| 汽 qì | steam | 7 | 氵 汽 | 氵 | 氵 | 气 | 氵 气 | |
| *条(條) tiáo | (a classifier) | 7 | 丿 ク 夂 条 | 木 | 木 | | 夂 木 | |
| 服 fú | clothing*; obey | 8 | 月 ... 服 | 月 | 月 ( yuè, *flesh*) | | 月 𠬝 | |
| 往 wàng | toward | 8 | 彳 往 | 彳 | 彳 | 王 | 彳 主 | |
| 拐 guǎi | to turn | 8 | 扌 扣 拐 | 扌 | 扌 | | 扌 口 力 | |
| 直 zhí | straight | 8 | 直 | 十 | 十 | | 十 且 | |
| *怎 zěn | how | 9 | 丿 𠂉 𠂇 乍 乍 怎 | 心 | 心 | 乍 zhà | 乍 心 | |
| 南 nán | south | 9 | 十 ... 南 | 十 | 十 | | 十 冂 ¥ | |
| 拿 ná | to hold | 10 | 人 亼 合 拿 | 人 | 合, 手 | | 合 手 | |

| | | | | | | | | |
|---|---|---|---|---|---|---|---|---|
| 街 jiē | street | 12 | 彳 彳土 彳圭 街 | 彳 | 行 | | 彳 土 土 亍 | |
| *舒 shū | comfortable | 12 | 𠂉 亽 舍 舍 舍 舒 舒 | 人 | | | 舍 予 | |

同: Think of this character as showing all the voices (口) in the room (冂) expressing unity (一): 同.
坐: Two persons sitting on the ground (土 soil).
拿: Using a hand (手) to close (合 close, shut) it is the way to hold something.

## Radicals

The new radicals introduced in this chapter are 工, 夕, 火, and 禾.

### 1. 工

As a character 工 *gōng* means "work." As a radical it can be used in various parts of a character to form a compound character. The compound characters in this chapter that contain this radical are 功 and 左.

| Character | Basic Meaning | No. of Str. | Stroke Order | Mean. Clue | Phon. Clue | Compo-nents | Struct-ure |
|---|---|---|---|---|---|---|---|
| 功 gōng | achievement, merit | 5 | 工 功 | 力 (lì *strength*) | 工 gōng | 工 力 | |
| 左 zuǒ | left | 5 | 一 ナ 左 | | | ナ 工 | |

### 2. 夕

As a character 夕 *xī* means "dusk." The compound characters in this chapter that contain this radical are 外 and 多.

| Character | Basic Meaning | No. of Str. | Stroke Order | Mean. Clue | Phon. Clue | Compo-nents | Struct-ure |
|---|---|---|---|---|---|---|---|
| *外 wài | outside | 5 | 夕 夘 外 | 丨 (wall), 丶 (outside) | | 夕 卜 | |
| 多 duō | many | 6 | 夕 多 | 夕 + 夕 = more than one, many | | 夕 夕 | |

### 3. 火

As a character 火 *huǒ* means "fire." As a radical it is used in compound characters related to fire and light. The compound characters in this chapter that contain this radical are 灯 and 炒.

| Character | Basic Meaning | No. of Str. | Stroke Order | Mean. Clue | Phon. Clue | Compo-nents | Struct-ure |
|---|---|---|---|---|---|---|---|
| 灯(燈) dēng | lamp | 6 | 火 灯 灯 | 火 | 丁 dīng | 火 丁 | ⿰ |
| 炒 chǎo | stir fry | 8 | 火 炒 | 火 | 少 | 火 少 | ⿰ |

### 4. 禾

禾 *hé* can be a character meaning "grain." As a radical, it is used as the left-hand part in compound characters. The compound characters in this chapter that contain this radical are 和 and 租.

| Character | Basic Meaning | No. of Str. | Stroke Order | Mean. Clue | Phon. Clue | Compo-nents | Struct-ure |
|---|---|---|---|---|---|---|---|
| 和 hé | and | 8 | 一 禾 和 | | | 禾 口 | ⿰ |
| 租 zū | to hire, to rent | 10 | 丿 二 千 禾 禾 租 | | | 禾 且 | ⿰ |

## EXERCISES

### I. Character Exercises

**1. Form new characters by using different components of the following characters.**

**Example:** 工 (from 功) + 𠂇 (from 有) → 左

| 租， 右， 服， 她， 炒， 打 |
|---|

______ (from ______ ) + ______ (from ______ ) → ______

______ (from ______ ) + ______ (from ______ ) → ______

______ (from ______ ) + ______ (from ______ ) → ______

______ (from ______ ) + ______ (from ______ ) → ______

______ (from ______ ) + ______ (from ______ ) → ______

2. How many words/phrases can you form using the following characters?

开，　公，　功，　坐，　火，　上，　车，　课

______________________________

3. Write as many of the characters you have learned as possible that can be divided into top and bottom parts, for example, 怎.

______________________________

4. 从 is constructed from two of the character 人. Write down other characters you have learned with a similar formation.

______________________________

5. What is the common component shared by the following group?

同，　和，　点，　拿，　拐 → (　　　)

6. Solve the character riddles:

a. 不左不右: ____________

b. 你没有他有, 天没有地有: ____________

c. 一口 bites off half of 多: ____________

## II. Vocabulary Exercises

1. Write the Pinyin for the following characters, then form a word with each character.

a. 直 (　　　) ____________　　b. 住 (　　　) ____________

真 (　　　) ____________　　往 (　　　) ____________

c. 会 (　　　) ____________

公 (　　　) ____________

2. Write two different words using each of the following characters:

a. 电 → __________ __________

b. 学 → __________ __________

c. 车 → __________ __________

III. Structure Exercises

1. Rearrange the elements to make a grammatical sentence.

a. 去，公共汽车，得，火车zhàn，大学，从，坐

→ ______________________________________________

b. 着，地图，找，难，拿，不，了，就

→ ______________________________________________

2. You have invited your class for a dinner at your house. Write a paragraph in Chinese characters to describe how to go to your house.

______________________________________________

______________________________________________

______________________________________________

______________________________________________

______________________________________________

______________________________________________

## Supplementary Reading

### Reading 1

高志明： 你好！ 请问火车zhàn在哪儿？

行人[1]： 在前边。

高志明：　怎么走？

行人：　一直往前走，dào了十字lù口往左拐就是了。

高志明：　谢谢你！

行人：　不用谢。

1. 行人：pedestrian

## COMPREHENSION QUESTIONS

1. 高志明想去哪儿？

______________________________

2. 请问，去火车zhàn怎么走？

______________________________

## Reading 2

### 老子[1]

你们知道老子是shéi吗？ 老子是中国一个很有名的人。因为他在图书馆做事，suǒ以他看的书很多，知道的东西也很多。因为他知道的东西很多，suǒ以他xiě的《道déjīng》[2] 很有思想[3]，也很有意思。《道déjīng》这本书也叫《老子》。这本书只有五千个字。

1. 老子：founder of Daoism
2. 《道déjīng》：classic Daoist work attributed to Laozi
3. 思想：thought, idea

## COMPREHENSION QUESTIONS

1. 老子是shéi?

2. 老子xiě的那本书叫什么名字?

## Character Practice

| | | | | | | | | | |
|---|---|---|---|---|---|---|---|---|---|
| 心 | 心 | | | | | | | | |
| 开 | 开 | | | | | | | | |
| 天 | 天 | | | | | | | | |
| 火 | 火 | | | | | | | | |
| 正 | 正 | | | | | | | | |
| 来 | 来 | | | | | | | | |
| 走 | 走 | | | | | | | | |
| 公 | 公 | | | | | | | | |

| 从 | 从 | | | | | | | | |
|---|---|---|---|---|---|---|---|---|---|
| 同 | 同 | | | | | | | | |
| 坐 | 坐 | | | | | | | | |
| 汽 | 汽 | | | | | | | | |
| 条 | 条 | | | | | | | | |
| 服 | 服 | | | | | | | | |
| 往 | 往 | | | | | | | | |
| 拐 | 拐 | | | | | | | | |
| 直 | 直 | | | | | | | | |
| 怎 | 怎 | | | | | | | | |
| 南 | 南 | | | | | | | | |
| 拿 | 拿 | | | | | | | | |
| 街 | 街 | | | | | | | | |

| 舒 | 舒 | | | | | | | | |
|---|---|---|---|---|---|---|---|---|---|
| 功 | 功 | | | | | | | | |
| 左 | 左 | | | | | | | | |
| 外 | 外 | | | | | | | | |
| 多 | 多 | | | | | | | | |
| 灯 | 灯 | | | | | | | | |
| 炒 | 炒 | | | | | | | | |
| 和 | 和 | | | | | | | | |
| 租 | 租 | | | | | | | | |

# CHAPTER TWELVE
# 第 十 二 课

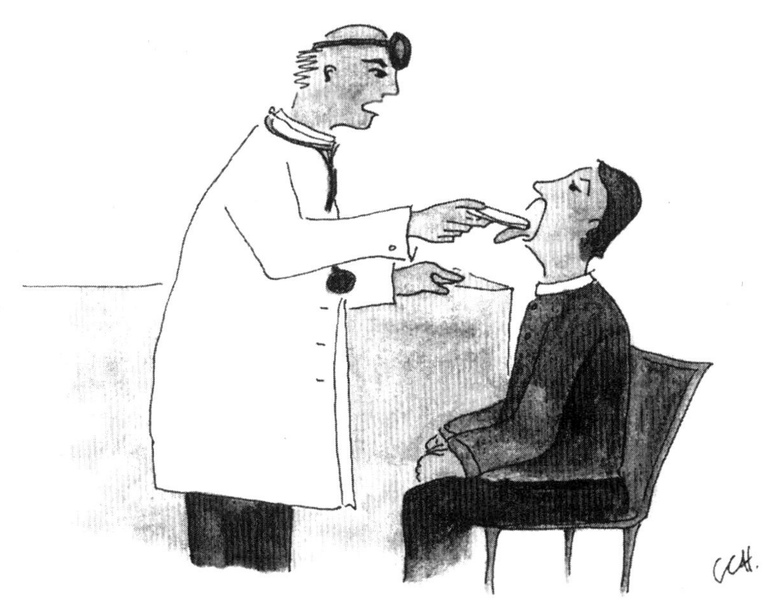

**Text**

我最不xǐ欢看病了。看病要花很多钱，吃了药病也不一定会好。可是，今天上午我去医院看医生了。

昨天白京以来找我liáo天，我们喝了很多酒，也吃了很多好吃的东西。晚上，我就不舒服了。我头疼，肚子疼，哪儿都不舒服。

我太太说："不好了，你病了！"她先给我喝了一点儿水，然后再给我吃了药。可是，我还哪儿都不舒服。我想："我以前喝酒都没有不舒服，今天怎么了？"我太太说我晚上喝太多酒，吃太多东西了，是吃坏了，suǒ以不舒服。她说："今天太晚了。你喝杯水，休息吧。明天一定要去看我同学的哥哥高医生。"

今天早上我还头疼。我不想吃东西，就去看医生了。

我从我家前边儿的车zhàn坐公车去医院，车上很挤，没有地方坐。我在北京街下车。医院在中国银行的左边儿，高医生是这家医院有名的医生。医院里看病的人很多，我等了很久才开始看。高医生说我没发烧，我的病没大问tí。他告诉我这几天不要吃肉，也不要喝酒。除了喝水和喝汤以外，只可以吃米饭。他要我回家休息休息，还要我吃药。今天下午我吃了药，还喝了一点儿汤，xiàn在已经好了。我不知道老白是不是也病了。我还没给他打电话呢。他xiàn在不在家，我得给他打手机。

**生词 New Words**

| | | |
|---|---|---|
| 最 | zuì | (Adv) most |
| 病 | bìng | (N) illness; (V) be ill |
| 看病 | kàn bìng | (VO) to see a doctor |
| 医生 | yīshēng | (N) physician, doctor |
| 看医生 | kàn yīshēng | (VO) (same as 看病) |
| 花 | huā | (V) spend (money or time) |
| 钱 | qián | (N) money |
| 了 | le | (P) (indicates completed action) |
| 药 | yào | (N) medicine |
| 吃药 | chī yào | (VO) take medicine |
| 一定 | yídìng | (Adv) definitely |
| 今天 | jīntiān | (TW) today |
| 上午 | shàngwǔ | (TW) in the morning |

| | | |
|---|---|---|
| 医院 | yīyuàn | (PW) hospital |
| 昨天 | zuótiān | (TW) yesterday |
| 就 | jiù | (Adv) then (earlier than expected) |
| 头 | tóu | (N) head |
| 疼 | téng | (V) feel pain |
| 肚子 | dùzi | (N) stomach |
| 先 | xiān | (Adv) first |
| 一点儿 | yìdiǎnr | (Q) a bit, a little |
| 水 | shuǐ | (N) water |
| 然后 | ránhòu | (Conj) and then |
| 再 | zài | (Adv) and then |
| 怎么了? | Zěnme le? | (Ex)What's going on? What's the matter? |
| 吃坏了 | chī huàile | (Ex) stomach problem from taking the wrong food |
| 晚 | wǎn | (SV) be late |
| 杯 | -bēi | (Cl) cup/glass of |
| 休息 | xiūxi | (V) rest |
| 明天 | míngtiān | (TW) tomorrow |
| 早上 | zǎo.shang | (TW) in the morning |
| 车zhàn | chēzhàn | (PW) bus stop |
| 挤 | jǐ | (SV) be crowded |
| 北京街 | Běijīng Jiē | (PW) name of a street |
| 下 | xià | (V) get off, disembark |
| 银行 | yínháng | (PW) bank (financial institution) |
| 等 | děng | (V) wait |
| 久 | jiǔ | (SV) take/be a long time |
| 才 | cái | (Adv) then (later than expected) |
| 开始 | kāishǐ | (V) begin |
| 发烧 | fā shāo | (VO) have fever |
| 天 | -tiān | (TD) day(s) |
| 除了……以外…… | chúle…yǐwài… | (Pat) besides, except for |
| 回 | huí | (V) return |
| 下午 | xiàwǔ | (TW) in the afternoon |
| 已经 | yǐjīng | (Adv) already |
| 还……呢 | hái…ne | (Pat) (continuation of an action) |
| 手机 | shǒujī | (N) cell phone |

## COMPREHENSION QUESTIONS

1. Read the text of this chapter and answer the following questions.

   a. 我为什么最不xǐ欢去看医生?

   ______________________________

   b. 为什么我今天上午去了?

   ______________________________

   c. 我哪儿不舒服?

   ______________________________

   d. 医院在哪儿?

   ______________________________

   e. 医生对我怎么说?

   ______________________________

   f. 老白不在家, 我怎么找他?

   ______________________________

2. Play the roles of 我 and 我太太 in pairs.

3. In groups, draw a map of where the hospital is located.

北京街

4. In groups, make a list of 高医生's advice.

5. In pairs, create a telephone conversation with 老白. 问他怎么了。Then write the dialogue down, using as many Chinese characters as possible.

老白: ______________________________

我: ______________________________

老白: ______________________________

我: ______________________________

老白: ______________________________

我: ______________________________

老白: ______________________________

我: ______________________________

## Writing Help

### Independent Characters

| Character | Basic Meaning | No. of Str. | Stroke Order | Radical | Compo-nents | Struct-ure |
|---|---|---|---|---|---|---|
| 久 jiǔ | long time | 3 | ノ ク 久 | 丿 | ノ 入 | |
| 才 cái | then | 3 | 一 寸 才 | 一 | 才 | |
| *已 yǐ[1] | already | 3 | ㇆ コ 已 | 己 | 已 | |

1. Please note that 已 is one of three characters that look remarkably similar, the other two being the 己 *jǐ* of 自己 *zìjǐ*, "self" (taught in Chapter 19) and 巳 *sì*, the sixth of twelve units in one of the traditional systems of counting. These three characters differ in the degree of closure of the vertical, left-hand stroke of the upper box. The 已 of 已经 taught in this chapter has a halfway closed line, while the 己 *jǐ* of 自己 *zìjǐ* taught in Chapter 19 lacks this left-hand line altogether, and the less commonly seen character 巳 has a completely closed box on top.

### Compound Characters

The following are the new compound characters in this chapter with radicals you have learned: 今, 头, 发, 休, 回, 花, 肚, 坏, 杯, 定, 始, 经, 药, 院, 昨, 挤, 除, 息, 烧, 最, and 等.

| Character | Basic Meaning | No. of Str. | Stroke Order | Radical | Mean. Clue | Phon. Clue | Compo-nents | Struct-ure |
|---|---|---|---|---|---|---|---|---|
| 今 jīn | today | 4 | 今 | 人 | | | 人 ㇇ | |
| 头(頭) tóu | head | 5 | 丶 ⺀ 头 | 大 | 大 | | ⺀ 大 | |
| 发(發) fā | to emit | 5 | ⺊ 𠂇 发 发 | 又 | | | 𠂇 又 | |
| *休 xiū | to rest | 6 | 亻 休 | 亻 | 人,木 (a person leaning on a tree to rest.) | | 人 木 | |
| 回 huí | to return | 6 | 冂 冋 回 | 口 | | | 口 口 | |
| 花 huā | flower, to spend | 7 | 艹 艹亻 花 | 艹 | 艹 | 化 huà | 艹 化 | |
| *肚 dù | stomach | 7 | 月 肚 | 月 | 月 | 土 tǔ | 月 土 | |

| | | | | | | | | |
|---|---|---|---|---|---|---|---|---|
| 坏(壞) huài | bad | 7 | 扌 坏 | 土 | 土(tǔ, *soil*) | | 土 不 | ◫ |
| *杯 bēi | cup | 8 | 木 杯 | 木 | 木 | | 木 不 | ◫ |
| 定 dìng | to decide | 8 | 宀 定 | 宀 | 宀 | | 宀 正 | ⊟ |
| *始 shǐ | beginning | 8 | 女 始 始 | 女 | 女 | | 女 厶口 | ◫ |
| 经(經) jīng | to go through | 8 | 纟 纫 纵 经 | 纟 | | 圣 jīn g | 纟ス 工 | ◫ |
| 药(藥) yào | medicine | 9 | 艹 苎 药 | 艹 | 艹 | 约 yuē | 艹 纟 勺 | ◫ |
| 院 yuàn | courtyard | 9 | 阝 阝 院 院 | 阝 | | 元 yuán | 阝 完 | ◫ |
| *昨 zuó | yesterday | 9 | 日 昨 | 日 | 日 | 乍 zhà | 日 乍 | ◫ |
| 挤(擠) jǐ | crowded | 9 | 扌 挤 挤 挤 | 扌 | 扌 | 齐 qí | 扌 齐 | ◫ |
| 除 chú | to remove | 9 | 阝 阝 除 除 | 阝 | | | 阝 余 | ◫ |
| *息 xī | to rest | 10 | 自 息 | 心 | 自, 心(to concentrate your heart on yourself) | | 自 心 | ⊟ |
| 烧(燒) shāo | to cook | 10 | 火 灯 炒 烧 烧 烧 | 火 | 火 | 尧 yáo | 火 戈 兀 | ◫ |
| 最 zuì | most | 12 | 日 旦 早 旱 旱 旱 最 | 日 | | | 日 耳 又 | ⊟ |
| 等 děng | to wait | 12 | ⺮ 笙 等 | 竹 | | | ⺮ 土 寸 | ⊟ |

杯: Neither a glass nor a cup is made of wood.
等: Waiting under the bamboo shade in front of a temple.

## Radicals

The new radicals introduced in this chapter are 匚, 灬, 疒, and 钅.

### 1. 匚

This is used in compound characters as the left three-quarter enclosure. The compound character in this chapter that contains this radical is 医.

| Character | Basic Meaning | No. of Str. | Stroke Order | Mean. Clue | Phon. Clue | Components | Structure |
|---|---|---|---|---|---|---|---|
| *医(醫) yī | medicine (profession) | 7 | 一 丆 七 至 医 医 医 | 匚 | | 匚矢 | 匚 |

### 2. 灬

灬 is used as the bottom part in compound characters to indicate fire or dots. The compound characters in this chapter that contains this radical are 点 and 然.

| Character | Basic Meaning | No. of Str. | Stroke Order | Mean. Clue | Phon. Clue | Components | Structure |
|---|---|---|---|---|---|---|---|
| 点(點) diǎn | dot | 9 | 占 点 点 点 点 | 灬 | | 占灬 | ⊟ |
| *然 rán | to burn | 12 | 丿 ク 夕 夕 肰 肰 然 | 灬 | | 夕犬灬 | ⊞ |

### 3. 疒

This radical is used as the left-top semi-enclosure in compound characters to indicate a meaning related to illness or disease. The compound characters in this chapter that contain this radical are 病 and 疼.

| Character | Basic Meaning | No. of Str. | Stroke Order | Mean. Clue | Phon. Clue | Components | Structure |
|---|---|---|---|---|---|---|---|
| 病 bìng | ill; illness | 10 | 丶 亠 广 广 疒 疒 疒 病 病 病 | 疒 | 丙 bǐng | 疒 丙 | 厂 |
| 疼 téng | painful | 10 | 疒 疚 疼 | 疒 | 冬 dōng | 疒 冬 | 厂 |

4. 钅

As a character it means "gold" and is written as 金 *jīn*. As a radical it used as the left part in a compound character and is written as 钅 to form characters related to metal or money. The compound characters in this chapter that contain this radical are 钱 and 银.

| Character | Basic Meaning | No. of Str. | Stroke Order | Mean. Clue | Phon. Clue | Compo- nents | Struct- ure |
|---|---|---|---|---|---|---|---|
| 钱(錢) qián | money; surname | 10 | ノ ⺈ 𠂉 ⺋ 钅 钅一 钅二 钱 钱 钱 | 钅 | 戋( indicat- ing 'ian') | 钅 戋 | ◫ |
| 银(銀) yín | silver | 11 | 钅 银 | 钅 | | 钅 艮 | ◫ |

## EXERCISES

### I. Character Exercises

1. **Form new characters by using different components of the following characters.**

   **Example:** 工 (from 功) + 𠂇 (from 有) → 左

   很, 住, 定, 杯, 学, 姐, 钱

   ______ (from ______ ) + ______ (from ______ ) → ______

   ______ (from ______ ) + ______ (from ______ ) → ______

   ______ (from ______ ) + ______ (from ______ ) → ______

   ______ (from ______ ) + ______ (from ______ ) → ______

   ______ (from ______ ) + ______ (from ______ ) → ______

2. **Add different parts to 阝 to form as many characters as you can:**

   ______________________________________________

3. **Correct the following characters if they are wrong:**

a. 一经 → ____________ b. 上果 → ____________

c. 饭馆几 → ____________ d. 书服 → ____________

e. 东西 → ____________

4. **Correct the wrong characters in the following sentences:**

令天上午找去医院着医生了。→ ______________________

医生要我体息体息。→ ______________________

5. **Solve the character riddles:**

a. 大口吃小口: ____________

b. '买' 有 '卖' 有，人人都有: ____________

c. 有它 (*tā*, "it") 就卖，没它 (*tā*, "it")就买: ____________

## II. Vocabulary Exercises

1. **Write different characters next to the Pinyin in each group of homonyms, then form a word/phrase with each character:**

a. zài: ______________________ b. yī: ______________________

zài: ______________________ yī: ______________________

c. yào: ______________________ d. míng: ______________________

yào: ______________________ míng: ______________________

2. Use each of the following characters to form as many words as possible:

a. 天 → ______________________________

b. 看 → ______________________________

c. 午 → ______________________________

d. 车 → ______________________________

III. Structure Exercises

1. Correct any errors in the following sentences:

a. 我正在看了一本英文书。

→ ______________________________

b. 他一个早上开车了。

→ ______________________________

c. 他还不在吃午饭呢。

→ ______________________________

d. 我吃饭了就去看你。

→ ______________________________

e. 他们先daò了学校，才去银行。

→ ______________________________

f. 他昨天就去北京呢。

→ ______________________________

2. Complete the following sentences:

a. 你 _____ 住在北京吗?

我 _____ 住在北京 _____。

b. 我哥哥在南京念 ____ 两个月的书，就去东京 _____。

c. 你吃 ______ 午饭 ____ 吗?

_____ ______ 吃呢，太忙了。我 ______ 念英文呢，你呢?

我 _____ ______ 吃呢。我 ______ 不饿。

## Supplementary Reading

### Reading 1

打车

开chū租汽车的：你好！ 你去哪儿?

打车的：北京医院。

开chū租汽车的：行。上车吧！

打车的：谢谢。

开chū租汽车的：Dào了。十二块。

打车的：给你二十块。

开chū租汽车的：你有两块钱吗？ 我给你十块。

打车的：对不qǐ，我没有两块钱。

开chū租汽车的：没事儿。我找你八块。

打车的：谢谢。

COMPREHENSION QUESTIONS

1. 从上车的地方dào北京医院打车要多shǎo钱?

2. 打车的给开chū租汽车的多shǎo钱?

Reading 2

## Xǐ欢喝酒的商人

有的人很xǐ欢喝酒，也很会喝酒。他们喝pí酒，也喝白酒。五六个人就néng喝四五十píng pí酒。很多人都说："要是想gēn会喝酒的人做生意，就得先学喝酒。"Gēn他们做生意，他们请你喝酒，你一定要喝。要是你不喝，他们心里会想你不是真心想gēn他们做生意。

COMPREHENSION QUESTIONS

1. 要是想gēn会喝酒的人做生意，就得先学什么?

2. 要是你不喝，他们会gēn你做生意吗?

## Character Practice

| | | | | | | | | | |
|---|---|---|---|---|---|---|---|---|---|
| 久 | 久 | | | | | | | | |
| 才 | 才 | | | | | | | | |
| 已 | 已 | | | | | | | | |
| 今 | 今 | | | | | | | | |
| 头 | 头 | | | | | | | | |
| 发 | 发 | | | | | | | | |
| 休 | 休 | | | | | | | | |
| 回 | 回 | | | | | | | | |
| 花 | 花 | | | | | | | | |
| 肚 | 肚 | | | | | | | | |
| 坏 | 坏 | | | | | | | | |
| 杯 | 杯 | | | | | | | | |
| 定 | 定 | | | | | | | | |

| 始 | 始 | | | | | | | | |
|---|---|---|---|---|---|---|---|---|---|
| 经 | 经 | | | | | | | | |
| 药 | 药 | | | | | | | | |
| 院 | 院 | | | | | | | | |
| 昨 | 昨 | | | | | | | | |
| 挤 | 挤 | | | | | | | | |
| 除 | 除 | | | | | | | | |
| 息 | 息 | | | | | | | | |
| 烧 | 烧 | | | | | | | | |
| 最 | 最 | | | | | | | | |
| 等 | 等 | | | | | | | | |
| 医 | 医 | | | | | | | | |
| 点 | 点 | | | | | | | | |

| 然 | 然 | | | | | | | | |
|---|---|---|---|---|---|---|---|---|---|
| 病 | 病 | | | | | | | | |
| 疼 | 疼 | | | | | | | | |
| 钱 | 钱 | | | | | | | | |
| 银 | 银 | | | | | | | | |

# CHAPTER THIRTEEN

# 第 十 三 课

**Text**

去年秋天，方美春和同学们到北京来学汉语。来北京以前，他们都已经学了一年的汉语。以前，谁也没有来过中国。他们到北京的第二天就开始上课了。除了星期六和星期日以外，他们天天都有课。上午从八点十分到十一点半上中文课，下午从一点三刻到四点钟有练习课。下课以后还要做很多作业。他们最ài去图书馆做作业，因为那儿很安jìng。同学们个个都很用功，天天都很忙。

到了星期六，星期日人人都很高兴。他们可以在家liáo天，做饭，也可以去看电yǐng，去商diàn买东西，去玩儿。来北京以前，方美春没有做过饭，现在她做的中国炒饭人人都说好吃。她常常请同学们和老师来她这儿吃饭。人人都ài吃她做的中国炒饭。美春打电话告诉妈妈，说明年春天回家的时候她做炒饭给妈妈吃。上个月二十号星期天是方美春的生日，她的nán朋友海明说因为是美春的生日，别在家做饭了，他要请美春和朋友们去一家好的饭馆儿吃晚饭。他听说银行对面的那家xīn的英国饭馆儿外边儿，里边儿都不错。他希望去那儿。美春说当然可以。不过，英国饭馆儿一定没有炒饭。美春拿了很多炒饭去饭馆儿。美春的同学，朋友差不多都来了。你知道一共来了多少人？ 二十多个！ 他们还请了英国老板一块儿来吃。海明高兴地说："真不错，我还没在英国饭馆儿吃过中国炒饭呢。"英国老板还说以后要gēn美春学做中国炒饭。

**生词 New Words**

| | | |
|---|---|---|
| 方美春 | Fāng Měichūn | (N) a personal name |
| 去年 | qùnián | (TW) last year |
| 秋天 | qiūtiān | (TW) autumn, fall |
| 到 | dào | (CV) to |
| ……以前 | …yǐqián | (Pat) before… |
| 年 | -nián | (TD) year(s) |
| 谁 | shéi/shuí | (Pr) who |
| 过 | -guo | (P) (used after a verb to indicate an experience) |
| 到 | dào | (V) arrive |
| 第 | dì- | (Pre) (indicates numerical order) |
| 星期 | xīngqī | (TW) week |
| 星期日/天 | xīngqīrì/tiān | (TW) Sunday |
| 点 | -diǎn | (Cl) (number) o'clock |
| 分 | -fēn | (Cl) minute |
| 半 | bàn | (NU) half, semi- |
| 刻(钟) | kè (zhōng) | (Cl) quarter hour, fifteen minutes |
| 钟 | zhōng | (N) clock (also time as measured in hours/minutes) |

| | | |
|---|---|---|
| 练习 | -liànxí | (V/N) practice |
| 下课 | xià kè | (VO) finish class |
| ……以后 | …yǐhòu | (Pat) after… |
| 作业 | zuòyè | (N) schoolwork, homework |
| 安jìng | ānjìng | (SV) be peaceful and quiet |
| 个个, 人人, 天天 | Cl Cl (gège, etc.) | (Pat) every… |
| 用功 | yònggōng | (SV) be diligent |
| 高兴 | gāoxìng | (SV) be happy |
| 电yǐng | diànyǐng | (N) movie |
| 饭 | fàn | (N) meal, cooked rice, food, cuisine |
| 玩儿 | wánr | (V) have a good time, play |
| 现在 | xiànzài | (TW) presently, now |
| 常常 | chángcháng | (Adv) frequently, often |
| 老师 | lǎoshī | (N) teacher |
| 这儿,这里 | zhèr, zhèlǐ | (PW) here, this place |
| 明年 | míngnián | (TW) next year |
| 春天 | chūntiān | (TW) spring |
| ……的时候 | …de shí.hòu | (Pat) at the time of… |
| 上(个)月 | shàng(ge)yuè | (TW) last month |
| 号 | -hào | (Cl) day of the month |
| 生日 | shēngrì | (N) birthday |
| 海明 | Hǎimíng | (N) a personal name |
| 别 | bié | (Conj) don't (imperative) |
| 听说 | tīngshuō | (V) hear it said that… |
| 不错 | búcuò | (SV) be pretty good |
| 对面 | duìmiàn | (PW) side directly opposite |
| 里边儿 | lǐ.biānr | (PS/ PW) inside |
| 希望 | xīwàng | (V) hope, wish |
| 当然 | dāngrán | (Adv) of course |
| 不过 | bú guò | (Conj) still, however |
| 差不多 | chàbuduō | (Ex) almost, just about, good enough |
| 多少? | duōshǎo? | (Q) how many? how much? |
| 地 | -de | (P) (marks the manner in which a single instance of an action is carried out) |
| Adv 地V | Adv de V | (Pat) indicates single instance manner of an action |
| 以后 | yǐhòu | (TW) afterward |

## COMPREHENSION QUESTIONS

Read the text of this chapter and answer the following questions.

1. 去年秋天以前，方美春和他的同学去过北京吗?

2. 去北京以前他们学了多久的中文?

3. 他们天天都要上课吗?

4. 他们几点上中文课?

5. 下午有什么课?

6. 他们最xǐ欢去哪儿做作业?

7. 为什么同学们天天都很忙?

8. 为什么到了星期六同学们都很高兴? 他们星期六，星期日做什么?

9. 方美春做的什么菜人人都xǐ欢吃?

10. 谁是方美春的nán朋友?

11. 生日那天,他们去哪儿吃饭?

12. 还请了什么人?

______________________________________________

13. 说说方美春生日的晚饭。

______________________________________________

## Writing Help

### Independent Characters

| Character | Basic Meaning | No. of Str. | Stroke Order | Radical | Compo-nents | Struct-ure |
|---|---|---|---|---|---|---|
| *习(習) xí | to study | 3 | 乛 刁 习 | 乙 | 乛 冫 | □ |
| 月 yuè | month | 4 | 月 | 月 | 月 | □ |
| *业(業) yè | line of business | 5 | 丨 丨丨 丨丨丶 丨丨丶丿 业 | 业 | 丨丨 丶丿 一 | □ |
| 年 nián | year | 6 | 丿 𠂉 𠂉一 𠂉丨 𠂉丰 年 | 丿 | 年 | □ |
| *里(裏) lǐ | inside | 7 | 曰 里 | 里 | 田 土 | □ |

### Compound Characters

The following are the new compound characters in this chapter with radicals you have learned: 号, 过, 安, 兴, 作, 时, 听, 练, 秋, 星, 钟, 春, 面, 差, 候, 谁, 第, 望, 期, and 错.

| Character | Basic Meaning | No. of Str. | Stroke Order | Radical | Mean. Clue | Phon. Clue | Compo-nents | Struct-ure |
|---|---|---|---|---|---|---|---|---|
| 号(號) hào | to call | 5 | 口 口一 号 | 口 | 口 | | 口 丂 | ⿱ |
| 过(過) guò | to pass | 6 | 辶 过 | 辶 | 辶 | | 辶 寸 | ⿺ |
| 安 ān | peace(ful) | 6 | 宀 安 | 宀 | 宀, 女 | | 宀 女 | ⿱ |
| *兴(興) xìng | to prosper | 6 | 丶 丷 ⺍ 𫠠 兴 | 八 | | | 𫠠 八 | ⿱ |
| 作 zuò | to do/make | 7 | 亻 作 | 亻 | 亻 | 乍 zhà | 亻 乍 | ⿰ |

| | | | | | | | | |
|---|---|---|---|---|---|---|---|---|
| 时(時) shí | time | 7 | 日 时 | 日 | 日, 寸(cùn, *inch*) | | 日 寸 | |
| 听(聽) tīng | to listen | 7 | 口 听 | 口 | 口 | 斤 jīn | 口 斤 | |
| 练(練) liàn | to practice | 8 | 纟 纩 纻 纺 练 练 | 纟 | | | 纟 东 | |
| *秋 qiū | autumn | 9 | 禾 秋 | 禾 | 禾(hé, *grains* ) 火 | | 禾 火 | |
| 星 xīng | star | 9 | 日 星 | 日 | 日 | 生 | 日 生 | |
| 钟(鐘) zhōng | clock; surname | 9 | 丿 𠂉 𠂉 钅 钟 | 钅 | 钅 | 中 | 钅 中 | |
| *春 chūn | spring | 9 | 一 二 三 龵 夫 春 | 日 | 日 | | 夫 日 | |
| 面 miàn | side | 9 | 一 丆 丙 而 而 面 | 一 | | | 丆 回 | |
| 差 chà | difference | 9 | 𦍌 差 | 羊 | | | 𦍌 工 | |
| *候 hòu | to wait for | 10 | 亻 亻 仁 候 | 亻 | | | 亻 丨 工 矢 | |
| 谁(誰) shéi | who | 11 | 讠 讠 讠 讠 谁 谁 谁 | 讠 | 讠 | | 讠 亻 隹 | |
| *第 dì | order, grade | 11 | ⺮ 第 | 竹 | | 弟 | ⺮ 弔 | |
| 望 wàng | to gaze into the distance | 11 | 亠 亡 望 望 | 月 | | 王 | 亡 月 王 | |
| *期 qī | period | 12 | 一 十 卄 卄 甘 甘 其 其 期 | 月 | 月 | 其 qī | 其 月 | |
| 错(錯) cuò | error, mistake | 13 | 钅 钅 钅 钅 钅 错 | 钅 | | | 钅 昔 | |

安: The presence of a woman under the roof provides a sense of peace.
兴: Lots of things growing on the ground 一 with roots underneath 八: prosperous.
时: A small part, 寸, of a full day, 日, is time.
秋: Grains 禾 under the hot sun 火 become ready for harvest: autumn.

## Radicals

The new radicals introduced in this chapter are 刂, 巾, 小, and 王.

### 1. 刂

刂 is a variant form of the character 刀 *dāo* (knife). As a radical it often is found on the right-hand side of a character, indicating "knife" or a related meaning. The compound characters in this chapter that contain this radical are 别, 刻, and 到.

| Character | Basic Meaning | No. of Str. | Stroke Order | Mean. Clue | Phon. Clue | Compo-nents | Struct-ure |
|---|---|---|---|---|---|---|---|
| 别 bié | other, not | 7 | 口 另 别 | 另 (lìng, another), 刂 (separating one from another) | | 口 力 刂 | ⿰ |
| 刻 kè | quarter of an hour; carve | 8 | 亠 亡 亥 亥 刻 | 刂 | | 亥 刂 | ⿰ |
| 到 dào | to arrive | 8 | 一 ㄠ 厶 至 到 | 至 (zhì, reach) | | 厶 土 刂 | ⿰ |

### 2. 巾

巾 *jīn*, towel, can be used as a character as well as a radical. The compound characters in this chapter that contain this radical are 师, 希, and 常.

| Character | Basic Meaning | No. of Str. | Stroke Order | Mean. Clue | Phon. Clue | Compo-nents | Struct-ure |
|---|---|---|---|---|---|---|---|
| *师(師) shī | teacher | 6 | 丨 刂 刂 师 师 | | | 刂 一 巾 | ⿰ |
| *希 xī | to expect | 7 | ノ ㄨ 㐅 产 产 肴 希 | | | ㄨ 布 | ⿱ |
| 常 cháng | often; surname | 11 | 丨 丬 丬 ⺌ 尚 常 | | | ⺌ 口 巾 | ⿳ |

3. 小

This character can also be used as a radical. The compound characters in this chapter that contain this radical are 少 and 当.

| Character | Basic Meaning | No. of Str. | Stroke Order | Mean. Clue | Phon. Clue | Compo-nents | Struct-ure |
|---|---|---|---|---|---|---|---|
| 少 shǎo | few | 4 | 小 少 | | 小 | 小 丿 | ⊟ |
| 当 dāng | to undertake | 6 | 丨 丬 𭕄 当 | | | ⺌ 彐 | ⊟ |

4. 王

王 as a character means "king." As a radical it is used in compound characters related to jade or something precious. The compound characters in this chapter that contain this radical are 玩 and 现.

| Character | Basic Meaning | No. of Str. | Stroke Order | Mean. Clue | Phon. Clue | Compo-nents | Struct-ure |
|---|---|---|---|---|---|---|---|
| 玩 wán | to play | 8 | 王 玗 玩 | 王 | 元 yuán | 王元 | ◫ |
| *现(現) xiàn | now | 8 | 王 现 | | 见 | 王见 | ◫ |

玩: It is a rich man's hobby to collect and play with jade.

## EXERCISES

### I. Character Exercises

1. **Form new characters by using different components of the following characters.**

**Example:** 工 (from 功) + ナ (from 有) → 左

| 昨, 定, 找, 过, 功, 别, 休 |
|---|

_____ (from _____ ) + _____ (from _____ ) → _____

_____ (from _____ ) + _____ (from _____ ) → _____

_____ (from _____ ) + _____ (from _____ ) → _____

_____ (from _____ ) + _____ (from _____ ) → _____

_____ (from _____ ) + _____ (from _____ ) → _____

2. Write as many as possible of the characters you have learned that can be divided into left-hand and right-hand parts. For example, 谁.

_______________________________________________

3. Fill in the blanks according to the Pinyin given:

a. 用 gōng → 用 ________ b. zuò 业 → ________ 业

4. Solve the character riddle:

听说一半多一点: ________________

II. Vocabulary Exercises

1. Write the Pinyin for the following characters, then form a word with each character:

a. 学 ( ) ________________ b. 作 ( ) ________________

字 ( ) ________________ 做 ( ) ________________

2. Form as many words or phrases as you can using the characters below:

| 星, 老, 望, 面, 日, 期, 么, 希, 下, 听, 怎, 兴, 对, 在,<br>上, 始, 说, 现, 秋, 作, 午, 课, 天, 业, 师, 开, 高 |
|---|

_______________________________________________

_______________________________________________

_______________________________________________

_______________________________________________

3. **What are the differences between the two? Please explain each phrase in English.**

a 六月 ______________________ b. 十一月 ______________________

六个月 ______________________ 十一个月 ______________________

c. 几月? ______________________

几个月? ______________________

## Supplementary Reading

### Reading 1

高小春: 文海,你上哪儿去?

王文海: 上课。

高小春: 你几点上课?

王文海: 两点。

高小春: 现在几点?

王文海: 差十分两点。

高小春: 那,你快走吧!

王文海: 再见。

高小春: 再见。

COMPREHENSION QUESTIONS

1. 王文海几点上课?

______________________________

2. 王文海gēn高小春说话的时候是几点?

______________________________

Reading 2

## 没事儿

中国人常用"没事儿"。你gēn朋友说好七点在电yǐng院等他。你七点半才到。你说:"对不qǐ,我来晚了。"他说:"没事儿。"朋友请你到饭馆儿吃饭。可是,你忘了去。第二天你给朋友打电话,你说:"对不qǐ,昨天晚上我忘了你请我吃饭这事儿。"你朋友说:"没事儿。"你们知道这里的两个"没事儿"是什么意思吗?在这里,"没事儿"就是"没关系、没什么"的意思。

COMPREHENSION QUESTIONS

1. 你gēn你的中国朋友说"对不qǐ",他会对你说什么?

______________________________

2. "没事儿"这jù话是什么意思?

______________________________

## Character Practice

| | | | | | | | | | |
|---|---|---|---|---|---|---|---|---|---|
| 习 | 习 | | | | | | | | |
| 月 | 月 | | | | | | | | |
| 业 | 业 | | | | | | | | |
| 年 | 年 | | | | | | | | |
| 里 | 里 | | | | | | | | |
| 号 | 号 | | | | | | | | |
| 过 | 过 | | | | | | | | |
| 安 | 安 | | | | | | | | |
| 兴 | 兴 | | | | | | | | |
| 作 | 作 | | | | | | | | |
| 时 | 时 | | | | | | | | |
| 听 | 听 | | | | | | | | |
| 练 | 练 | | | | | | | | |

| 秋 | 秋 | | | | | | | | |
|---|---|---|---|---|---|---|---|---|---|
| 星 | 星 | | | | | | | | |
| 钟 | 钟 | | | | | | | | |
| 春 | 春 | | | | | | | | |
| 面 | 面 | | | | | | | | |
| 差 | 差 | | | | | | | | |
| 候 | 候 | | | | | | | | |
| 谁 | 谁 | | | | | | | | |
| 第 | 第 | | | | | | | | |
| 望 | 望 | | | | | | | | |
| 期 | 期 | | | | | | | | |
| 错 | 错 | | | | | | | | |
| 别 | 别 | | | | | | | | |

| | | | | | | | | | |
|---|---|---|---|---|---|---|---|---|---|
| 刻 | 刻 | | | | | | | | |
| 到 | 到 | | | | | | | | |
| 师 | 师 | | | | | | | | |
| 希 | 希 | | | | | | | | |
| 常 | 常 | | | | | | | | |
| 少 | 少 | | | | | | | | |
| 当 | 当 | | | | | | | | |
| 玩 | 玩 | | | | | | | | |
| 现 | 现 | | | | | | | | |

# CHAPTER FOURTEEN
# 第 十 四 课

## Text

前天是星期六，早上九点左右，方美春还没起床呢，她的男朋友海明就给她打电话，海明说想请她去城里玩儿。他说他十点在城里的大商场书店门口等她。从方美春住的地方去城里的那个大商场差不多要一个钟头，要是人多，车挤的话，就要一个多钟头。方美春起床以后，没吃早饭就chū门了。她先坐公共汽车去城里，然后走lù去商场。下车的时候，已经十点差五分了。她想，“哎呀，我晚了。海明一定已经在商场门口等我了。我得走得快一点儿。”从车zhàn到商场美春平常要走一刻钟，那天她走得很快，十点过五分她就到了。海明已经在那儿等了半天了，他九点三刻就来了。海明问美春想去哪儿。美春说：“快冬天了，我想买一条冬天chuān的裙子。”他们上商场的二楼，那儿有很多好看的衣服，有好多裙子，什么颜sè的都有,有红的、粉红的、灰的、黄的、浅蓝的、白的、深绿的。海明问美春ài什么颜sè的，美春说：“这么多颜sè，我不知道我xǐ欢什么了。”海明说：“那你就一条一条chuānchuan吧。看看你chuān哪一条最好看。”美春chuān了好几条，花了一个多钟头，一条也不xǐ欢。有的不好看，有的太guì。她说：“我饿了，我没吃早饭，现在快中午了，咱们去那个有名的韩国饭馆儿吃顿午饭吧。午饭以后去别的商场看看。”海明说：“你一个人去吧，我在前面的咖啡馆儿看书。你买了裙子来找我。”

美春去了三家商店，都没有她xǐ欢的裙子。她去咖啡馆儿找海明。海明正喝着咖啡在看书，他看书看得很快，已经看了几十页了。他真不懂，买一条裙子怎么这么难。美春别的事都做得很快，就是买东西tè别慢。

美春说：“我累了，咱们回家吧。明天再来。”海明不高兴地说：“我明天不来了，我要预备下星期的考试。我们今天chū门不是来买东西的，也不是来看书的，而是来玩儿的。你要是不买裙子，咱们今天就可以去玩儿了。你jiāng来买东西别找我，还是找别人一块儿去吧。”

## 生词 New Words

| | | |
|---|---|---|
| 前天 | qiántiān | (TW) the day before yesterday |
| 左右 | zuǒyòu | (Adv) about, more or less |
| 起床 | qǐ chuáng | (VO) get out of bed; get up |
| 男 | nán | (Pre) male (human) |
| 里 | lǐ | (PS/PW) inside |
| 商场 | shāngchǎng | (PW) market; bazaar |
| 书店 | shūdiàn | (PW) bookshop |
| 钟头 | zhōng.tóu | (N) hour |
| 要是……(的话)就 | yào.shì...(de huà) jiù | (Pat) if...then |
| chū门 | chū mén | (VO) go out, leave home (for a bit) |
| 差 | chà | (V) lacking, less than |
| 得 | de | (P) (marks the manner or extent of an action) |
| (VO)V 得…… | (VO)V de... | (Pat) (indicates customary manner or the extent of an action) |
| 快 | kuài | (SV) be fast, be quick |
| 平常 | píngcháng | (Adv) usually |
| 过 | guò | (V) surpassing, more than, pass by |
| 半天 | bàntiān | (TD) for a long time |
| 冬天 | dōngtiān | (TW) winter |
| 裙子 | qúnzi | (N) dress; skirt (Cl -*tiáo* 条) |
| 楼 | -lóu | (Cl) floor |
| 衣服 | yīfu | (N) clothing (Cl -*jiàn* 件) |
| 好 | hǎo | (Adv) quite, very |
| 颜sè | yán.sè | (N) color |
| 红 | hóng | (SV) be red |
| 粉红 | fěnhóng | (SV) be pink |
| 灰 | huī | (SV) be grey |
| 黄 | huáng | (SV) be yellow |
| 浅 | qiǎn | (SV) be shallow; be light |
| 蓝 | lán | (SV) be blue |
| 白 | bái | (SV) be white |
| 深 | shēn | (SV) be deep; be dark; be profound |
| 绿 | lǜ | (SV) be green |
| 那 | nà | (Conj) in that case |
| 看 | kàn | (V) consider, be of the opinion |
| 好 | hǎo | (SV) several |

| | | |
|---|---|---|
| 中午 | zhōngwǔ | (TW) noon |
| 咱们 | zánmen | (Pr) we, us (inclusive of listener) |
| 韩国 | Hán.guó | (PW) Korea |
| 顿 | -dùn | (Cl) used with 饭 to mean "meal" |
| 别的 | biéde | (N) other |
| 咖啡馆儿 | kāfēiguǎnr | (PW) café |
| 商店 | shāngdiàn | (PW) shop; store (Cl -*jiā* 家) |
| 在 | zài | (Adv) be…ing |
| 页 | -yè | (Cl) page |
| 懂 | dǒng | (V) understand |
| 难 | nán | (SV) be difficult |
| 事 | shì | (N) matter, affair |
| tè别 | tèbié | (SV) be special |
| 慢 | màn | (SV) be slow |
| 累 | lèi | (SV) be physically drained, be tired |
| 预备 | yùbei | (V) prepare |
| 下星期 | xiàxīngqī | (TW) next week |
| 不是……(而)是…… | búshì…(ér)shì… | (Pat) it's not…but rather |
| jiāng来 | jiānglái | (TW) in the future, future |
| 还是 | háishì | (Adv) still (best to…) |
| 别人 | biéren | (N) other people |

## COMPREHENSION QUESTIONS

1. **Read the text of this chapter and then complete the following timetable according to the context:**

| Time<br>时间 | Person<br>人 | Action<br>做什么 |
|---|---|---|
| **9:00 a.m.** | | |
| **9:45 a.m.** | | |
| **9:55 a.m.** | | |
| **10:05 a.m.** | | |

2. **Indicate if the following statements are true or false according to the text:**

a. (　　　) 美春想买一条裙子。

b. (　　　) 海明知道美春xǐ欢什么颜sè。

c. (　　　) 美春不xǐ欢她chuān的那几条裙子。

d. (　　　) 美春xǐ欢吃日本菜。

e. (　　　) 他们一块去咖啡馆儿喝茶。

f. (　　　) 海明要买一本书。

g. (　　　) 海明看书看得很慢。

h. (　　　) 美春什么事都做得很快，买东西也很快。

i. (　　　) 海明明天没有事。

j. (　　　) 海明今天很想跟美春一块去玩儿。

k. (　　　) 因为她买东西买得太慢，海明jiāng来不要跟美春去买东西了。

# Writing Help

## Independent Characters

| Character | Basic Meaning | No. of Str. | Stroke Order | Radical | Compo-nents | Struct-ure |
|---|---|---|---|---|---|---|
| 平 píng | flat | 5 | 一 丆 ㄇ 亚 平 | 一 | 干 丷 | □ |
| *页(頁) yè | page | 6 | 页 | 页 | 页 | □ |
| 而 ér | but | 6 | 一 丆 丙 而 而 | 一 | 而 | □ |

## Compound Characters

The following are the new compound characters in this chapter with radicals you have learned: 冬, 场, 红, 灰, 浅, 咱, 难, 黄, 深, 绿, 韩, 裙, 蓝, 楼, 慢, and 懂.

| Character | Basic Meaning | No. of Str. | Stroke Order | Radical | Mean. Clue | Phon. Clue | Compo -nents | Struct- ure |
|---|---|---|---|---|---|---|---|---|
| *冬 dōng | winter | 5 | 夂 冬 | 冫 | | | 夂 冫 | |
| 场(場) chǎng | site, gathering place | 6 | 土 场 | 土 | 土 | 𠃓 (indicat-ing 'ang') | 土 𠃓 | |
| 红(紅) hóng | red | 6 | 纟 红 | 纟 | 纟 | 工 gōng | 纟 工 | |
| 灰 huī | grey | 6 | 𠂇 𠂇 𠂇 灰 | 火 | 𠂇 (cover), 火 | | 𠂇 火 | |
| 浅(淺) qiǎn | shallow | 8 | 氵 氵 氵 浅 浅 浅 | 氵 | 氵 | 戋 (indicat-ing 'ian') | 氵 戋 | |
| 咱 zán | I, me | 9 | 口 咱 | 口 | 口 | | 口 自 | |
| 难(難) nán | difficult | 10 | 又 对 对 对 难 难 难 | 又 | | | 又 隹 | |
| 黄 huáng | yellow; surname | 11 | 艹 龷 龷 龷 黄 黄 黄 黄 | 艹 | 艹 | | 艹 一 由 八 | |
| 深 shēn | deep | 11 | 氵 氵 氵 深 | 氵 | 氵 | 罙 (indicat-ing 'en') | 氵 冖 八 木 | |
| 绿(綠) lǜ | green | 11 | 纟 纟 纟 纟 纟 纟 纟 绿 绿 | 纟 | 纟 | 录 lù | 纟 录 | |
| *韩(韓) hán | Korea | 12 | 一 十 十 古 古 古 卓 卓 卓 卓 韩 韩 | 十 | | | 十 日 十 韦 | |
| *裙 qún | skirt | 12 | 衤 衤 衤 衤 衤 裙 | 衤 | 衤 | 君 jūn | 衤 尹 口 | |
| 蓝(藍) lán | blue | 13 | 艹 艹 艹 艹 艹 艹 艹 蓝 | 艹 | 艹 | 监 (indicat-ing 'ian') | 艹 监 | |

| | | | | | | | | |
|---|---|---|---|---|---|---|---|---|
| 楼(樓) lóu | build, floor | 13 | 木 木 杧 柈 柈 楼 楼 | 木 | 木 | 娄 lóu | 木米女 | |
| 慢 màn | slow | 14 | 忄 忄 愠 慢 | 忄 | 忄 | 曼 màn | 忄日四又 | |
| 懂 dǒng | to understand | 15 | 忄 忄 忄 忄 懂 懂 | 忄 | 忄 | 董 dǒng | 忄艹重(千里) | |

监: Though this character is pronounced *jiān* when it functions as an independent character, as a phonetic component it often indicates the *ian* sound.

## Radicals

The new radicals introduced in this chapter are 广, 田, 米, 页, and 走.

### 1. 广

广 *guǎng* as a character means "extensive." As a radical it is used as the left half enclosure in a compound character. The compound characters in this chapter that contain this radical are 床 and 店.

| Character | Basic Meaning | No. of Str. | Stroke Order | Mean. Clue | Phon. Clue | Compo-nents | Struct-ure |
|---|---|---|---|---|---|---|---|
| 床 chuáng | bed | 7 | 丶 亠 广 床 | 木 | | 广 木 | |
| 店 diàn | shop | 8 | 亠 亠 广 庐 店 | 占 (zhàn, *to occupy*) | | 广 占 | |

店: Think of a shop as occupying an enclosed space.

### 2. 田

田 *tián* as a character means "field." As a radical it indicates "field" or "hard work." The compound characters in this chapter that contain this radical are 男, 备, and 累.

| Character | Basic Meaning | No. of Str. | Stroke Order | Mean. Clue | Phon. Clue | Compo-nents | Struct-ure |
|---|---|---|---|---|---|---|---|
| *男 nán | male | 7 | 丨 冂 冂 冊 田 男 | 田, 力 (lì, *strength*) | | 田 力 | |
| 备(備) bèi | ready | 8 | 夂 备 | | | 夂 田 | |
| 累 lèi | tired | 11 | 田 罒 罒 罒 累 | 田, 糸 (*silk*) | | 田 糸 | |

累: It is tiring work to raise silkworms in a field.

3. 米

This character can also be used as a radical in compound characters related to rice or things made of rice. The compound character in this chapter that contains this radical is 粉.

| Character | Basic Meaning | No. of Str. | Stroke Order | Mean. Clue | Phon. Clue | Compo-nents | Struct-ure |
|---|---|---|---|---|---|---|---|
| 粉 fěn | (rice) powder | 10 | 米 粉 | 米 | 分 | 米分 | ⿰ |

4. 页

This can also be used as a radical in compound characters. The compound characters in this chapter that contain this radical are 预, 顿, and 颜.

| Character | Basic Meaning | No. of Str. | Stroke Order | Mean. Clue | Phon. Clue | Compo-nents | Struct-ure |
|---|---|---|---|---|---|---|---|
| *预(預) yù | in advance | 10 | ㇇ マ 子 予 预 | | 予 yú | 予 页 | ⿰ |
| *顿(頓) dùn | (classifier) | 10 | 一 匚 屯 屯 顿 | | 屯 tún | 屯 页 | ⿰ |
| *颜(顏) yán | color | 15 | 亠 立 产 颜 | | 彦 yàn | 彦 页 | ⿰ |

5. 走

This character can also be used as a radical in compound characters indicating movement. The compound character in this chapter that contains this radical is 起.

| Character | Basic Meaning | No. of Str. | Stroke Order | Mean. Clue | Phon. Clue | Compo-nents | Struct-ure |
|---|---|---|---|---|---|---|---|
| 起 qǐ | to get up | 10 | 土 走 走 起 起 | 走 | 己 jǐ | 走 己 | ⿺ |

## EXERCISES

### I. Character Exercises

1. Form new characters by using different components of the following characters.

Example: 工 (from 功) + ナ (from 有) → 左

| 法，钱，息，场，点，床，备 |
|---|

_____ (from _____ ) + _____ (from _____ ) → _____

_____ (from _____ ) + _____ (from _____ ) → _____

_____ (from _____ ) + _____ (from _____ ) → _____

_____ (from _____ ) + _____ (from _____ ) → _____

_____ (from _____ ) + _____ (from _____ ) → _____

2. Correct the following characters if they are wrong:

a. 篮色 → ______________  b. 钱绿色 → ______________

c. 分红 → ______________  d. 起店 → ______________

### II. Vocabulary Exercises

1. Write different characters next to the Pinyin in each group of homonyms. Then form a word/phrase with each character:

a. zuò ( ) ______________________________

zuò ( ) ______________________________

b. wèi ( ) ______________________________

wèi ( ) ______________________________

c. nán ( ) ______________________________

nán ( ) ______________________________

2. Write the Pinyin for the following characters. Then form a word with each character:

a. 而 (          ) ____________________

b. 面 (          ) ____________________

c. 慢 (          ) ____________________

3. How many words/phrases can you form with the following characters?

a. 天 → ______________________________________________________________

b. 午 → ______________________________________________________________

c. 上 → ______________________________________________________________

III. Structure Exercises

1. Complete the following sentences:

a. 他说英文 _________________，我不懂。

b. 法国菜，他 ________ 最 ________，我们都xǐ欢吃。

c. 小方很用功，他说汉语 _________________。

d. 老王开车 _________________，所以我们都不坐他的车。

## Supplementary Reading

### Reading 1

老板：　怎么yàng?　这件衬衫行吗?

万小冬：　有点儿大。有小一点儿的吗?

老板：　这件是中号的，行吗?

万小冬：　我不xǐ欢黄sè。有别的颜sè的吗?

老板：　还有浅蓝sè的。

万小冬：　给我看看。

老板：　你看看。不错吧!

万小冬：　多少钱?

老板：　六百五十块。

万小冬：　这么guì!　便宜一点儿，行吗?　五百块。

老板：　不行。最少六百块。

万小冬：　好吧，好吧。给你六百块。

#### COMPREHENSION QUESTIONS

1. 万小冬要买什么?

______________________________

2. 万小冬花了多少钱买了那件浅蓝.sè的衬衫?

______________________________

**Reading 2**

这是学文给美春xiě的一fēng电子yóu件[1]。

* * *

美春:

下星期六是我的生日，我想请你到北京饭馆吃晚饭。北京饭馆在城里。你可以先坐火车到城里，然后走lù去饭馆儿。火车zhàn对面是图书馆。从图书馆那儿一直往前走，到了银行那儿往左拐，再往前走两条街。北京饭馆就在xié店和牛仔kù店的中jiān。你也可以打的去北京饭馆。打的很舒服，也很方便，可是很guì。

我也请了王小兰。小兰gāng从英国回来。我想你一定很想gēn她liáo天。除了小兰以外,我还请了白京以和志明。白京以还是xǐ欢qí自行车。他说从他家qí车到北京饭馆只要半个小时。对了，志明是你的línjū。你gēn他一块儿来吧。

学文

8月21日

* * *

美春看了信就给志明打电话，她问志明去不去。志明说:“当然去。可是我最不xǐ欢坐火车。我们坐chū租汽车去吧!”美春说:“好呀!”

---

[1]电子yóu件：e-mail

COMPREHENSION QUESTIONS

1. 学文为什么请客？ 学文请了几个人？ 他们是谁？

_______________________________________________

2. Identify the location of the 北京饭馆 on the map below based on the information given in the above passage. Circle the correct answer.

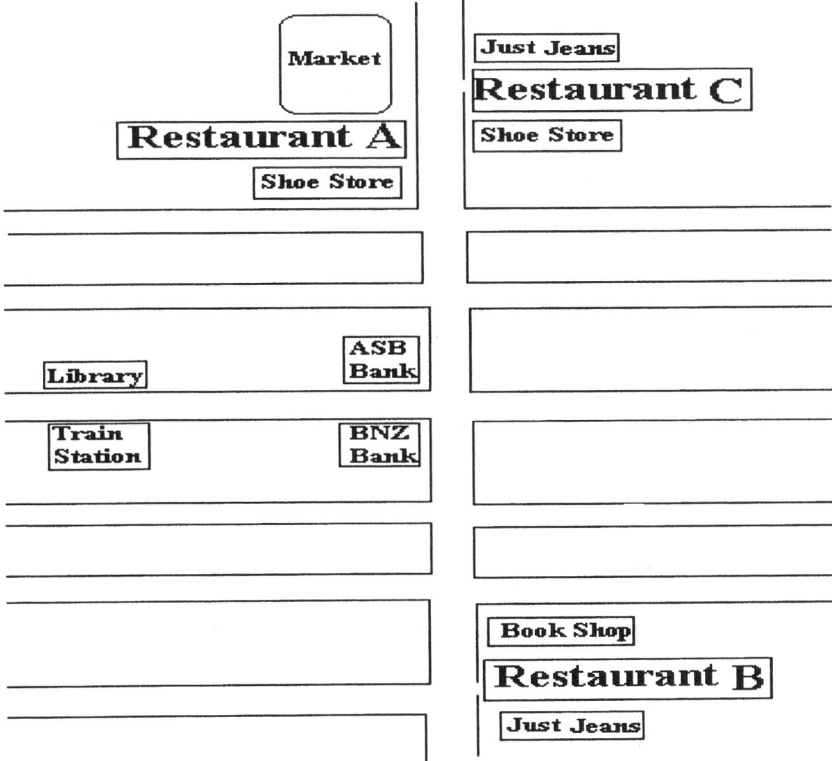


北京饭馆在哪儿？

a. Restaurant A　　b. Restaurant B　　c. Restaurant C

## Character Practice

| | | | | | | | | | |
|---|---|---|---|---|---|---|---|---|---|
| 平 | 平 | | | | | | | | |
| 页 | 页 | | | | | | | | |
| 而 | 而 | | | | | | | | |
| 冬 | 冬 | | | | | | | | |
| 场 | 场 | | | | | | | | |
| 红 | 红 | | | | | | | | |
| 灰 | 灰 | | | | | | | | |
| 浅 | 浅 | | | | | | | | |
| 咱 | 咱 | | | | | | | | |
| 难 | 难 | | | | | | | | |
| 黄 | 黄 | | | | | | | | |
| 深 | 深 | | | | | | | | |

| 绿 | 绿 | | | | | | | | |
|---|---|---|---|---|---|---|---|---|---|
| 韩 | 韩 | | | | | | | | |
| 裙 | 裙 | | | | | | | | |
| 蓝 | 蓝 | | | | | | | | |
| 楼 | 楼 | | | | | | | | |
| 慢 | 慢 | | | | | | | | |
| 懂 | 懂 | | | | | | | | |
| 床 | 床 | | | | | | | | |
| 店 | 店 | | | | | | | | |
| 男 | 男 | | | | | | | | |
| 备 | 备 | | | | | | | | |
| 累 | 累 | | | | | | | | |

| 粉 | 粉 | | | | | | | | |
|---|---|---|---|---|---|---|---|---|---|
| 预 | 预 | | | | | | | | |
| 顿 | 顿 | | | | | | | | |
| 颜 | 颜 | | | | | | | | |
| 起 | 起 | | | | | | | | |

# CHAPTER FIFTEEN
# 第 十 五 课

### Text

钱希平在城东住了七年了，后天要搬家了。因为从今年开始他在一个新的学校教书，这个学校在城南。从城东到城南开汽车要开一个半钟头。他们那儿 xià 天很热，冬天很冷，还常常下雪，春天不是刮风，就是下雨，出门很不方便。天天来回的车票也要七，八块钱，不便宜。钱希平的太太说他们一定要搬去城南住。

钱希平的新家在城南一个公寓楼里，他们的公寓在三楼。新 fáng 子很大：有四个 wòfáng，一个书 fáng，一个客厅，一个饭厅，还有一个很大的厨 fáng 和两个厕所。公寓楼里有电梯，可是他们一家平常都不会去用，他家就在三楼，不必用电梯。用楼梯，走上楼，走下楼就可以了。城南的fáng子真是guì，买这fáng子花了钱希平五十六万块钱。

要搬新家了，钱希平还要买很多家具。他的父母，哥哥，姐姐都想他买了fáng子也许没钱了，所以大家要买几件家具送给他。下个月是钱希平40岁的生日，新的家具是大家送给他的生日lǐwù。家具都很好看，钱希平最xǐ欢的是他姐姐送的饭桌，是日本做的。

住进新家以后，钱希平上班，下班都不用坐车了。孩子们上学，太太上街买东西也很方便。后边儿就是城里最高的南山。星期六，星期天还可以dài孩子们去爬山。孩子们都爱爬山。他早上不必很早起来，下午下班后，走lù十分钟就可以到家了！ 他太太做晚饭的时候，钱希平还可以gēn孩子们玩儿huò者休息休息。他晚上可以这么早回家，一家人都很高兴。

**生词 New Words**

| | | |
|---|---|---|
| 钱希平 | Qián Xīpíng | (N) a personal name |
| 后天 | hòutiān | (TW) the day after tomorrow |
| 要……了 | yào...le | (Pat) about to... |
| 搬家 | bān jiā | (VO) move house, relocate |
| 今年 | jīnnián | (TW) this year |
| 新 | xīn | (SV) be new |
| 学校 | xuéxiào | (PW) school |

| | | |
|---|---|---|
| 南 | nán | (PS) the south |
| 汽车 | qìchē | (N) automobile |
| xià天 | xiàtiān | (TW) summer |
| 热 | rè | (SV) be hot |
| 冷 | lěng | (SV) be cold |
| 下雪 | xià xuě | (VO) snow |
| 不是……就是…… | búshì…jiùshì… | (Pat) if not…then it's |
| 刮风 | guā fēng | (VO) have wind gusts |
| 下雨 | xià yǔ | (VO) rain |
| 出门 | chū mén | (VO) go out, leave home (for a bit) |
| 车票 | chēpiào | (N) bus ticket (Cl -*zhāng* 张) |
| 搬 | bān | (V) move (some large object) |
| 公寓楼 | gōngyù lóu | (PW) apartment building |
| 公寓 | gōngyù | (PW) apartment |
| 书fáng | shūfáng | (PW) den, (private) library |
| 客厅 | kètīng | (PW) living room |
| 饭厅 | fàntīng | (PW) dining room |
| 厨fáng | chúfáng | (PW) kitchen |
| 厕所 | cèsuǒ | (PW) toilet |
| 电梯 | diàntī | (N) elevator |
| 用 | yòng | (V) use |
| 楼梯 | lóutī | (N) stairs |
| 上 | shàng | (V) go or come up |
| 下 | xià | (V) go or come down |
| 是 | shì | (Pat) (used to emphasize the doer, time, or place of an action;) |
| 家具 | jiājù | (N) furniture (Cl -jiàn 件) |
| 好看 | hāokàn | (SV) good-looking; have an interesting story |
| 也许 | yěxǔ | (Adv) perhaps |
| 大家 | dàjiā | (N) everyone |
| 好些 | hǎo.xiē | (Q) several; many |
| 所以…… | suǒ.yǐ… | (Pat) therefore… |
| 下个月 | xiàgeyuè | (TW) next month |
| 岁 | -suì | (Cl) age |
| 饭桌 | fànzhuō/cānzhuō | (N) dining table |
| 是……的 | shì…de | (Pat) (used to emphasize the doer, time, or place of an action) |

| | | |
|---|---|---|
| 进 | jìn | (V) enter |
| 上班 | shàng bān | (VO) go to work |
| 下班 | xià bān | (VO) finish work |
| 上学 | shàng xué | (VO) go to school |
| 上街 | shàng jiē | (VO) go out (onto the city streets) |
| 山 | shān | (N) hill, mountain |
| 爬山 | pá shān | (VO) climb a mountain |
| 爱 | ài | (V) love |
| 早 | zǎo | (SV) be early |
| 起来 | qǐlái | (V) rise (up); get up |
| huò者 | huò.zhě | (Conj) or (in a statement) |

## COMPREHENSION QUESTIONS

**Read the text of this chapter and answer the following questions.**

1. 钱希平为什么要搬家?

______________________________

2. 他的新家在哪儿? 说说他的新家。

______________________________

3. 谁送东西给钱希平? 送了xiē什么?

______________________________

4. 钱希平最xǐ欢的是什么?

______________________________

5. 搬进新家后，他们星期六，星期天做什么?

______________________________

# Writing Help

## Independent Characters

| Character | Basic Meaning | No. of Str. | Stroke Order | Radical | Compo-nents | Struct-ure |
|---|---|---|---|---|---|---|
| 山 shān | mountain | 3 | 丨 ㇄ 山 | 山 | 山 | |
| 风(風) fēng | wind | 4 | 丿 几 风 风 | 风 | 几 㐅 | |
| 雨 yǔ | rain | 8 | 冂 帀 雨 雨 雨 雨 | 雨 | 雨 | |

## Compound Characters

The following are the new compound characters in this chapter with radicals you have learned: 许, 冷, 进, 刮, 具, 者, 校, 热, 桌, 班, 梯, 寓, and 搬.

| Character | Basic Meaning | No. of Str. | Stroke Order | Radical | Mean. Clue | Phon. Clue | Compo-nents | Struct-ure |
|---|---|---|---|---|---|---|---|---|
| 许(許) xǔ | to permit | 6 | 讠 许 | 讠 | 讠 | 午 | 讠 午 | |
| 冷 lěng | cold | 7 | 冫 冷 冷 | 冫 | 冫 | 令 lìng | 冫 令 | |
| 进(進) jìn | to enter | 7 | 一 二 井 井 进 | 辶 | 辶 | 井 jǐng | 辶 井 | |
| 刮 guā | to scrape | 8 | 千 舌 刮 | 刂 | 刂 | | 舌 刂 | |
| *具 jù | tool | 8 | 具 | 八 | | | 且 八 | |
| *者 zhě | this | 8 | 者 | 日 | | | 耂 日 | |
| *校 xiào | school | 10 | 木 木亠 校 | 木 | 木 | 交 jiāo | 木 亠 父 | |
| 热(熱) rè | hot | 10 | 扌 执 执 执 热 热 热 | 灬 | 灬 | | 扌 丸 灬 | |
| *桌 zhuō | table | 10 | 丨 ⺊ 占 桌 | 木 | 木 | 卓 zhuó | ⺊ 日 木 | |
| 班 bān | class; team | 10 | 王 王丿 珏 班 | 王 | | | 王 丿 王 | |

| *梯 tī | ladder | 11 | 木 梯 | 木 | 木 | 弟 | 木 弟 | ⿰ |
|---|---|---|---|---|---|---|---|---|
| *寓 yù | residence | 12 | 宀 宀 宀 宀 宀 寓 寓 寓 寓 | 宀 | 宀 | 禺 yù | 宀 禺 | ⿱ |
| 搬 bān | to move | 13 | 扌 扌 扌 扌 扌 扌 搬 | 扌 | 扌 | 般 bān | 扌 舟 殳 | ⿲ |

## Radicals

The new radicals introduced in this chapter are 厂, 山, 斤, 爪, 西, and 雨.

### 1. 厂

厂 *chāng*, "factory," can be used as a character as well as a radical. As a radical it is used as the left semi-enclosure in compound characters, indicating the cover. The compound characters in this chapter that contain this radical are 厅, 厕, and 厨.

| Character | Basic Meaning | No. of Str. | Stroke Order | Mean. Clue | Phon. Clue | Compo-nents | Struct-ure |
|---|---|---|---|---|---|---|---|
| *厅(廳) tīng | hall | 4 | 一 厂 厅 | 厂 | 丁 dīng | 厂 丁 | ⿸ |
| *厕(廁) cè | toilet | 8 | 厂 厕 厕 | 厂 | 则 zé | 厂 刂 | ⿸ |
| *厨(廚) chú | kitchen | 12 | 厂 厂 厂 厂 厂 厨 | 厂, 豆(dòu, *bean*) | | 厂 豆 寸 | ⿸ |

### 2. 山

This character can also be used as a radical in compound characters indicating hills or mountains. The compound characters in this chapter that contain it are 出 and 岁.

| Character | Basic Meaning | No. of Str. | Stroke Order | Mean. Clue | Phon. Clue | Compo-nents | Struct-ure |
|---|---|---|---|---|---|---|---|
| 出 chū | to go out | 5 | 丨 屮 屮 出 出 | 山,山 | | 山 山 | ⿱ |
| *岁(歲) suì | year ; age | 6 | 丨 山 山 岁 | 山(as old as a hill) | | 山 夕 | ⿱ |

出: Primitive man lived in caves among the mountains. When he wanted to go out, he needed to get out of the mountain.

### 3. 斤

As a character *(jīn)*, this is a Chinese unit of weight (equal to one half kilogram). It means "axe" when it is used as a radical. The compound characters in this chapter that contain this radical are 所 and 新.

| Character | Basic Meaning | No. of Str. | Stroke Order | Mean. Clue | Phon. Clue | Compo- nents | Struct- ure |
|---|---|---|---|---|---|---|---|
| *所 suǒ | hall | 8 | 𠂆 戶 所 | 户 (hù, *house*) | | 户 斤 | ⿰ |
| 新 xīn | new | 13 | 亠 立 立 亲 新 | | 亲 qīn | 立 木 斤 | ⿰ |

### 4. 爪

As a character 爪 (*zhuā*) means "paw." As a radical it can either be written as 爪, in which case it is found on the left of a compound character, or it can be written as 爫, in which case it is found on the top of the compound character. The compound characters in this chapter that contain this radical are 爬 and 爱.

| Character | Basic Meaning | No. of Str. | Stroke Order | Mean. Clue | Phon. Clue | Compo- nents | Struct- ure |
|---|---|---|---|---|---|---|---|
| 爬 pá | to crawl | 8 | ㇒ 𠂆 爪 爪 爬 | 爪 | 巴 bā | 爪 巴 | ⿺ |
| 爱(愛) ài | to love | 10 | ㇒ ⺈ ⺈ 爫 爫 爱 | 友 | | 爫 冖 友 | ⿱ |

### 5. 西

This character can also be used as a radical in compound characters. The compound character in this chapter that contains this radical is 票.

| Character | Basic Meaning | No. of Str. | Stroke Order | Mean. Clue | Phon. Clue | Compo- nents | Struct- ure |
|---|---|---|---|---|---|---|---|
| 票 piào | ticket | 11 | 覀 覀 票 | 示(shì, *to show*) | | 西 示 | ⿱ |

6. **雨**

雨 can also be used as a radical in compound characters indicating rain-related weather. The compound character in this chapter that contains this radical is 雪.

| Character | Basic Meaning | No. of Str. | Stroke Order | Mean. Clue | Phon. Clue | Components | Structure |
|---|---|---|---|---|---|---|---|
| 雪 xuě | snow | 11 | 雨 雪 雪 雪 | 雨 | | 雨 ⺕ | ⊟ |

## EXERCISES

### I. Character Exercises

1. **Form new characters by using different components of the following characters.**

   **Example:** 工 (from 功) + 𠂇 (from 有) → 左

   | 外，孩，梯，出，筷，许，刮 |
   |---|

   _____ (from _____ ) + _____ (from _____ ) → _____

   _____ (from _____ ) + _____ (from _____ ) → _____

   _____ (from _____ ) + _____ (from _____ ) → _____

   _____ (from _____ ) + _____ (from _____ ) → _____

   _____ (from _____ ) + _____ (from _____ ) → _____

2. **Write 2 characters containing 戈, and then form a word or a phrase with each character:**

   a. (        ) ______________________________

   b. (        ) ______________________________

3. **Solve the character riddle:**

   有一半，又有一半: _______________

## II. Vocabulary Exercises

1. Combine a character from column A with one from column B, and then write the word in brackets. No character can be used more than one time.

| A | B | |
|---|---|---|
| 刮 | 山 | (          ) |
| 公 | 雨 | (          ) |
| 下 | 桌 | (          ) |
| 厕 | 班 | (          ) |
| 家 | 许 | (          ) |
| 爬 | 风 | (          ) |
| 搬 | 梯 | (          ) |
| 饭 | 家 | (          ) |
| 上 | 具 | (          ) |
| 也 | 所 | (          ) |
| 楼 | 寓 | (          ) |

2. How many words/phrases can you form with the following characters?

   a. 公 → ______________________________

   b. 所 → ______________________________

3. Write different characters next to the Pinyin in the following set of homonyms, and then form a word/phrase with each character:

   ér (          ) ______________________________

   ér (          ) ______________________________

4. Add a radical to the following to form a new character, and then use it in a word/phrase:

主 → (     ) ______________________________

5. Write down the antonym of each of the following words. Then transcribe the new words into Pinyin:

a. 旧 → (     ) ______________

b. 慢 → (     ) ______________

III. Structure Exercises

1. Fill in each blank by choosing the most appropriate word or phrase from the alternatives provided in the box. You must not use any word or phrase more than once. There are more choices than blanks.

a.

| 会，可以，可是，从，往，到，了，已经 |
|---|
| 常常，得，以前，以后，告诉，知道，就 |

昨天中午王乐来找我喝酒，我们喝 ________ 很多酒。当然，也吃了很多好吃的东西。昨天晚上，我 ________ 不舒服了。我太太说:“不好了，你病了!”她给我喝了很多杯水，给我吃了药。________ 一点儿也没有用。我想:“我 ________ 喝酒都好好的，今天怎么了?”我坐在床上才好一点儿。我太太说我中午喝太多酒，吃太多东西了。她说我今天什么都不néng吃，只 ________ 吃米饭，喝水。我不想吃米饭，就喝了一点儿汤。________ 了晚上我只好去看医生了。

b.

| 做，作业，后面，男，半，搬，客厅，去， |
|---|
| 跟，来，huò者，而是，进，出，以后，休息 |

钱希平在我家楼上住了两年，明天上午十点 ________ 他要 ________ 家了。他是我的好朋友。他的新fáng子有一个大 ________，还有一个书fáng，孩子们下课 ________，就可以在那里写 ________。新家的 ________ 就是山，星期天还可以 ________ 孩子们 ________ 爬山，________ 在家 ________。住 ________ 新fáng子，钱希平一家一定很高兴。

## Supplementary Reading

### Reading 1

小平：学文，听说你搬家了。

学文：是呀！ 我在城里买了一个公寓。

小平：在几楼？

学文：十楼。

小平：你住这么高呀！

学文：有电梯。上下楼都很方便。

小平：我在中国住的公寓就没电梯。

学文：你住几楼？

小平：六楼。

学文：六楼！天天都要走楼梯，那一定很不方便。

小平：可不是。

### COMPREHENSION QUESTIONS

1. 学文为什么搬家？

___

2. 小平在中国的时候，为什么天天都要走楼梯？

___

## Reading 2

### 《家 春 秋》

《家》、《春》、《秋》这三本小说是中国一位很有名的作家[1] xiě的。这位作家在上海和南京上中学，在法国上大学。从1929年到1937年xiě了很多很有名的小说，《家》这本小说也是在那时候xiě的。他从1938年到1940年xiě了《春》和《秋》这两本小说。《家》、《春》、《秋》这三本小说写的是高家人的故事。很多人都xǐ欢看这位作家写xiě小说。

1. 这位作家的名字叫Bājīn (巴金, 1904–2005)。

#### COMPREHENSION QUESTIONS

1. 《家》这本小说是在什么时候xiě的？《春》和《秋》呢？

_______________________________________________

2. 《家》、《春》、《秋》这三本小说xiě的是谁家的故事？

_______________________________________________

## Character Practice

| 山 | 山 | | | | | | | | |
|---|---|---|---|---|---|---|---|---|---|
| 风 | 风 | | | | | | | | |

| | | | | | | | | | |
|---|---|---|---|---|---|---|---|---|---|
| 雨 | 雨 | | | | | | | | |
| 许 | 许 | | | | | | | | |
| 冷 | 冷 | | | | | | | | |
| 进 | 进 | | | | | | | | |
| 刮 | 刮 | | | | | | | | |
| 具 | 具 | | | | | | | | |
| 者 | 者 | | | | | | | | |
| 校 | 校 | | | | | | | | |
| 热 | 热 | | | | | | | | |
| 桌 | 桌 | | | | | | | | |
| 班 | 班 | | | | | | | | |
| 梯 | 梯 | | | | | | | | |
| 寓 | 寓 | | | | | | | | |

| 搬 | 搬 | | | | | | | | |
|---|---|---|---|---|---|---|---|---|---|
| 厅 | 厅 | | | | | | | | |
| 厕 | 厕 | | | | | | | | |
| 厨 | 厨 | | | | | | | | |
| 出 | 出 | | | | | | | | |
| 岁 | 岁 | | | | | | | | |
| 所 | 所 | | | | | | | | |
| 新 | 新 | | | | | | | | |
| 爬 | 爬 | | | | | | | | |
| 爱 | 爱 | | | | | | | | |
| 票 | 票 | | | | | | | | |
| 雪 | 雪 | | | | | | | | |

# CHAPTER SIXTEEN
# 第 十 六 课

## Text

钱希平搬进新家以后请了二十多个朋友去他家吃饭。他太太忙了三天，做了十几个菜。钱希平还买了很多酒，有白酒，红酒跟米酒，当然还有名pái儿的啤酒。两个孩子也跑来跑去地搬东西。钱希平有一个男孩子，一个女孩子。男孩子十三岁了，去年刚上中学。女孩今年才八岁，是小学生。下午五点左右，客人们都来了。希平的老同学黄家深一进门就大shēng地说："啊，希平，你真不错，能住上这么好的fáng子，我不知道什么时候才能有这么多钱买得起这么好的fáng子呢。孩子们呢？ 来，来，来，这是给你们的。"家深来都给孩子们带来他们xǐ欢的东西，跟他们玩儿。这次他给孩子们一人一本小说。孩子们也很xǐ欢家深。因为家深dài眼镜，所以孩子们叫他眼镜叔叔。

钱希平请客人们吃他太太做的菜。钱太太做的菜很地道，好些菜在饭馆里都吃不着呢。大家也喝了不少酒。家深太xǐ欢喝酒了。那天，客人当中他喝得最多了，筷子都拿不住了。他太太对他说："你喝得不少了，你不能再喝了。"可是他说："没关系！ 我还能喝得下好几杯酒呢！ 你看，我的眼睛还能看得很清楚，看得见桌子上的菜，我的耳朵还能听得很清楚你们在讲什么。来，来，喝酒！ 喝酒！ 好酒啊。"钱希平说："对，对，对！ 大家慢慢儿吃，多吃点儿，多喝点儿，别客气。我们的邻jū出门去了，不在家，吵一点儿没关系。"

二十几个朋友吃吃喝喝，吃完饭，又liáo天，到半夜才高兴地回家去睡觉。可是第二天早上谁都起不来了，家深睡醒起来已经下午两点了。

## 生词 New Words

| | | |
|---|---|---|
| 跟 | gēn | (Conj) and (usually joins nouns) |
| 名pái儿 | míngpáir | (N) famous brand, nameplate |
| 啤酒 | píjiǔ | (N) beer |
| 跑 | pǎo | (V) run |
| V来V去 | V-lái-V-qù | (Pat) indicates a thorough repetition |
| 女 | nǚ- | (Pre) (female human) |
| 刚 | gāng | (TW) just, just now |
| 小学生 | xiǎoxué.shēng | (N) elementary school pupil |
| 老 | lǎo | (SV) be old (usually of person or living things for a long time) |
| <u>黄家深</u> | <u>Huáng Jiāshēn</u> | (N) a personal name |
| 一……就…… | yī…jiù… | (Pat) as soon as |
| 门 | mén | (N) door |
| 大shēng | dà shēng | (Adv) loud |
| 啊 | á | (P) (indicates surprise, sudden realization) |
| 能 | néng | (Aux) can |
| 上 | -shàng | (VC) come/go up |
| 起 | -qǐ | (VC) afford to |
| 次 | -cì | (VCl) times |
| 带 | dài | (V) take or bring along, lead around |
| 跟 | gēn | (CV) (together) with |
| 又 | yòu | (Adv) once again |
| 给 | gěi | (V) give, give to |
| 眼镜 | yǎnjìng | (N) eyeglasses (Cl *-fù* 副) |
| 着 | -zháo | (VC) successfully complete |
| 当中 | dāngzhōng | (PS/PW) the middle (more abstract) |
| 住 | -zhù | (VC) make secure or firm |
| 少 | shǎo | (SV) lack, be deficient, lose, be missing |
| 没关系 | méi guānxi | (Ex) never mind; it doesn't matter |
| 下 | -xià | (VC) come/go down |
| 眼睛 | yǎn.jīng | (N) eye |
| 清楚 | qīng.chǔ | (SV) be clear |
| 见 | -jiàn | (VC) perceive |
| 桌子 | zhuōzi | (N) table |
| 耳朵 | ěrduo | (N) ear |
| 听 | tīng | (V) listen |
| 讲 | jiǎng | (V) speak, say |

| | | |
|---|---|---|
| 啊 | a | (P) (tells listener he or she really should have known that) |
| 邻jū | línjū | (N) neighbor |
| 吵 | chǎo | (SV) be noisy |
| 完 | -wán | (VC) finish, complete |
| 半夜 | bànyè | (N) midnight |
| 睡觉 | shuì jiào | (VO) sleep, "go to bed" |
| 来 | -lái | (VC) come |
| 睡 | shuì | (V) sleep |
| 醒 | xǐng | (V) wake (up) |

## COMPREHENSION QUESTIONS

**1. Read the text of this chapter and find the following grammatical categories in the text:**

a. Resultative complements (action + result)

b. Verbs (including stative verbs and auxiliary verbs)

c. Circle each 了, and then classify its function and meaning.

**2. Answer the following questions:**

a. 钱希平为什么请他的朋友去他家吃饭?

b. 那天有多少朋友到钱希平的家吃饭?

c. 他太太忙了几天，预备了多少菜?

d. 钱希平买了什么酒?

e. 钱希平有几个孩子? 他们几岁了?

f. 黄家深送什么东西给钱希平的孩子?

g. 孩子们为什么叫黄家深眼镜叔叔呢?

______________________________

h. 钱太太的菜做得好不好?

______________________________

i. 家深为什么筷子都拿不住了?

______________________________

j. 黄家深认为自己喝没喝太多酒? 你怎么知道?

______________________________

k. 为什么钱希平说吵一点儿没关系?

______________________________

l. 朋友们什么时候回家?

______________________________

m. 为什么他们第二天早上都起不来了?

______________________________

n. 家深第二天几点才睡醒?

______________________________

## Writing Help

### Independent Characters

| Character | Basic Meaning | No. of Str. | Stroke Order | Radical | Compo-nents | Struct-ure |
|---|---|---|---|---|---|---|
| 又 yòu | again | 2 | ㇇ 又 | 又 | 又 | □ |
| *耳 ěr | ear | 6 | 一 丅 丌 丌 丌 耳 | 耳 | 耳 | □ |
| *系 xì | be related to | 7 | 一 玄 系 | 丿 | 丿 糸 | ⊟ |

## Compound Characters

The following are the new compound characters in this chapter with radicals you have learned: 刚, 次, 朵, 讲, 邻, 吵, 完, 夜, 带, 啊, 能, 啤, 清, 睛, 楚, 睡, and 镜.

| Character | Basic Meaning | No. of Str. | Stroke Order | Radical | Mean. Clue | Phon. Clue | Compo- nents | Struct- ure |
|---|---|---|---|---|---|---|---|---|
| 刚(剛) gāng | just now | 6 | 冂 冈 刚 | 刂 | | 冈 gāng | 冈 刂 | ⿰ |
| 次 cì | times | 6 | 冫 冫 次 | 冫 | | | 冫 欠 | ⿰ |
| *朵 duǒ | (classifier) | 6 | 几 朵 | 木 | 木 | | 几 木 | ⿱ |
| 讲(講) jiǎng | to talk | 6 | 讠 讲 | 讠 | 讠 | 井 jǐng | 讠 井 | ⿰ |
| *邻(鄰) lín | next to | 7 | 今 令 邻 | 阝 | | 令 lìng | 令 阝 | ⿰ |
| 吵 chǎo | noise | 7 | 口 吵 | 口 | 口 | 少 | 口 少 | ⿰ |
| 完 wán | finish | 7 | 完 | 宀 | | 元 yuán | 宀 元 | ⿱ |
| 夜 yè | night | 8 | 亠 广 疒 疒 疒 夜 | 亠 | 夕 (xī, *dusk*) | | 亠 亻、夕 | |
| 带 dài | to bring | 9 | 一 十 卄 卅 卅 带 | 巾 | | | 卅 冖 巾 | |
| 啊 á | (particle) | 10 | 口 吓 啊 | 口 | 口 | 阿 a | 口 阿 | ⿲ |
| 能 néng | can | 10 | 厶 肙 能 能 | 月 | | | 厶 月 匕 匕 | |
| *啤 pí | beer (啤酒) | 11 | 口 咱 啤 啤 | 口 | 口 | 卑 bēi | 口 白 千 | ⿰ |
| 清 qīng | clear | 11 | 氵 清 | 氵 | 氵 | 青 qīng | 氵 青 | ⿰ |

| | | | | | | | | |
|---|---|---|---|---|---|---|---|---|
| *睛 jīng | eye | 13 | 目 睛 | 目 | 目 | 青 qīng | 目 青 | |
| *楚 chǔ | clear | 13 | 木 林 林 楚 | 木 | | | 木木疋 | |
| 睡 shuì | to sleep | 13 | 目 目 目 盱 盱 盱 盱 睡 睡 | 目 | 目 | 垂 chuí | 目 垂 | |
| *镜(鏡) jìng | mirror | 16 | 钅 钅 镕 镜 | 钅 | 钅 | 竟 jìng | 钅 立日儿 | |

## Radicals

The new radicals introduced in this chapter are 见, 酉, and 足.

### 1. 见

见 can be used as a radical in compound characters indicating "eye" or "sight." The compound character in this chapter that contains this radical is 觉.

| Character | Basic Meaning | No. of Str. | Stroke Order | Mean. Clue | Phon. Clue | Components | Structure |
|---|---|---|---|---|---|---|---|
| *觉(覺) jiào | to sleep | 9 | ⺍ 觉 | 见 | | ⺍ 见 | |

### 2. 酉

As a character 酉 *yǒu* means "liquor." As a radical it is often used in compound characters indicating related meanings. The compound character in this chapter that contains this radical is 醒.

| Character | Basic Meaning | No. of Str. | Stroke Order | Mean. Clue | Phon. Clue | Components | Structure |
|---|---|---|---|---|---|---|---|
| 醒 xǐng | to wake up | 16 | 酉 酲 醒 | | 星 | 酉日生 | |

3. 足

This character can be both a character and a radical. As a character it means "foot" and is written as 足 *zú*. As a radical it is written as ⻊ and used as the left-hand part of a compound character to form characters related to activities of the foot or with a meaning of foot. The compound characters in this chapter that contain this radical are 跑 and 跟.

| Character | Basic Meaning | No. of Str. | Stroke Order | Mean. Clue | Phon. Clue | Compo- nents | Struct- ure |
|---|---|---|---|---|---|---|---|
| 跑 pǎo | to run | 12 | 口 ⻊ 跑 | 足 | 包 bāo | 足包 | ◫ |
| 跟 gēn | with | 13 | ⻊ 跟 | 足 | 艮 gěn | ⻊ 艮 | ◫ |

## Exercises

I. Character Exercises

**1. Form new characters by using different components of the following characters.**

**Example:** 工 (from 功) + 𠂇 (from 有) → 左

讲，清，灰，觉，很，醒，吵，跑，字

_____ (from _____ ) + _____ (from _____ ) → _____

_____ (from _____ ) + _____ (from _____ ) → _____

_____ (from _____ ) + _____ (from _____ ) → _____

_____ (from _____ ) + _____ (from _____ ) → _____

_____ (from _____ ) + _____ (from _____ ) → _____

2. How many words/phrases can you form with the following characters?

a. 习 → ______________________________

b. 半 → ______________________________

c. 名 → ______________________________

3. Circle each of the characters below that has been constructed using a radical + phonetic strategy:

| 耳， | 啊， | 睡， | 朵， | 清， | 镜， | 晴， | 吵， | 讲， | 次， |
|---|---|---|---|---|---|---|---|---|---|
| 完， | 邻， | 能， | 夜， | 楚， | 带， | 醒， | 觉， | 系， | 又 |

4. Write as many characters you know as possible that contain a component of 小.

______________________________

II. Vocabulary Exercises

1. Write the Pinyin for the following characters. Then form a word with each character:

a. 炒 (　　　) ______________

　 吵 (　　　) ______________

b. 请 (　　　) ______________

　 清 (　　　) ______________

2. **Write different characters next to the Pinyin in each group of homonyms. Then form a word/phrase with each character:**

a. wàng ( ) ________________

wàng ( ) ________________

b. chú ( ) ________________

chú ( ) ________________

c. gōng ( ) ________________

gōng ( ) ________________

3. **Combine a character from column A with one from column B, and then write the word in the parentheses. No character can be used more than one time.**

| A | B | |
|---|---|---|
| 眼 | 夜 | ( ) |
| 半 | 牌 | ( ) |
| 名 | 师 | ( ) |
| 老 | 镜 | ( ) |

III. Structure Exercises

1. **Fill in the blanks with the proper PVC or RVC:**

a. 小王的家你找 ________ 吗?

b. 我没有地图，以前也没有去过他家，我想我 ________。

c. 要是我看 ________ 他，叫他来找你。

d. 好吧。你们一块儿来我家吃晚饭吧。我买了很多菜，一个人吃________。大家来吃吧。

e. 我的汉语书不见了，________。

## Supplementary Reading

### Reading 1

白开水

我xǐ欢到我家对面的那家中国饭馆儿吃牛肉炒饭、喝中国茶。王医生知道了就对我说："吃牛肉的时候最好不要喝茶。"今天我又去那家饭馆儿吃牛肉炒饭。我跟老板说："我不要喝茶。请给我热水。"老板听了半天，还是不知道我要什么。我又说："你看，那是茶，是热的。我要水，热的水。"老板听懂了。他说："哦，你要白开水。"我明白了。在中国饭馆儿里，热的水不叫热水，叫白开水。

COMPREHENSION QUESTIONS

1. 吃牛肉炒饭的时候，我为什么不要喝茶？

_______________

2. 吃牛肉炒饭的时候，我不要喝茶，我喝什么？

_______________

## Reading 2

### 头疼

以前有一个叫美欢的女孩子。她常常去看医生。Měi一次去看医生，她都跟医生说她头疼。有一天，她又去看医生了。医生想了一想，对她说:"你太忙了。家里的事能做的就做，做不了的就别做了。"

几天后，美欢的妈妈来了。她对医生说"我的头真疼。"医生给她看病了。医生对她说:"你太累了。家里的事能做的就做吧，做不了的就别做了。"

过了几个星期，医生在饭馆儿看到美欢和她妈妈。医生对她们说:"你们的头还疼吗?"。美欢说:"我和妈妈的头都不疼了。可是，现在我bàba的头疼了。"

#### COMPREHENSION QUESTIONS

1. 美欢为什么常常去看医生?

___

2. 美欢的bàba为什么头疼?

___

## Character Practice

| | | | | | | | | | |
|---|---|---|---|---|---|---|---|---|---|
| 又 | 又 | | | | | | | | |
| 耳 | 耳 | | | | | | | | |
| 系 | 系 | | | | | | | | |
| 刚 | 刚 | | | | | | | | |
| 次 | 次 | | | | | | | | |
| 朵 | 朵 | | | | | | | | |
| 讲 | 讲 | | | | | | | | |
| 邻 | 邻 | | | | | | | | |
| 吵 | 吵 | | | | | | | | |
| 完 | 完 | | | | | | | | |
| 夜 | 夜 | | | | | | | | |
| 带 | 带 | | | | | | | | |
| 啊 | 啊 | | | | | | | | |

| 能 | 能 | | | | | | | | |
|---|---|---|---|---|---|---|---|---|---|
| 啤 | 啤 | | | | | | | | |
| 清 | 清 | | | | | | | | |
| 睛 | 睛 | | | | | | | | |
| 楚 | 楚 | | | | | | | | |
| 睡 | 睡 | | | | | | | | |
| 镜 | 镜 | | | | | | | | |
| 觉 | 觉 | | | | | | | | |
| 醒 | 醒 | | | | | | | | |
| 跑 | 跑 | | | | | | | | |
| 跟 | 跟 | | | | | | | | |

# CHAPTER SEVENTEEN
# 第 十 七 课

**Text**

商先生是Xīn西兰的华人。他六十岁才开始学汉语。他很用功，不过，他老是学不好，记不住生词。他说一个星期要记五十多个生词太多，太难了。十多，二十岁的人都记不了这么多生词，他怎么能记得住呢!

他早上起来，又是记生词，又是写汉字。他把他学过的汉字都仔细地写在纸上。他一有kòng儿就拿出来看。他还把汉字放在他床边儿的书桌上，睡觉以前看几遍，睡醒了又看一下。他说只要天天学，他就一定能把汉语学好，能把生词记住。

商先生想明年去中国看他九十多岁的阿姨。他已经有五十年没看到他阿姨了。

商先生家里这儿是汉字，那儿也是汉字。他太太跟他的朋友说她看不懂汉字，一看到汉字就生气，家里楼上，楼下的fáng间里都是汉字，真气死人。去年，她也开始学汉语了。商先生和商太太一块儿去图书馆借书，还书。不到半年的时间，他们已经会说好多汉语，会写好多汉字了，他们还学会了bāo饺子。他们想来想去，为什么要等到明年才去中国呢？ 现在就去吧！ 现在是秋天，北京很凉快。到了中国可以好好儿练习练习汉语，吃现成的中国饺子了。

上个月，商先生和商太太带了一个放着他们所有的汉语书和别的行李的大箱子到中国去了。

他们下了飞机，商先生用汉语跟飞机场的小姐说话。他jǐn张极了，小姐听不懂他说的汉语。商先生就用铅笔在一张纸上写："找想卖中国自酒，你这儿有买吗？"那小姐看了半天还是看不懂他的意思。你知道为什么吗？ 商先生把"我"字写成了"找"字，把"白"字写成"自"字，还把"买"字写成"卖"字，把"卖"字写成"买"字了。你想，小姐能看懂商先生写什么吗？

## 生词 New Words

| | | |
|---|---|---|
| 商先生 | Shāng Xiānshēng | (N) Mr. Shang |
| 华人 | Huárén | (N) person of Chinese ethnicity |
| 老 | lǎo | (Adv) always, invariably |
| 好 | -hǎo | (VC) satisfactorily complete |
| 记 | jì | (V) remember |
| 生词 | shēngcí | (N) new words, new vocabulary |
| 了 | -liǎo | (VC) able to |
| 又……又…… | yòu…yòu… | (P) both…and… |
| 写 | xiě | (V) write |
| 写字 | xiě zì | (VO) write |
| 把 | bǎ | (CV) take |
| 仔细 | zǐxì | (Adv) careful |
| 纸 | zhǐ | (N) paper (Cl *-zhāng* 张) |
| 放 | fàng | (V) put, place |
| 床边儿 | chuáng.biānr | (PS/PW) next to bed |
| 书桌 | shūzhuō | (N) desk |
| 遍 | -biàn | (VCL) times |
| ……一下 | …yíxià | (Adv) a bit (after a verb) |
| 只要 | zhǐyào | (Conj) all you need to do is |
| 阿姨 | āyí | (N) aunt (mother's sister) |
| 到 | -dào | (VC) (reach a point) |
| 懂 | -dǒng | (VC) understand |
| 生气 | shēngqì | (SV) be angry |
| 楼上 | lóu.shàng | (PS/PW) upstairs |
| 楼下 | lóu.xià | (PS/PW) downstairs |
| fáng间 | fángjīan | (N) room (of house; Cl *-gè* 个, 间) |
| 真气死人! | Zhēn qìsǐ rén! | (Ex) How infuriating! |
| 借 | jiè | (V) borrow; lend |
| 还 | huán | (V) return (something) |
| 时间 | shíjiān | (N) time |
| 会 | -huì | (VC) master |
| 饺子 | jiǎozi | (N) "Chinese ravioli," Chinese dumpling |
| 凉快 | liáng.kuài | (SV) be (comfortably) cool (said of weather) |
| 好好儿 | hǎohaor | (Adv) earnestly; all out |
| 现成 | xiànchéng | (Attr) ready-made |
| 所有的 | suóyǒude | (N) every, all of something |
| 行李 | xínglǐ | (N) luggage (Cl *-jiàn* 件) |

| | | |
|---|---|---|
| 箱子 | xiāngzi | (N) (large) box, trunk, chest |
| 飞机 | fēijī | (N) airplane |
| 飞机场 | fēijīchǎng | (PW) airport |
| 说话 | shuō huà | (VO) speak |
| jǐn张 | jǐnzhāng | (SV) be nervous, be tense |
| ……极了 | …jíle | (Adv) extremely |
| 铅笔 | qiānbǐ | (N) pencil |
| 张 | -zhāng | (Cl) (for flat objects like tables, paper, paintings) |
| 意思 | yìsi | (N) meaning |
| 成 | -chéng | (VC) (indicates transformation) |

## COMPREHENSION QUESTIONS

1. **Read the text of this chapter, and for each statement below indicate whether it is true or false:**

   a. (　　) 商先生六十六岁才开始学汉语。

   b. (　　) 他很用功，不过，他老是学不好，记不住生词。

   c. (　　) 他说一个星期要记一百五十个生词太多了。

   d. (　　) 他天天晚上睡觉前，记生词，写汉字。

   e. (　　) 他把他学过的汉字和生词都仔细地写在书上，他天天早上都拿出来看。

   f. (　　) 他还把写好的汉字放在书桌上，睡觉以前看几遍，睡醒了再看一下。

   g. (　　) 他说只要天天学，他一定能把汉语学好。

   h. (　　) 商先生想后年去中国看他九十多岁的妈妈。

   i. (　　) 他已经有四十年没看到他妈妈了。

   j. (　　) 商太太很不xǐ欢家里都是汉字。

   k. (　　) 商太太也学习汉语了，可是，她只会说汉语，不会写汉字。

   l. (　　) 他们很xǐ欢吃饺子，可是不会包。

m. (　　　) 他们明年要去中国。

n. (　　　) 他们要去中国学汉语，吃中国饺子。

o. (　　　) 他们带了他们所有的衣服去中国。

p. (　　　) 他们坐飞机去中国。

q. (　　　) 在飞机上，商先生用汉语跟一位小姐练习汉语。

r. (　　　) 小姐听不懂他的话，也看不懂他写的汉字。

**2. Answer the following questions:**

a. 商先生什么时候开始学汉语? ______________________

b. 他为什么学不好，记不住生词? ______________________

c. 商先生怎么记生词? ______________________

d. 他们明年想去哪儿? 做什么? 为什么? ______________________

e. 商太太跟商先生的朋友说什么? ______________________

f. 她为什么生气? ______________________

g. 商太太什么时候开始学汉语? ______________________

h. 他们一块儿去哪儿? 做什么? ______________________

i. 不到半年的时间，他们学会了什么? ______________________

j. 他们什么时候要去中国? 为什么? ______________________

k. 大箱子里有什么? ______________________________

l. 商先生用汉语跟谁说话? ______________________________

m. 为什么小姐听不懂他的汉语? ______________________________

n. 为什么小姐看不懂商先生写什么? ______________________________

## Writing Help

### Independent Characters

| Character | Basic Meaning | No. of Str. | Stroke Order | Radical | Compo-nents | Struct-ure |
|---|---|---|---|---|---|---|
| 飞(飛) fēi | to fly | 3 | 飞 飞 飞 | 乙 | 飞 | |
| 死 sǐ | death | 6 | 一 歹 死 | 歹 | 歹 匕 | |
| 成 chéng | to succeed | 6 | 一 厂 万 成 成 成 | 戈 | [illegible] 戈 | |

### Compound Characters

The following are the new compound characters in this chapter with radicals you have learned: 记, 华, 把, 纸, 阿, 李, 极, 细, 放, 姨, 饺, 借, 凉, 铅, 遍, and 箱.

| Character | Basic Meaning | No. of Str. | Stroke Order | Radical | Mean. Clue | Phon. Clue | Compo-nents | Struct-ure |
|---|---|---|---|---|---|---|---|---|
| 记(記) jì | to remember | 5 | 讠 讠 讠 记 | 讠 | 讠 | 己 jǐ | 讠 己 | |
| *华(華) huá | China | 6 | 化 华 | 十 | 十 | 化 huà | 化 十 | |

| | | | | | | | | |
|---|---|---|---|---|---|---|---|---|
| 把 bǎ | to hold* | 7 | 扌 把 | 扌 | 扌 | 巴 bā | 扌 巴 | |
| 纸(紙) zhǐ | paper | 7 | 纟 纟 纟 纟 纸 | 纟 | 纟 | 氏 shì | 纟 氏 | |
| 阿 ā | (particle) | 7 | 阝 阿 | 阝 | | | 阝 可 | |
| 李 lǐ | plum; surname | 7 | 木 李 | 木 | 木 | | 木 子 | |
| 极 jí | extreme | 7 | 木 木 杒 极 | 木 | | 及 jí | 木 及 | |
| 细(細) xì | fine, slender | 8 | 纟 细 | 纟 | 纟 | | 纟 田 | |
| 放 fàng | to put | 8 | 方 放 | 攵 | | 方 | 方 攵 | |
| 姨 yí | aunt | 9 | 女 女 女 女 女 女 姨 | 女 | 女 | 夷 yí | 女 夷 | |
| *饺(餃) jiǎo | dumpling | 9 | 饣 饣 饺 | 饣 | 饣 | 交 jiāo | 饣 交 | |
| 借 jiè | to borrow; to lend | 10 | 亻 亻 亻 亻 亻 借 | 亻 | 亻 | | 亻 龷 日 | |
| 凉 liáng | cool | 10 | 冫 凉 | 冫 | 冫 | | 冫 京 | |
| 铅(鉛) qiān | lead | 10 | 钅 钅 铅 | 钅 | 钅 | | 钅 几 口 | |
| *遍 biàn | times | 12 | 户 户 扁 扁 扁 遍 | 辶 | | 扁 biǎn | 辶 扁 | |
| *箱 xiāng | box | 15 | ⺮ 箱 箱 | 竹 | 竹 | 相 xiāng | ⺮ 木 目 | |

## Radicals

The new radicals introduced in this chapter are 冖, 门, and 弓.

### 1. 冖

This radical is used as the top part of a compound character. The compound character in this chapter that contains this radical is 写.

| Character | Basic Meaning | No. of Str. | Stroke Order | Mean. Clue | Phon. Clue | Compo-nents | Struct-ure |
|---|---|---|---|---|---|---|---|
| 写(寫) xiě | to write | 5 | 冖 冖 写 写 | | | 冖 与 | |

### 2. 门

门 can be both a character and a radical. As a radical it is used to form characters related to the meaning "door." The compound character in this chapter that contains this radical is 间.

| Character | Basic Meaning | No. of Str. | Stroke Order | Mean. Clue | Phon. Clue | Compo-nents | Struct-ure |
|---|---|---|---|---|---|---|---|
| *间(間) jiān | gap | 7 | 门 间 | 门, 日 (seeing the sun through an open door) | | 门 日 | |

### 3. 弓

弓 *gōng* means "bow" as a character. The compound character in this chapter that contains this radical is 张.

| Character | Basic Meaning | No. of Str. | Stroke Order | Mean. Clue | Phon. Clue | Compo-nents | Struct-ure |
|---|---|---|---|---|---|---|---|
| 张(張) zhāng | (classifier)*; surname | 8 | 弓 弓 弓 弓 张 张 张 | | 长 zhǎng/ cháng | 弓 长 | |

## EXERCISES

### I. Character Exercises

1. **Form new characters by using different components of the following characters.**

   **Example:** 工 (from 功) + 𠂇 (from 有) → 左

| 跟， 饱， 铅， 浅， 想， 筷， 男 |
|---|

______ (from ______ ) + ______ (from ______ ) → ______

______ (from ______ ) + ______ (from ______ ) → ______

______ (from ______ ) + ______ (from ______ ) → ______

______ (from ______ ) + ______ (from ______ ) → ______

______ (from ______ ) + ______ (from ______ ) → ______

2. **Form five characters each using each of the following components:**

   a. 田 → ________________________________

   b. 扌 → ________________________________

   c. 木 → ________________________________

   d. 纟 → ________________________________

   e. 竹 → ________________________________

   f. 钅 → ________________________________

   g. 辶 → ________________________________

3. Circle the misused characters in the following sentences, and write the correct ones:

a. 他们一快儿去学校介书。→ ____________

b. 谢啊姨坐气车来找家。→ ____________

c. 多吃点吵牛内把。→ ____________

## II. Vocabulary Exercises

1. Combine a character from column A with one from column B, and then write the word in the parentheses. No character can be used more than one time.

| A | B | |
|---|---|---|
| 飞 | 思 | ( ) |
| 仔 | 桌 | ( ) |
| 书 | 快 | ( ) |
| 意 | 机 | ( ) |
| 凉 | 细 | ( ) |

2. Write the characters corresponding to the Pinyin and containing the following radicals. Then form a word/phrase with each of the characters:

a. 纟 zhǐ ( ) ____________

xì ( ) ____________

b. 钅 qiān ( ) ____________

qián ( ) ____________

c. 昔 jiè ( ) ____________

cuò ( ) ____________

## III. Writing Exercises

1. Write a short paragraph on the topic 商先生是怎么学汉语的。

2. 要是你去中国，你要带什么？ Make a list.

## Supplementary Reading

### Reading 1

四hé院

人们说起四hé院就会想起北京。什么是四hé院呢？ 四hé院是北京一千年前就有的fáng子。四hé院的中心[1]是院子，院子的四面都有fáng子，所以叫四hé院。住在四hé院北边fáng子的是家中的老人，大儿子住在东边儿，二儿子住在西边儿。女儿住在后院。四hé院很tè别，你去北京的时候应该去看一下。

1. 中心：center

COMPREHENSION QUESTIONS

1. 北京什么时候开始就有四hé院？

______________________________

2. 四hé院的四面有什么？

______________________________

## Reading 2

### 三毛

三毛 (1943–1991) 是中国一位很有名的女作家。三毛从小就xǐ欢看书。她看的第一本书是张乐平画和写的小人书[1]。那时候她才三岁。三毛英文名字叫Echo。她的名字不叫三毛。三毛是她的笔名。因为她很xǐ欢张乐平画的三毛的故事，所以在她开始写作以后，就用三毛这个笔名。三毛去过很多国家，她懂得好几个国家的语言。

1. 那本小人书叫《三毛liúlàng记》。

COMPREHENSION QUESTIONS

1. 三毛是谁？ 三毛从小就xǐ欢做什么？

______________________________

2. 三毛为什么用三毛这个笔名？

______________________________

## Character Practice

| | | | | | | | | | |
|---|---|---|---|---|---|---|---|---|---|
| 飞 | 飞 | | | | | | | | |
| 死 | 死 | | | | | | | | |
| 成 | 成 | | | | | | | | |
| 记 | 记 | | | | | | | | |
| 华 | 华 | | | | | | | | |
| 把 | 把 | | | | | | | | |
| 纸 | 纸 | | | | | | | | |
| 阿 | 阿 | | | | | | | | |
| 李 | 李 | | | | | | | | |
| 极 | 极 | | | | | | | | |
| 细 | 细 | | | | | | | | |
| 放 | 放 | | | | | | | | |
| 姨 | 姨 | | | | | | | | |

| | | | | | | | | | |
|---|---|---|---|---|---|---|---|---|---|
| 饺 | 饺 | | | | | | | | |
| 借 | 借 | | | | | | | | |
| 凉 | 凉 | | | | | | | | |
| 铅 | 铅 | | | | | | | | |
| 遍 | 遍 | | | | | | | | |
| 箱 | 箱 | | | | | | | | |
| 写 | 写 | | | | | | | | |
| 间 | 间 | | | | | | | | |
| 张 | 张 | | | | | | | | |

# CHAPTER EIGHTEEN
# 第 十 八 课

**Text**

我住在南京路，南京路很安静，一点儿都不吵，也不热闹。我们家对面有一家小小的卖衣服的商店。那家商店的两个老板，一个姓常，一个姓张。我们叫他们常伯伯和张伯伯。我有空儿常常去那儿玩儿。

常伯伯很高也很瘦，他以前住在黄河北边。张伯伯没有常伯伯高，他不胖也不瘦。张伯伯以前住在长江的南边儿。他说长江比黄河长，常伯伯说长江跟黄河一样长。我说："我知道，我们老师说长江比黄河长。"张伯伯听了很高兴。

常伯伯和张伯伯都有五十多岁了。他们对做生意不太有兴趣，对做衣服很有兴趣，店里的衣服都是他们做的。他们店里卖的衣服又舒服又便宜，只是不够时máo。他们说别的店卖的衣服虽然时máo，可是比他们的几乎贵两倍。有钱的人才买得起。

我父母都是老师。他们的薪水不是很高。可是，上个月的考试我的成绩tè别好。他们给我买了两条名pái儿的牛仔裤。我现在穿的这条裤子比常伯伯店里最贵的裤子贵三分之一。张伯伯问我为什么不在他们店里买裤子。我说我穿的这条裤子跟他们店里卖的完全不同。我的裤子又时máo又是名pái儿的。我现在穿的这条还不是最贵的，我还有一条比这条更贵的呢！

**生词 New Words**

| | | |
|---|---|---|
| 路 | lù | (N) road (Cl *-tiáo* 条) |
| 南京路 | Nánjīng Lù | (PW) name of a street |
| 安静 | ānjìng | (SV) be peaceful and quiet |
| 热闹 | rè.nào | (SV) be bustling |
| 常伯伯 | Cháng Bóbo | (N) Uncle Chang |
| 张伯伯 | Zhāng Bóbo | (N) Uncle Zhang |
| 有空儿 | yǒu kòngr | (VO) have free time |
| 瘦 | shòu | (SV) be thin, be lean |
| 黄河 | Huánghé | (PW) the Yellow River |
| 胖 | pàng | (SV) be fat (of humans) |
| 长江 | Chángjiāng | (PW) the Yangtze River |
| 比 | bǐ | (CV) compared to |
| 长 | cháng | (SV) be long |
| 一样 | yíyàng | (Adv) similarly |
| 做生意 | zuò shēng.yì | (VO) engage in commerce |

| | | |
|---|---|---|
| 兴趣 | xìng.qù | (N) interest (in something) |
| 够 | gòu | (V) be enough, sufficient, adequate |
| 时máo | shímáo | (SV) be fashionable |
| 虽然……可是…… | suīrán…kě.shì… | (Pat) although…however |
| 几乎 | jīhū | (Adv) almost; nearly |
| 贵 | guì | (V) be expensive |
| 倍 | -bèi | (Cl) -fold, number of times |
| 薪水 | xīnshuǐ | (N) salary |
| 成绩 | chéngjì | (N) grades; result; achievement |
| 牛仔裤 | niúzǎikù | (N) denim jeans (Cl *-tiáo* 条) |
| 裤子 | kùzi | (N) pants, trousers (Cl *-tiāo* 条) |
| 穿 | chuān | (V) wear; put on (clothing) |
| Y 分之 X | Y fēn zhī X | (Pat) (indictates X/Y fraction) |
| 完全 | wánquán | (Adv) completely |
| 不同 | bùtóng | (SV) be different |
| 更 | gèng | (Adv) even more |

## COMPREHENSION QUESTIONS

1. **Read the text of this chapter, and for each statement below indicate whether it is true or false:**

   a. (　　　) 常伯伯和张伯伯差不多一样大。

   b. (　　　) 他们对做生意tè别有兴趣。

   c. (　　　) 他们店里卖的东西很便宜。

   d. (　　　) 别的店卖的衣服很时máo也很便宜。

   e. (　　　) 上个月我考试的成绩很好，我的父母买了lǐwù送给我。

   f. (　　　) 我名pái儿的裤子比常伯伯店里的裤子贵得多。

   g. (　　　) 我穿的裤子跟常伯伯店里卖的不一样。

2. **Ask each other the following questions about the above text. Then sketch the answers below:**

   a. 商店在哪儿，我家在哪儿？

   b. 我认识的<u>张伯伯</u>和<u>常伯伯</u>。

   c. <u>张伯伯</u>和<u>常伯伯</u>以前住在哪儿？

## Writing Help

### Independent Characters

| Character | Basic Meaning | No. of Str. | Stroke Order | Radical | Compo-nents | Struct-ure |
|---|---|---|---|---|---|---|
| *之 zhī | 的 | 3 | 丶 ⺈ 之 | 丶 | 之 | □ |
| 长(長) cháng | long | 5 | 长 | 丿 | 长 | □ |
| 乎 hū | (particle) | 5 | 丿 ⺈ 𠂌 乊 乎 | 丿 | 乎 | □ |

### Compound Characters

The followings are the new compound characters in this chapter with radicals you have learned: 江, 全, 更, 闹, 河, 胖, 虽, 样, 倍, 够, 绩, 裤, 路, 瘦, 趣, and 薪.

| Character | Basic Meaning | No. of Str. | Stroke Order | Radical | Mean. Clue | Phon. Clue | Compo-nents | Struct-ure |
|---|---|---|---|---|---|---|---|---|
| 江 jiāng | river; surname | 6 | 氵 氵 汀 江 | 氵 | 氵 | | 氵 工 | ◫ |
| 全 quán | whole | 6 | 人 全 | 人 | | | 人 王 | ⊟ |
| 更 gèng | even | 7 | 更 | 一 | | | 一 曰 乂 | ⊟ |
| 闹(鬧) nào | noise | 8 | 门 闩 闹 | 门 | 门, 市 | | 门 市 | ⊓ |
| 河 hé | river | 8 | 氵 河 | 氵 | 氵 | 可 | 氵 可 | ◫ |
| 胖 pàng | fat | 9 | 月 胖 | 月 | 月 | 半 | 月 半 | ◫ |
| 虽(雖) suī | although | 9 | 口 吕 吊 虽 虽 | 口 | | | 口 虫 | ⊟ |
| *样(樣) yàng | shape | 10 | 木 样 | 木 | | 羊 yáng | 木 羊 | ◫ |
| *倍 bèi | double | 10 | 亻 位 倍 | 亻 | | | 亻 立 口 | ◫ |

| | | | | | | | | |
|---|---|---|---|---|---|---|---|---|
| 够 gòu | enough | 11 | 句 够 | 夕 | 句(jù, *sentence*), 多( Many sentences are enough) | | 句 夕 夕 | |
| *绩(績) jī | to accomplish | 11 | 纟 纟 纟 纟 纟 绩 | 纟 | 纟 | | 纟 责 | |
| *裤(褲) kù | trousers | 12 | 衤 衤 衤 裤 | 衤 | 衤 | 库 kù | 衤 广 车 | |
| 路 lù | road | 13 | 口 ㄗ ㄗ 𧾷 𧾷 路 | 足 | 足 | | 𧾷 各(夂口) | |
| 瘦 shòu | skinny | 14 | 疒 疒 疒 疒 疒 疒 疒 疒 瘦 | 疒 | 疒 | 叟 sǒu | 疒 叟 | |
| *趣 qù | to call | 15 | 走 趄 趣 | 走 | | 取 qǔ | 走 耳 又 | |
| *薪 xīn | salary (from 'firewood') | 16 | 艹 薪 | 艹 | 艹 | 新 | 艹 亲 斤 | |

闹: It can be remembered as a market (市 *shì*) inside the door = noisy 闹.

## Radicals

The new radicals introduced in this chapter are 贝, 比 , 穴, and 青.

### 1. 贝

贝 *bèi* as a character means "shell." As shells were used in earliest times in China as money, 贝 is used as a radical to indicate money or precious things. The compound character in this chapter that contains that radical is 贵.

| Character | Basic Meaning | No. of Str. | Stroke Order | Mean. Clue | Phon. Clue | Compo-nents | Struct-ure |
|---|---|---|---|---|---|---|---|
| 贵(貴) guì | expensive, precious | 9 | 口 中 虫 贵 贵 | 贝 | | 中 一 贝 | |

### 2. 比

比 can be a character and a radical.

| Character | Basic Meaning | No. of Str. | Stroke Order | Mean. Clue | Phon. Clue | Compo-nents | Struct-ure |
|---|---|---|---|---|---|---|---|
| 比 bǐ | to compare | 4 | ⺊ ⺊ 比 比 | | | ⺊ 匕 | |

### 3. 穴

As an independent character 穴 *xuè* means "cave, hole." As a radical it is used in some compound characters indicating related meanings. The compound characters in this chapter that contain this radical are 空 and 穿.

| Character | Basic Meaning | No. of Str. | Stroke Order | Mean. Clue | Phon. Clue | Compo-nents | Struct-ure |
|---|---|---|---|---|---|---|---|
| 空 kòng | empty | 8 | 宀 穴 空 | 穴(hole) | 工 gōng | 宀八工 | ⊟ |
| 穿 chuān | to wear | 9 | 穴 穴 穴 穿 穿 | | | 穴 牙 | ⊟ |

### 4. 青

青 *qīng* as a character means "glassy green." The compound character in this chapter that contains this radical is 静 jìng. Some characters learned before contain this component as well. What are they?

| Character | Basic Meaning | No. of Str. | Stroke Order | Mean. Clue | Phon. Clue | Compo-nents | Struct-ure |
|---|---|---|---|---|---|---|---|
| 静(靜) jìng | quiet | 14 | 青 青 青 静<br>静 静 静 | | 青 qīng | 青 争 | ◫ |

## EXERCISES

### I. Character Exercises

**1. Form new characters by using different components of the following characters.**

**Example:** 工 (from 功) + 𠂇 (from 有) → 左

| 空， 深， 看， 阿， 学， 今， 静， 现 |
|---|

______ (from ______ ) + ______ (from ______ ) → ______

______ (from ______ ) + ______ (from ______ ) → ______

______ (from ______ ) + ______ (from ______ ) → ______

______ (from ______ ) + ______ (from ______ ) → ______

______ (from ______ ) + ______ (from ______ ) → ______

2. **Write the characters corresponding to the Pinyin and containing the following radicals. Then form a word/phrase with each of the characters.**

a. 氵 jiāng ( ) ______

hé ( ) ______

b. 疒 bìng ( ) ______

shòu ( ) ______

3. **Form four characters using each of the following components:**

a. 王 → ______

b. 目→ ______

c. 人 → ______

d. 又 → ______

e. 页 → ______

## II. Vocabulary Exercises

**Combine a character from column A with one from column B, and then write the word in parentheses. No character can be used more than one time.**

| A | B | |
|---|---|---|
| 虽 | 绩 | ( ) |
| 成 | 静 | ( ) |
| 热 | 全 | ( ) |
| 薪 | 闹 | ( ) |
| 安 | 然 | ( ) |
| 完 | 水 | ( ) |

## Supplementary Reading

### Reading 1

#### 大山

你们知道谁是 Mark Rowswell 吗? Mark Rowswell 的中文名字叫大山。他是加拿大人。1988 年他去中国。他在北京大学念书。他在北京的时候,因为常常上电视说笑话,所以人人都知道他的名字。大山说中文说得非常好。要是你只听他说话,不看他的脸,你一定想他是中国人。大山的 bàba 的 bàba 也住过中国。他 bàba 的 bàba 是医生。1922 年他在中国的一家医院做事。因为地方的名字不同了,大山找了十年才找到那家医院。大山虽然是外国人,但中国的报纸说他不是外人。

COMPREHENSION QUESTIONS

1. 谁是大山? 为什么他在中国很有名?

______________________________

2. 大山为什么花了这么多时间才找到他 bàba 的 bàba 工作的那家医院?

______________________________

3. 为什么中国的报纸说大山不是外人?

______________________________

## Reading 2

### 小人之过也，必文

2000多年前的中文跟现在的很不一样。“小人之过也，必文。”这句话是2000年前写的。你知道这句话是什么意思吗？“小人之过也，必文。”的意思是“小人做错了事，一定不想给别人知道。”这里“过”是“做错了的事”的意思。“之”就是“的”。“文”是“不要给别人知道”。虽然“小人书”是“小孩子看的书”，可是“小人”不是“小孩子”的意思。这里“小人”说的是不好的人，常常做坏事。

### COMPREHENSION QUESTIONS

1. “小人之过也，必文。”这是什么意思？

______________________________

2. “小人之过也，必文。”这里的小人是什么意思？

______________________________

## Character Practice

| | | | | | | | | | |
|---|---|---|---|---|---|---|---|---|---|
| 之 | 之 | | | | | | | | |
| 长 | 长 | | | | | | | | |
| 乎 | 乎 | | | | | | | | |
| 江 | 江 | | | | | | | | |
| 全 | 全 | | | | | | | | |
| 更 | 更 | | | | | | | | |
| 闹 | 闹 | | | | | | | | |
| 河 | 河 | | | | | | | | |
| 胖 | 胖 | | | | | | | | |
| 虽 | 虽 | | | | | | | | |
| 样 | 样 | | | | | | | | |
| 倍 | 倍 | | | | | | | | |
| 够 | 够 | | | | | | | | |

| | | | | | | | | | |
|---|---|---|---|---|---|---|---|---|---|
| 绩 | 绩 | | | | | | | | |
| 裤 | 裤 | | | | | | | | |
| 路 | 路 | | | | | | | | |
| 瘦 | 瘦 | | | | | | | | |
| 趣 | 趣 | | | | | | | | |
| 薪 | 薪 | | | | | | | | |
| 贵 | 贵 | | | | | | | | |
| 比 | 比 | | | | | | | | |
| 空 | 空 | | | | | | | | |
| 穿 | 穿 | | | | | | | | |
| 静 | 静 | | | | | | | | |

# CHAPTER NINETEEN

# 第 十 九 课

## Text

钟名然今年二月从北京来新西兰学英语。来了新西兰以后，他就住在我家。钟名然很用功，这几个月，他英语已经说得很不错了。因为天天很jǐn张，所以哪儿都没时间去玩儿。

他听说雪山城的风景很好看，很想到那儿去旅游。考完试，他比较有空儿，想轻松一下，就给同学谢里打电话。谢里是法国人。他在雪山城找了个假期工作。他说他可以带钟名然去雪山城玩。钟名然听了很高兴。

七月，新西兰是冬天。雪山城很冷，他们得多带几件衣服去。可不是吗？电shì上说，雪山城那儿下大雪呢，路上都是白sè的，就是穿上两件毛衣，一件外衣也许还不够暖和呢！钟名然越看越冷，马上去商店买大衣。

雪山城lí我家很远，一共有700多公里，中间还有一条大河。你知道坐火车到雪山城要多久吗？至少得要六个小时，真不近。那儿比我们这儿冷得多了。虽然不刮大风，可是会下雪。雪山城的风景tè别好看，很多外国人都xǐ欢去那儿旅游。

钟名然和谢里到了雪山城，出了火车站就坐出租汽车去饭店。车站lí饭店不远，可是路上的车很多，好多学生假期都来这儿玩，堵车堵得很利害。他们很晚才到饭店。第二天，钟名然很早就起来了。可是谢里晚上跟他朋友去喝酒，所以睡得比较晚。钟名然想谢里可能早上起不来了，就自己出去玩儿了。谢里醒了以后找不到钟名然，他很着急。他穿上大衣马上就去找钟名然。他知道钟名然最爱吃西瓜，就到饭店附近的水果摊去找钟名然。看！钟名然正在水果摊旁边儿仔细地挑着西瓜呢！

## 生词 New Words

| | | |
|---|---|---|
| 钟名然 | Zhōng Míngrán | (N) a personal name |
| 新西兰 | Xīnxīlán | (PW) New Zealand |
| 英语 | Yīngyǔ | (N) English (language) |
| 雪山城 | Xuéshānchéng | (PW) Snowy Mountain Town |
| 风景 | fēngjǐng | (N) scenery |
| 旅游 | lǚyóu | (V) tour |
| 比较 | bǐjiào | (Adv) comparatively |
| 轻松 | qīngsōng | (SV) be relaxed |
| 谢里 | Xiè Lǐ | (N) a personal name |
| 假期 | jiàqī | (TW) vacation; holiday period |
| 工作 | gōngzuò | (N) job |
| 可不是吗? | Kě búshì ma? | (Ex) Isn't that so? |
| 外衣 | wàiyī | (N) jacket (Cl -件) |
| 暖和 | nuǎnhuo | (SV) be (comfortably) warm (said of weather) |
| 越……越…… | yuè...yuè... | (Pat) more and more |
| 马上 | mǎshàng | (Adv) right away |
| 远 | yuǎn | (SV) be far |
| 公里 | gōnglǐ | (Cl) kilometers |
| 中间 | zhōng.jiān | (PS) the middle |
| 河 | hé | (N) river (Cl *-tiáo* 条) |
| 火车 | huǒchē | (N) train |
| 多久? | duō jiǔ? | (QW) how long? |
| 至少 | zhìshǎo | (Adv) at the very least |
| 小时 | xiǎoshí | (N) hour |
| 近 | jìn | (SV) be near |
| 风 | fēng | (N) wind |
| 出 | chū | (V) go/come out |
| 火车站 | huǒchēzhàn | (PW) train station |
| 出租汽车 | chūzū qìchē | (N) taxi |
| 饭店 | fàndiàn | (PW) hotel |
| 车站 | chēzhàn | (PW) (train/bus) station |
| 堵车 | dǔ chē | (VO) jam up (of traffic) |
| 利害 | lì.hài | (SV) be formidable, be fierce |
| 可能 | kěnéng | (Adv) possibly |
| 自己 | zìjǐ | (Pr) self |
| 着急 | zháojí | (SV) be anxious |

| | | |
|---|---|---|
| 西瓜 | xīguā | (N) watermelon |
| 附近 | fùjìn | (PW) vicinity |
| 水果摊 | shuǐguǒtān | (PW) fruit stall |
| 旁边儿 | páng.biānr | (PS/PW) the side |
| 挑 | tiāo | (V) choose; select |

## COMPREHENSION QUESTIONS

1. Read the text of this chapter and answer the following questions.
   a. 钟名然是哪国人?

   ______________________________

   b. 他为什么来新西兰?

   ______________________________

   c. 他住哪儿?

   ______________________________

   d. 他为什么没有去别的地方玩儿?

   ______________________________

   e. 考完试，他想去哪儿玩?

   ______________________________

   f. 为什么?

   ______________________________

   g. 他给谁打电话?

   ______________________________

   h. 谢里是谁?

   ______________________________

i. 谢里怎么说?

________________________________________

j. 雪山城的天气(weather)怎么样?

________________________________________

k. 钟名然看了电shì以后做什么?

________________________________________

l. ‘我’家lí雪山城有多远?

________________________________________

m. 那儿的风景怎么样? 谁xǐ欢去那儿?

________________________________________

n. 钟名然怎么去饭店?

________________________________________

o. 那天晚上谢里做了什么?

________________________________________

p. 第二天早上谢里为什么很着急?

________________________________________

q. 钟名然去哪儿了? 在做什么?

________________________________________

2. Create a telephone conversation between 钟名然 and 谢里, discussing the plan to visit 雪山城. Write the conversation using as many Chinese characters as possible.

钟名然: ____________________________________

谢里：＿＿＿＿＿＿＿＿＿＿＿＿＿＿＿＿＿＿＿＿＿＿

钟名然：＿＿＿＿＿＿＿＿＿＿＿＿＿＿＿＿＿＿＿＿＿

谢里：＿＿＿＿＿＿＿＿＿＿＿＿＿＿＿＿＿＿＿＿＿＿

钟名然：＿＿＿＿＿＿＿＿＿＿＿＿＿＿＿＿＿＿＿＿＿

谢里：＿＿＿＿＿＿＿＿＿＿＿＿＿＿＿＿＿＿＿＿＿＿

钟名然：＿＿＿＿＿＿＿＿＿＿＿＿＿＿＿＿＿＿＿＿＿

谢里：＿＿＿＿＿＿＿＿＿＿＿＿＿＿＿＿＿＿＿＿＿＿

## Writing Help

### Independent Characters

| Character | Basic Meaning | No. of Str. | Stroke Order | Radical | Compo-nents | Struct-ure |
|---|---|---|---|---|---|---|
| *工 gōng | work | 3 | 一 丅 工 | 工 | 工 | ☐ |
| 马(馬) mǎ | horse | 3 | 马 | 马 | 马 | ☐ |
| *己 jǐ[1] | oneself | 3 | ㇕ ㇕ 己 | 己 | 己 | ☐ |
| 瓜 guā | melon | 5 | 𠂆 瓜 瓜 | 瓜 | 瓜 | ☐ |
| 至 zhì | until | 6 | 至 | 土 | 至 | ☐ |

1. See Chapter 12 for a comparison of the subtle contrast in appearance between 己 *jǐ* above and 已 *yǐ* introduced there.

## Compound Characters

The following are the new compound characters in this chapter with radicals you have learned: 利, 远, 近, 附, 松, 果, 急, 挑, 害, 假, 堵, 景, 游, 越, 暖, and 摊.

| Character | Basic Meaning | No. of Str. | Stroke Order | Radical | Mean. Clue | Phon. Clue | Compo-nents | Struct-ure |
|---|---|---|---|---|---|---|---|---|
| 利 lì | benefit | 7 | 禾 利 | 刂 | 刂 | | 禾 刂 | ⿰ |
| 远(遠) yuǎn | far | 7 | 二 亍 元 远 | 辶 | 辶 | 元 yuán | 辶 元 | ⿺ |
| 近 jìn | near | 7 | 斤 近 | 辶 | 辶 | 斤 jīn | 辶 斤 | ⿺ |
| 附 fù | to attach | 7 | 阝 阝亻 附 | 阝 | | 付 fù | 阝 亻 寸 | ⿲ |
| 松 sōng | pine tree; relaxed* | 8 | 木 松 | 木 | 木 | 公 | 木 公 | ⿰ |
| *果 guǒ | fruit | 8 | 曰 果 | 木 | 田, 木 (a tree grows in the field) | | 木 田 | ⿱ |
| 急 jí | to hurry | 9 | ⺈ ⺈ ⺈ ⺈ 急 | 心 | 心 | | ⺈ 彐 心 | ⿳ |
| 挑 tiāo | to pick | 9 | 扌 扌 扌 扌 挑 挑 挑 | 扌 | | 兆 ('iao') | 扌 兆 | ⿰ |
| 害 hài | to harm | 10 | 宀 宀 宀 宀 害 | 宀 | | | 宀 口 丰 | ⿳ |
| 假 jià | holiday | 11 | 亻 亻 亻 亻 亻 假 | 亻 | 亻 | 叚 jiǎ | 亻 叚 | ⿲ |
| 堵 dǔ | to block up | 11 | 扌 堵 | 土 | 土 | | 土 者 | ⿰ |
| *景 jǐng | scenery | 12 | 曰 景 | 日 | 日 | 京 | 日 京 | ⿱ |
| 游(遊) yóu | to swim | 12 | 氵 汸 汸 游 | 氵 | 氵 | 斿 yóu | 氵 方 𠂉 子 | ⿲ |

| Character | Basic Meaning | No. of Str. | Stroke Order | Mean. Clue | Phon. Clue | Components | Structure |
|---|---|---|---|---|---|---|---|
| 越 yuè | to cross | 12 | 走 走 走 越 越 越 | 走 | 走 | 戉 yuè | 走 戉 | |
| 暖 nuǎn | warm | 13 | 日 日 日 日 日 暖 | 日 | 日 | 爰 yuán | 日 爰 | |
| *摊(攤) tān | stall; stand (commercial) | 13 | 扌 扠 摊 | 扌 | 扌 | 难 | 扌 又 隹 | |

兆: Though this character is pronounced *zhào* when it functions as an independent character, as a phonetic component it often indicates the *iao* sound.

## Radicals

The new radicals introduced in this chapter are 车, 方, and 立.

### 1. 车

When this character functions as a radical in a compound character, it is usually found to its left. The compound characters in this chapter containing this radical are 轻 and 较.

| Character | Basic Meaning | No. of Str. | Stroke Order | Mean. Clue | Phon. Clue | Components | Structure |
|---|---|---|---|---|---|---|---|
| 轻(輕) qīng | light (not heavy) | 9 | 车 轻 | | 圣 jīng | 车 圣 | |
| 较(較) jiào | to compare | 10 | 车 较 较 | | 交 jiāo | 车 交 | |

### 2. 方

方 *fāng* as a character means "square" or "direction." It can be used in compound characters with related meanings. The compound characters in this chapter that contain this radical are 旁 and 旅.

| Character | Basic Meaning | No. of Str. | Stroke Order | Mean. Clue | Phon. Clue | Components | Structure |
|---|---|---|---|---|---|---|---|
| *旁 páng | beside | 10 | 亠 立 立 旁 | 方 | 方 | 立 冖 方 | |
| *旅 lǚ | to travel, trip | 10 | 方 方 方 方 旅 旅 | | | 方 𠂉 民 | |

### 3. 立

立 can be used as a character as well as a radical. As a character it means to stand *(lì)*. When it is used as a radical in compound characters, it indicates a related meaning. The compound character in this chapter containing this radical is 站.

| Character | Basic Meaning | No. of Str. | Stroke Order | Mean. Clue | Phon. Clue | Compo-nents | Struct-ure |
|---|---|---|---|---|---|---|---|
| 站 zhàn | to stand | 10 | 立 站 | 立 | 占 zhàn | 立 占 | ◫ |

站: It is also a station where people stand around waiting.

## EXERCISES

### I. Character Exercises

**1. Form new characters by using different components of the following characters.**

**Example:** 工 (from 功) + 𠂇 (from 有) → 左

| 利, 完, 进, 急, 咱, 所 |
|---|

_____ (from _____ ) + _____ (from _____ ) → _____

_____ (from _____ ) + _____ (from _____ ) → _____

_____ (from _____ ) + _____ (from _____ ) → _____

_____ (from _____ ) + _____ (from _____ ) → _____

**2. How many words/phrases can you form using the following characters?**

a. 风 → ______________________________

b. 可 → ______________________________

c. 西 → ______________________________

d. 车 → ______________________________

3. Form five characters each using each of the following components:

   a. 月 → ____________________

   b. 扌 → ____________________

   c. 土 → ____________________

   d. 日 → ____________________

   e. 心 → ____________________

   f. 广 → ____________________

**4. Write as many characters as you can remember that contain the following radicals indicating the meanings in the parentheses:**

   a. 心 (heart/mind related)

   → ____________________

   b. 日 (sun/time related)

   → ____________________

   c. 扌 (hand-related activities)

   → ____________________

## II. Vocabulary Exercises

**1. Write two different pronunciations for each of the following characters, then make a word/phrase with each:**

   a. 和 (        ) ____________________

   (        ) ____________________

   b. 了 (        ) ____________________

   (        ) ____________________

   c. 仔 (        ) ____________________

   (        ) ____________________

## III. Structure Exercises

1. Complete the following sentences using the words in parentheses:

   a. 我 ______________________________。（累……不想去上课）

   b. 他的汉字 ______________________________。（写……好）

   c. 中文 ______________________________。（学……有意思）

   d. 英文 ____________ 我 ______________。（难……不想学）

   e. 他说得 __________ 我 ______________。（快……不懂）

   f. 你 ____________ 考试成绩 ____________。（用功……好）

## Supplementary Reading

### Reading 1

知之为知之，不知为不知

你们知道"知之为知之，不知为不知"是什么意思吗？ 这也是2000多年前写的中文。意思是"知道就说知道，不知道就说不知道，这样才能学到东西。"

COMPREHENSION QUESTIONS

1. "知之为知之，不知为不知"这句话是什么意思？

______________________________

2. "知之为知之，不知为不知"是什么时候写的？

______________________________

**Reading 2**

## 走马看花

以前有一个名叫大贵的男子，他长得很好看，可是tuǐ有点儿问题，所以走起路来不很方便。他想找一个漂亮的女孩子作他的太太。他请他的朋友华汉给他介绍一个女孩子。

华汉家对面住着一个很漂亮女孩子。她的名字叫小清。虽然小清长得很漂亮，可是耳朵长得不好看，所以一直没有男朋友。华汉想把小清介绍给大贵认识。

在八月八日的那一天，华汉让大贵qí马从小清家门口走过，又叫小清手里拿着花站在她家门口。小清看到qí在马上的大贵，心里很xǐ欢他。大贵也爱上了小清。后来小清作了大贵的太太。他们常常说起"走马看花"的那件事。现在这句话成了一句成语。意思是"只是很快地看了一遍，没仔细地看清楚。"

**COMPREHENSION QUESTIONS**

1. 为什么华汉要给大贵介绍女朋友?

_______________________________________________

2. "走马看花"是什么意思?

_______________________________________________

## Character Practice

| | | | | | | | | | |
|---|---|---|---|---|---|---|---|---|---|
| 工 | 工 | | | | | | | | |
| 马 | 马 | | | | | | | | |
| 己 | 己 | | | | | | | | |
| 瓜 | 瓜 | | | | | | | | |
| 至 | 至 | | | | | | | | |
| 利 | 利 | | | | | | | | |
| 远 | 远 | | | | | | | | |
| 近 | 近 | | | | | | | | |
| 附 | 附 | | | | | | | | |
| 松 | 松 | | | | | | | | |
| 果 | 果 | | | | | | | | |

| | | | | | | | | | |
|---|---|---|---|---|---|---|---|---|---|
| 急 | 急 | | | | | | | | |
| 挑 | 挑 | | | | | | | | |
| 害 | 害 | | | | | | | | |
| 假 | 假 | | | | | | | | |
| 堵 | 堵 | | | | | | | | |
| 景 | 景 | | | | | | | | |
| 游 | 游 | | | | | | | | |
| 越 | 越 | | | | | | | | |
| 暖 | 暖 | | | | | | | | |
| 摊 | 摊 | | | | | | | | |
| 轻 | 轻 | | | | | | | | |

| 较 | 较 | | | | | | | | |
|---|---|---|---|---|---|---|---|---|---|
| 旁 | 旁 | | | | | | | | |
| 旅 | 旅 | | | | | | | | |
| 站 | 站 | | | | | | | | |

# CHAPTER TWENTY
# 第 二 十 课

**Text**

江太太知道江兴成下午不去上班，没有事，就叫他上附近的超级市场替她买点儿东西。她说假期快到了，她想带孩子们去度假，所以要买点儿吃的，喝的，用的什么的。当然，还要买几斤现成的饺子。江太太还要他买东西的时候，不要被偷了钱和信用kǎ。江兴成刚出门他太太又叫住他，告诉他买东西回来的时候从高速公路去学校接孩子回家。江兴成不高兴地说："知道了。真讨厌！"

两个小时以后，江兴成带着四个孩子回来了。孩子们又吵又闹，江兴成要他们安静些。孩子们不但不听话，而且越来越吵了。大女儿一进家就要唱kǎ拉OK；二女儿要给同学打电话；小女儿要玩电nǎo；小儿子要看电shì上的足球sài。一会儿，二女儿跟小儿子打架了，儿子哭了，他的手被姐姐抓pò了，流血了。二女儿也生气了。江兴成说家里有了四个孩子真是吵死了，孩子们都应该去学校宿舍住。可是，假期的时候孩子们天天在家怎么办？自己还是天天去办公楼上班，不在家最好。

**生词 New Words**

| | | |
|---|---|---|
| 江兴成 | Jiāng Xìngchéng | (N) a personal name |
| 超级市场 | chāojí shìchǎng | (PW) supermarket |
| 度假 | dù jià | (VO) spend one's holiday |
| 斤 | -jīn | (Cl) unit of weight (½ kg, slightly more than a pound) |
| 被 | bèi | (CV) (marker for passive-voice sentence) |
| 偷 | tōu | (V) steal |
| 信用kǎ | xìnyòngkǎ | (N) credit card (Cl *-zhāng* 张) |
| 高速公路 | gāosù gōnglù | (N) highway; freeway |
| 接 | jiē | (V) meet; pick (somebody) up |
| 讨厌 | tǎoyàn | (SV) be a pain in the neck |
| 闹 | nào | (V) make noise; stir up trouble |
| 不但……而且…… | búdàn…érqiě… | (Pat) not only X, but also Y |
| 唱 | chàng | (V) sing |
| kǎ拉OK | kǎlā-ōukēi | (N) karaoke |
| 电nǎo | diànnǎo | (N) computer (lit. "electric brain") |
| 足球sài | zúqiúsài | (N) soccer match |
| 一会儿 | yìhuǐr | (TD) a while, a short time |
| 打架 | dǎ jià | (VO) scuffle |
| 哭 | kū | (V) cry, weep |
| 手 | shǒu | (N) hand |
| 抓 | zhuā | (V) grab; scratch; arrest |
| 流血 | liú xiě | (VO) bleed |
| 死 | -sǐ | (RVC) (indicates extremeness of state) |

| | | |
|---|---|---|
| 应该 | yīnggāi | (Aux) ought to |
| 宿舍 | sùshè | (PW) dormitory |
| 怎么办? | Zěnme bàn? | (Ex) What the heck do we do? |
| 办公楼 | bàngōnglóu | (PW) office building |

COMPREHENSION QUESTIONS

1. Read the text of this chapter, and for each statement below indicate whether it is true or false:

   a. (      ) 江太太知道江兴成下午要去上班，所以叫他替她买东西。

   b. (      ) 江太太要江兴成去买东西，因为她想带孩子们去度假。

   c. (      ) 江太太买东西的时候，被偷了钱和信用kǎ。

   d. (      ) 江兴成从高速公路去学校接孩子回家。

   e. (      ) 因为江兴成不xǐ欢他的太太说得太多，所以他说："真讨厌!"。

2. In pairs, fill in the boxes with the relevant information from the text:

| People | Description |
|---|---|
| 大女儿 | |
| 二女儿 | |
| 小女儿 | |
| 小儿子 | |

## Writing Help

### Independent Characters

| Character | Basic Meaning | No. of Str. | Stroke Order | Radical | Compo-nents | Struct-ure |
|---|---|---|---|---|---|---|
| *斤 jīn | ½ kg | 4 | 斤 | 斤 | 斤 | □ |
| 办(辦) bàn | to do | 4 | 刁 力 办 办 | 力 | 办 | □ |
| 且 qiě | also | 5 | 且 | 一 | 且 | □ |
| 血 xiě | blood | 6 | ノ 亻 仃 皿 血 | 血 | 血 | □ |

## Compound Characters

The following are the new compound characters in this chapter with radicals you have learned: 市, 讨, 厌, 级, 但, 足, 抓, 应, 拉, 该, 舍, 度, 架, 被, 速, 哭, 流, 偷, 接, 唱, 球, 宿, and 超.

| Character | Basic Meaning | No. of Str. | Stroke Order | Radical | Mean. Clue | Phon. Clue | Compo-nents | Struct-ure |
|---|---|---|---|---|---|---|---|---|
| *市 shì | market; city | 5 | 亠 市 | 亠 | 亠 | | 亠 巾 | |
| 讨(討) tǎo | to ask for | 5 | 讠 讨 | 讠 | 讠 | | 讠 寸 | |
| *厌(厭) yàn | disgusting | 6 | 厂 厌 厌 | 厂 | | | 厂 犬 | |
| 级(級) jí | degree, level | 7 | 纟 级 | 纟 | | 及 jí | 纟 及 | |
| 但 dàn | but | 7 | 亻 伯 但 | 亻 | | 旦 dàn | 亻 日 一 | |
| *足 zú | foot | 7 | 口 口 早 足 足 | 口 | | | 口 龰 | |
| 抓 zhuā | to grab | 7 | 扌 扩 折 抓 | 扌 | 扌 | 爪 zhuǎ | 扌 爪 | |
| 应(應) yīng | should | 7 | 广 庐 应 应 | 广 | | | 广 业 | |
| 拉 lā | to pull | 8 | 扌 拉 | 扌 | 扌 | | 扌 立 | |
| 该(該) gāi | should | 8 | 讠 计 访 该 | 讠 | 讠 | 亥 hài | 讠 亥 | |
| *舍 shè | inn | 8 | 人 仐 舍 | 人 | 人 | 舌 shé | 人 干 口 | |
| *度 dù | size | 9 | 广 庐 庐 庐 庐 度 | 广 | | | 广 廿 又 | |
| 架 jià | shelf; frame | 9 | 力 加 架 | 木 | 木 | 加 jiā | 力 口 木 | |
| 被 bèi | quilt*; by...-ed | 10 | 衤 被 | 衤 | 衤 | 皮 | 衤 皮 | |
| *速 sù | speed | 10 | 一 亩 申 束 速 | 辶 | 辶 | 束 shù | 辶 束 | |

| | | | | | | | | |
|---|---|---|---|---|---|---|---|---|
| 哭 kū | to cry | 10 | 口 吅 哭 哭 | 口 | 口, 犬 | | 口口犬 | |
| 流 liú | to flow | 10 | 氵 汁 浐 浐 浐 济 流 | 氵 | 氵 | | 氵 𠫓 儿 | |
| 偷 tōu | to steal | 11 | 亻 仒 佮 偷 偷 | 亻 | 亻 | | 亻 俞 | |
| 接 jiē | to meet | 11 | 扌 拉 接 | 扌 | 扌 | 妾 qiè | 扌 立 女 | |
| 唱 chàng | to sing | 11 | 口 吅 唱 | 口 | 口 | 昌 chāng | 口 日 曰 | |
| 球 qiú | ball | 11 | 王 玗 玗 玗 玗 球 球 球 | 王 | | 求 qiú | 王 求 | |
| *宿 sù | to stay overnight | 11 | 宀 宀亻 宿 | 宀 | 宀, 亻, 百 | | 宀 亻 百 | |
| 超 chāo | to surpass | 12 | 走 起 超 | 走 | 走 | 召 zhāo | 走 刀 口 | |

哭: It can be remembered as a person with arms stretched: 犬. The two 口 are like two eyes on the top, and one dot is a tear from the eye.

宿: It can be remembered as follows: hundreds 百 of people 人 living under one roof = dormitory.

## EXERCISES

### I. Character Exercises

**1. Form new characters by using different components of the following characters.**

**Example:** 工 (from 功) + 𠂇 (from 有) → 左

| 超, 较, 杯, 吧, 速, 抓 |
|---|

_____ (from _____ ) + _____ (from _____ ) → _____

_____ (from _____ ) + _____ (from _____ ) → _____

_____ (from _____ ) + _____ (from _____ ) → _____

_____ (from _____ ) + _____ (from _____ ) → _____

2. Form five characters each using each of the following components:

a. 寸 → ______

b. 走 → ______

c. 刂 → ______

3. Write two different pronunciations for each of the following characters. Then make a word/phrase with each.

a. 行 (    ) ______

(    ) ______

b. 得 (    ) ______

(    ) ______

c. 便 (    ) ______

(    ) ______

## II. Vocabulary Exercises

1. Form as many words or phrases as you can using the characters below:

讨，足，静，空，高，架，流，血，球
宿，安，应，厌，舍，有，该，打，速

______

______

______

______

1. **Write Pinyin next to each of the characters below. Then make a word or phrase with the character:**

a. 级 (　　) ______________

极 (　　) ______________

b. 块 (　　) ______________

快 (　　) ______________

2. **How many words/phrases can you form using the following characters?**

a. 家 → ______________________________

b. 子 → ______________________________

c. 高 → ______________________________

III. Structure Exercises

1. **Rearrange the elements below to form a grammatical sentence:**

a.

| 而且， | 卖， | 不但， | 吃， | 菜肉， | xǐ欢， | |
|---|---|---|---|---|---|---|
| <u>大女儿</u>， | 超级市场， | <u>小儿子</u>， | 饺子， | 也， | 的， | xǐ欢 |

______________________________________________

b.

| 的， | 上课， | 都， | 学校， | 假期， | 天天， | |
|---|---|---|---|---|---|---|
| 孩子们， | 用， | 不， | 时候， | 在， | 去， | 家 |

______________________________________________

## Supplementary Reading

### Reading 1

Xiāng 山

你知道Xiāng山在哪儿吗？ Xiāng山就在北京的西北部。因为Xiāng山那儿的风景很美，所以一年春夏秋冬都有很多人到那儿去玩儿。很多住在北京的人也xǐ欢在星期六和星期日带家人去爬山。春天Xiāng山的山上开了很多的花，花被风chuī下来的时候，很好看。夏天不但不热，而且很凉快。秋天的风景更漂亮。远远看去，红sè、黄sè、绿sè的山，美极了。冬天虽然冷，又下雪，可是Xiāng山还是很美，跟春天、夏天和秋天的美不一样。要是你们有机会去北京，一定要去Xiāng山玩儿。

COMPREHENSION QUESTIONS

1. Xiāng山在哪儿？

   ______________________________

2. Xiāng山一年春夏秋冬的风景都一样吗？有什么不同？

   ______________________________

## Reading 2

### 张大千

张大千（1899–1984）是一个很有名的画家。他从小就跟他妈妈学画画儿。他父母一共有十个孩子。他是第八个。他七岁开始上学，九岁开始学画画儿。十二岁就能画山水，花和人。他1917年跟他哥哥去日本学画画儿。1919年从日本回上海后就跟一位很有名的画家学书画[1]。他去过很多个国家，也住过很多个国家。他在美国住了八年。张大千画画儿画了六十多年，他很用功。在这么长的时间里，他画了三万多张画儿。

张大千不但xǐ欢画画儿，他也xǐ欢买画儿。听说有一次他已经跟朋友说好要买他朋友的fáng子，可是后来他看到有人要卖一幅很有名的画儿。他看了那幅画儿以后高兴得睡不着觉。过了几天，他跟他的朋友说他不买他的fáng子了，他把买fáng子的钱都拿去买画儿了。

1. 书画：painting and calligraphy

## COMPREHENSION QUESTIONS

1. 张大千是谁？ 他几岁就开始学画画儿？

_______________________________________________

2. 张大千画画儿画了多少年？ 他一共画了多少张画儿？

_______________________________________________

3. 张大千不但xǐ欢画画儿，而且还喜欢做什么？

_______________________________________________

## Character Practice

| 斤 | 斤 | | | | | | | | |
|---|---|---|---|---|---|---|---|---|---|
| 办 | 办 | | | | | | | | |
| 且 | 且 | | | | | | | | |
| 血 | 血 | | | | | | | | |
| 市 | 市 | | | | | | | | |
| 讨 | 讨 | | | | | | | | |
| 庆 | 庆 | | | | | | | | |

| 级 | 级 | | | | | | | | |
|---|---|---|---|---|---|---|---|---|---|
| 但 | 但 | | | | | | | | |
| 足 | 足 | | | | | | | | |
| 抓 | 抓 | | | | | | | | |
| 应 | 应 | | | | | | | | |
| 拉 | 拉 | | | | | | | | |
| 该 | 该 | | | | | | | | |
| 舍 | 舍 | | | | | | | | |
| 度 | 度 | | | | | | | | |
| 架 | 架 | | | | | | | | |
| 被 | 被 | | | | | | | | |
| 速 | 速 | | | | | | | | |
| 哭 | 哭 | | | | | | | | |

| 流 | 流 | | | | | | | | |
|---|---|---|---|---|---|---|---|---|---|
| 偷 | 偷 | | | | | | | | |
| 接 | 接 | | | | | | | | |
| 唱 | 唱 | | | | | | | | |
| 球 | 球 | | | | | | | | |
| 宿 | 宿 | | | | | | | | |
| 超 | 超 | | | | | | | | |

# Vocabulary Index
# 生词表

## A

| | | |
|---|---|---|
| 啊 | a | (P) (tells listener he or she really should have known that) (16) |
| 啊 | á | (P) (indicates surprise, sudden realization) (16) |
| ADV 地V | ADV de V | (Pat) indicates single instance manner of an action (13) |
| 爱 | ài | (V) love (15) |
| 哎呀 | āiya! | (Ex) oh! oh my! (6) |
| 安静 | ānjìng | (SV) be peaceful and quiet (13/18)[1] |
| 阿姨 | āyí | (N) aunt (mother's sister) (17) |

## B

| | | |
|---|---|---|
| 吧 | ba | (P) (indicates an assumption) (8) |
| 八 | bā | (Nu) eight (4) |
| 把 | bǎ | (CV) take (17) |
| 白 | bái | (SV) be white (14) |
| 百 | bǎi | (Nu) hundred (5) |
| 白京以 | Bái Jīngyǐ | (N) a personal name (11) |
| 搬 | bān | (V) move (some large object) (15) |
| 搬家 | bān jiā | (VO) move house, relocate (15) |
| 半 | bàn | (Nu) half, semi- (13) |
| 办公楼 | bàngōnglóu | (PW) office building (20) |
| 半天 | bàntiān | (TD) for a long time (14) |
| 半夜 | bànyè | (N) midnight (16) |
| 报 | bào | (N) newspaper (9) |
| 杯 | -bēi | (Cl) cup/glass of (12) |
| 被 | bèi | (CV) (marker for passive-voice sentence) (20) |
| 倍 | -bèi | (Cl) -fold, number of times (18) |

1. Whenever a vocabulary item first appears in a hybrid character-Pinyin format and later appears with all syllables represented by characters, then the convention will be to indicate both the chapter when the hybrid representaton first appears and the chapter when the full character version first appears. For example, 安静 first appears in hybrid form in Chapter 13 and in full charcter form in Chapter 18.

| | | |
|---|---|---|
| 北边儿 | běi.biānr | (PS/PW) the north (10) |
| 北京 | Běijīng | (PW) capital city of the People's Republic of China (9) |
| 北京街 | Běijīng Jiē | (PW) name of a street (9/12) |
| 本 | -běn | (Cl) volume (for books) (5) |
| 笨 | bèn | (SV) be stupid (8) |
| 笔 | bǐ | (N) pen, writing instrument (9) |
| 比 | bǐ | (CV) compared to (18) |
| 遍 | -biàn | (VCl) times (17) |
| 别 | bié | (Conj) don't (imperative) (13) |
| 别的 | biéde | (N) others (14) |
| 别人 | biéren | (N) other people (14) |
| 比较 | bǐjiào | (Adv) comparatively (19) |
| 冰水 | bīngshuǐ | (N) ice water (7) |
| 病 | bìng | (V) be ill (12) |
| 病 | bìng | (N) illness (12) |
| 伯伯 | bóbo | (N) uncle (father's elder brother) (7) |
| 伯母 | bómǔ | (N) aunt (wife of father's elder brother) (7) |
| 不 | bù-, bú-, bu- | (Adv) not (4) |
| 不必 | búbì | (Aux) need not, not have to (7) |
| 不错 | búcuò | (SV) be pretty good (13) |
| 不但……而且…… | búdàn...érqiě... | (Pat) not only X, but also Y (20) |
| 不过 | bú guò | (Conj) still, however (13) |
| 不是……(而)是…… | búshì...(ér)shìˇ... | (Pat) it's not...but rather (14) |
| 不是……就是…… | búshì...jiùshìˇ... | (Pat) if not...then it's (15) |
| 不同 | bùtóng | (SV) be different (18) |
| 不行 | bùxíng | (Ex) can't be done (6) |

## C

| | | |
|---|---|---|
| 才 | cái | (Adv) then (later than expected) (12) |
| 菜 | cài | (N) food; dishes (10) |
| 厕所 | cèsuǒ | (PW) toilet (15) |
| 茶 | chá | (N) tea (10) |
| 差 | chà | (V) lacking, less than (14) |
| 差不多 | chàbuduō | (Ex) almost, just about, good enough (13) |
| 长 | cháng | (SV) be long (18) |
| 唱 | chàng | (V) sing (20) |
| 常伯伯 | Cháng Bóbo | (N) Uncle Chang (18) |
| 常常 | chángcháng | (Adv) frequently, often (13) |
| 长江 | Chángjiāng | (PW) the Yangtze River (18) |

| | | |
|---|---|---|
| 吵 | chǎo | (SV) be noisy (16) |
| 炒 | chǎo | (V) stir-fry (11) |
| 超级市场 | chāojí shìchǎng | (PW) supermarket (20) |
| 叉子 | chāzi | (N) fork (Cl -*bǎ* 把) (10) |
| 车 | chē | (N) vehicle (Cl -*liàng*辆) (11) |
| 城 | chéng | (N) city, town (9) |
| 成 | -chéng | (VC) (indicates transformation) (17) |
| 成绩 | chéngjì | (N) grades; result; achievement (18) |
| 车票 | chēpiào | (N) bus ticket (Cl -张) (15) |
| 车站 | chēzhàn | (PW) bus stop (12/19) |
| 衬衫 | chènshān | (N) shirt (Cl -件) (9) |
| 吃 | chī | (V) eat; consume (7) |
| 吃饱了 | chībǎole | (Ex) to be full (8) |
| 吃坏了 | chī huàile | (Ex) stomach problem from taking the wrong food (12) |
| 吃药 | chī yào | (VO) take medicine (12) |
| 出 | chū | (V) go/come out (19) |
| 穿 | chuān | (V) wear; put on (clothing) (18) |
| 床边儿 | chuáng.biānr | (PS/PW) next to the bed (17) |
| 厨fáng | chúfáng | (PW) kitchen (15) |
| 除了……以外…… | chúle...yǐwài... | (Pat) besides, except for (12) |
| 出门 | chū mén | (VO) go out, leave home (for a bit) (14/15) |
| 春天 | chūntiān | (TW) spring (13) |
| 出租汽车 | chūzū qìchē | (N) taxi (11/19) |
| 词典 | cídiǎn | (N) dictionary (Cl -本) (5/6) |
| 次 | -cì | (VCl) times (16) |
| 从 | cóng | (CV) from (11) |
| 从……dào…… | cóng...dào... | (Pat) from...to... (11) |
| 聪明 | cōng.míng | (SV) be intelligent, be smart (8/19) |

## D

| | | |
|---|---|---|
| 大 | dà | (SV) be big, be large (4) |
| 打的 | dǎ dī | (VO) take a taxi (slang) (11) |
| 打电话 | dǎ diànhuà | (VO) make a phone call (10) |
| 带 | dài | (V) take or bring along, lead around (16) |
| 打架 | dǎ jià | (VO) scuffle (20) |
| 大家 | dàjiā | (N) everyone (15) |
| 大门 | dàmén | (N) main entrance (9) |
| 当然 | dāngrán | (Adv) of course (13) |
| 当中 | dāngzhōng | (PS/PW) the middle (more abstract) (10/16) |

| | | |
|---|---|---|
| 到 | dào | (V) arrive (13) |
| 到 | dào | (CV) to (13) |
| 到 | -dào | (VC) (reach a point) (17) |
| 刀子 | dāozi | (N) knife (Cl -把) (10) |
| 大人 | dàrén | (N) adult (10) |
| 大shēng | dà shēng | (Adv) loud (16) |
| 大学 | dàxué | (N) university (11) |
| 大学生 | dàxué.shēng | (N) university student (10) |
| 的 | de | (P) (indicates possession; used to join a modifying clause with the noun it modifies) (9) |
| 得 | de | (P) (marks the manner or extent of an action) (14) |
| 地 | -de | (P) (marks the manner in which a single instance of an action is carried out) (13) |
| 得 | děi | (Aux) must (6) |
| 灯 | dēng | (N) lamp, lights (11) |
| 等 | děng | (V) wait (12) |
| ……的时候 | ...de shíhòu | (Pat) at the time of... (13) |
| 第 | dì- | (Pre) (indicates numerical order) (13) |
| 点 | -diǎn | (Cl) o'clock (13) |
| 电nǎo | diànnǎo | (N) computer (20) |
| 电shì | diànshì | (N) television (6) |
| 电梯 | diàntī | (N) elevator (15) |
| 电yǐng | diànyǐng | (N) movie (13) |
| 地道 | dì.dào | (SV) be authentic (8) |
| 弟弟 | dìdi | (N) younger brother (6) |
| 地方 | dì.fāng | (PW) place, location (9) |
| 地图 | dìtú | (N) map (Cl -张); atlas (Cl -本) (8) |
| 懂 | dǒng | (V) understand (14) |
| 懂 | -dǒng | (VC) understand (17) |
| 东边儿 | dōng.biānr | (PS/PW) the east (9) |
| 冬天 | dōngtiān | (TW) winter (14) |
| 东西 | dōngxi | (N) thing (physical) (7) |
| 都 | dōu | (Adv) in all cases (8) |
| 堵车 | dǔ chē | (VO) jam up (of traffic) (19) |
| 对 | duì | (CV) to, toward (10) |
| 对 | duì | (SV) be correct (8) |
| 对面 | duìmiàn | (PW) side directly opposite (13) |
| 度假 | dù jià | (VO) spend one's holiday (20) |

| | | |
|---|---|---|
| 顿 | -dùn | (Cl) (used with 饭 to mean "meal") (14) |
| 多 | duō | (SV) many; be abundant (11) |
| 多久? | duō jiǔ? | (QW) how long? (19) |
| 多少? | duōshǎo? | (Q) how many? how much? (13) |
| 肚子 | dùzi | (N) stomach (12) |

## E

| | | |
|---|---|---|
| 饿 | è | (SV) be hungry (7) |
| 二 | èr | (Nu) two (4) |
| 耳朵 | ěrduo | (N) ear (16) |
| 儿子 | érzi | (N) son (5) |

## F

| | | |
|---|---|---|
| 法国 | Fǎ.guó | (PW) France (8) |
| 饭 | fàn | (N) meal; cooked rice; food; cuisine (13) |
| 饭店 | fàndiàn | (PW) hotel (19) |
| 放 | fàng | (V) put, place (17) |
| 方便 | fāngbiàn | (SV) be convenient (11) |
| fáng间 | fángjiān | (N) room (of a house; Cl -个, 间 ) (17) |
| 方美春 | Fāng Měichūn | (N) a personal name (13) |
| 饭馆儿 | fànguǎnr | (PW) restaurant (Cl -家) (7) |
| 方宜思 | Fāng Yísī | (N) a personal name (9) |
| fáng子 | fángzi | (N) house (9) |
| 饭厅 | fàntīng | (PW) dining room (15) |
| 饭桌 | fànzhuō/cānzhuō | (N) dining table (15) |
| 发烧 | fā shāo | (VO) have fever (12) |
| 法文 | Fǎwén | (N) French (language) (10) |
| 飞机 | fēijī | (N) airplane (17) |
| 飞机场 | fēijīchǎng | (PW) airport (17) |
| 分 | -fēn | (Cl) pennies (6) |
| 分 | -fēn | (Cl) minute (13) |
| 份 | -fèn | (Cl) (for issues of newspapers, magazines, and so on) (6) |
| 风 | fēng | (N) wind (19) |
| 风景 | fēngjǐng | (N) scenery (19) |
| 粉红 | fěnhóng | (SV) be pink (14) |
| 父母 | fùmǔ | (N) parents (6) |
| 附近 | fùjìn | (PW) vicinity (19) |

## G

| | | |
|---|---|---|
| 刚 | gāng | (TW) just; just now (16) |
| 高 | gāo | (SV) be tall or high (9) |
| 告诉 | gàosu | (V) tell; inform (6) |
| 高速公路 | gāosù gōnglù | (N) highway (20) |
| 高小美 | Gāo Xiǎoměi | (N) a personal name (10) |
| 高兴 | gāoxìng | (SV) be happy (13) |
| 个 | -gè | (Cl) (general classifier) (5) |
| 哥哥 | gēge | (N) older brother (6) |
| 个个, 人人, 天天 | Cl-Cl (gège, rénren, tiāntiān) | (Pat) every... (13) |
| 给 | gěi | (CV) for, to (10) |
| 给 | gěi | (V) give, give to (16) |
| 跟 | gēn | (CV) (together) with (16) |
| 跟 | gēn | (Conj) and (usually joins nouns) (16) |
| 更 | gèng | (Adv) even more (18) |
| 公共汽车/公车 | gōnggòng qìchē (gōngchē) | (N) public bus (11) |
| 功课 | gōngkè | (N) schoolwork; homework (11) |
| 公里 | gōnglǐ | (Cl) kilometer (19) |
| 公寓 | gōngyù | (PW) apartment (15) |
| 公寓楼 | gōngyù lóu | (PW) apartment building (15) |
| 工作 | gōngzuò | (N) job (19) |
| 够 | gòu | (V) be enough, sufficient, adequate (18) |
| 刮风 | guā fēng | (VO) have wind gusts (15) |
| 拐 | guǎi | (V) turn (11) |
| 贵 | guì | (V) be expensive (18) |
| 过 | -guo | (P) (used after a verb to indicate the experience) (13) |
| 过 | guò | (V) surpassing; more than; pass by (14) |
| 故事 | gùshi | (N) story, narrative account (10) |

## H

| | | |
|---|---|---|
| 还 | hái | (Adv) also, additionally (7) |
| 还......呢 | hái...ne | (Pat) (continuation of an action) (12) |
| 还是 | hái.shì | (Conj) or (9) |
| 还是 | háishì | (Adv) still (best to...) (14) |
| 孩子 | háizi | (N) child, youngster (10) |
| 海明 | Hǎimíng | (N) a personal name (13) |

| | | |
|---|---|---|
| 韩国 | Hán.guó | (PW) Korea (14) |
| 汗衫 | hànshān | (N) T-shirt (Cl -件) (9) |
| 汉语 | Hànyǔ | (N) Chinese (language) (7) |
| 汉字 | hànzì | (N) Chinese character(s) (7) |
| 好 | hǎo | (SV) be well, be good (6) |
| 好 | hǎo | (Adv) quite, very (14) |
| 好 | hǎo | (SV) several (14) |
| 好 | -hǎo | (VC) satisfactorily complete (17) |
| 号 | -hào | (Cl) day of the month (13) |
| 好吃 | hǎochī | (SV) be delicious (7) |
| 好好儿 | hǎohaor | (Adv) earnestly; all out (17) |
| 好喝 | hǎohē | (SV) be delicious to drink (7) |
| 好看 | hǎokàn | (SV) good-looking; have an interesting story (6/15) |
| 好些 | hǎo.xiē | (Q) several; many (15) |
| 好做 | hǎozuò | (SV) be easy to do (7) |
| 喝 | hē | (V) drink (7) |
| 和 | hé | (Conj) and, with (11) |
| 河 | hé | (N) river (Cl -条) (19) |
| 很 | hěn | (Adv) quite, very (6) |
| 红 | hóng | (SV) be red (14) |
| 后边儿 | hòu.biānr | (PS/PW) in back (10) |
| 后天 | hòutiān | (TW) the day after tomorrow (15) |
| 花 | huā | (V) spend (money or time) (12) |
| 话 | huà | (N) spoken language (5) |
| 画报 | huàbào | (N) illustrated periodical; picture magazine (6/9) |
| 还 | huán | (V) return (something) (17) |
| 黄 | huáng | (SV) be yellow (14) |
| 黄河 | Huánghé | (PW) the Yellow River (18) |
| 黄家深 | Huáng Jiāshēn | (N) a personal name (16) |
| 华人 | Huárén | (N) ethnic Chinese (17) |
| 灰 | huī | (SV) be grey (14) |
| 回 | huí | (V) return (12) |
| 会 | huì | (Aux) may, can (5) |
| 会 | -huì | (VC) master (17) |
| 火车 | huǒchē | (N) train (19) |
| 火车站 | huǒchēzhàn | (PW) train station (11/19) |
| huò者 | huò.zhě | (Conj) or (in a statement) (15) |

# J

| | | |
|---|---|---|
| 挤 | jǐ | (SV) be crowded (12) |
| 几 | jǐ? | (Q) how many? (classifier required) (5) |
| 几 | jǐ- | (Q) a few, several (classifier required) (5) |
| 记 | jì | (V) remember (17) |
| 家 | jiā | (N) family; home (6) |
| 家 | -jiā | (Cl) (for businesses) (7) |
| 家具 | jiājù | (N) furniture (Cl -件) (15) |
| 见 | -jiàn | (VC) perceive (16) |
| 件 | -jiàn | (Cl) (for clothing covering the upper half of the body) (9) |
| 讲 | jiǎng | (V) speak, say (16) |
| jiāng来 | jiānglái | (TW) in the future, future (14) |
| 江兴成 | Jiāng Xìngchéng | (N) a personal name (20) |
| 教 | jiāo | (V) teach (10) |
| 叫 | jiào | (V) be called, call (8) |
| 饺子 | jiǎozi | (N) "Chinese ravioli," Chinese dumpling (17) |
| 假期 | jiàqī | (TW) vacation; holiday period (19) |
| 家人 | jiārén | (N) family members (9) |
| 街 | jiē | (N) street (Cl -条) (11) |
| 接 | jiē | (V) meet; pick (somebody) up (20) |
| 借 | jiè | (V) borrow; lend (17) |
| 姐姐 | jiějie | (N) older sister (6) |
| 介绍 | jiè.shào | (V) introduce (10) |
| 几乎 | jīhū | (Adv) almost; nearly (18) |
| 机会 | jī.huì | (N) opportunity (10) |
| ……极了 | …jíle | (Adv) extremely (17) |
| 斤 | -jīn | (Cl) weight (slightly more than a pound) (20) |
| 近 | jìn | (SV) be near (19) |
| 进 | jìn | (V) enter (15) |
| 今年 | jīnnián | (TW) this year (15) |
| 今天 | jīntiān | (TW) today (12) |
| jǐn张 | jǐnzhāng | (SV) be nervous; be tense (17) |
| 九 | jiǔ | (Nu) nine (4) |
| 酒 | jiǔ | (N) liquor (7) |
| 久 | jiǔ | (SV) take/be a long time (12) |
| 旧 | jiù | (SV) be old (of objects, *not* living things) (8) |
| 就 | jiù | (Adv) only, just (9) |
| 就 | jiù | (Conj) then (11) |
| 就 | jiù | (Adv) then (earlier than expected) (12) |

## K

| | | |
|---|---|---|
| 咖啡 | kāfēi | (N) coffee (7) |
| 咖啡馆儿 | kāfēiguǎnr | (PW) café (14) |
| 开 | kāi | (V) open; operate; drive (a car) (11) |
| 开始 | kāishǐ | (V) begin (12) |
| kǎ拉OK | kǎlā-ōukēi | (N) karaoke (20) |
| 看 | kàn | (V) look; read (9) |
| 看 | kàn | (V) consider; be of the opinion (14) |
| 看病/看医生 | kàn bìng/kàn yīshēng | (VO) to see a doctor (12) |
| 考试 | kǎo shì | (VO) take a test or examination (10) |
| 考试 | kǎoshì | (N) test or examination (10) |
| 课 | kè | (N) lesson, class, course (10) |
| 刻(钟) | -kè (zhōng) | (Cl) quarter hour, fifteen minutes (13) |
| 可不是吗? | kě búshì ma? | (Ex) isn't that so? (19) |
| 可口可乐/可乐 | Kěkǒu Kělè/Kělè | (N) Coca-Cola (Cl *-guàn* 罐, *-píng* 瓶) (7) |
| 可能 | kěnéng | (Adv) possibly (19) |
| 客气 | kèqi | (SV) be polite (7) |
| 客人 | kèrén | (N) guest; shop/restaurant customer (7) |
| 可是 | kě.shì | (Conj) but, however (5/8) |
| 客厅 | kètīng | (PW) living room (15) |
| 可以 | kě.yǐ | (Aux) allowed to, can (5) |
| 口 | -kǒu | (Cl) (classifier for persons) (6) |
| 哭 | kū | (V) cry; weep (20) |
| 快 | kuài | (SV) be fast, be quick (14) |
| 块 | -kuài | (Cl) dollar (8) |
| 块 | -kuài | (Cl) a piece of (also used for 表) (9) |
| 快(要)……了 | kuài (yào)...le | (Pat) about to... (7) |
| 筷子 | kuàizi | (N) chopsticks (Cl -双) (10) |
| 裤子 | kùzi | (N) pants, trousers (Cl -条) (18) |

## L

| | | |
|---|---|---|
| 来 | lái | (V) come (11) |
| 来 | -lái | (VC) come (16) |
| 蓝 | lán | (SV) be blue (14) |
| 兰兰 | Lánlan | (N) a personal name (7) |
| 老 | lǎo | (SV) be old (usually of people or living things) (16) |
| 老 | lǎo | (Adv) always, invariably (17) |
| 老板 | lǎobǎn | (N) boss; owner (9) |

| | | |
|---|---|---|
| 老师 | lǎoshī | (N) teacher (10/13) |
| 了 | le | (P) (indicates a new situation) (7) |
| 了 | le | (P) (indicates completed action) (12) |
| 累 | lèi | (SV) be physically drained; be tired (14) |
| 冷 | lěng | (SV) be cold (15) |
| 里 | lǐ | (PS/PW) inside (14) |
| 里边儿 | lǐ.biānr | (PS/PW) inside (13) |
| 利害 | lì.hài | (SV) be formidable, be fierce (19) |
| 连……都/也…… | lián…dōu/yě… | (Pat) even… (10) |
| 两 | liǎng | (Q) two (classifier required) (5) |
| 凉快 | liáng.kuài | (SV) be (comfortably) cool (said of weather) (17) |
| 练习 | liànxí | (V/N) practice (13) |
| 了 | -liǎo | (VC) able to (17) |
| liáo天 | liáo tiān | (VO) chat (11) |
| 邻jū | línjū | (N) neighbor (16) |
| 六 | liù | (Nu) six (9) |
| 流血 | liú xiě/xuě | (VO) bleed (20) |
| 楼 | -lóu | (Cl) floor (14) |
| 楼上 | lóu.shàng | (PS/PW) upstairs (9/17) |
| 楼梯 | lóutī | (N) stairs (15) |
| 楼下 | lóu.xià | (PS/PW) downstairs (9/17) |
| 路 | lù | (N) road (Cl -条) (18) |
| 绿 | lǜ | (SV) be green (14) |
| 旅游 | lǚyóu | (V) tour (19) |

## M

| | | |
|---|---|---|
| 吗 | ma | (P) (indicates a question) (5) |
| 妈妈 | māma | (N) mother (6) |
| 马上 | mǎ.shàng | (Adv) right away (19) |
| 买 | mǎi | (V) buy (6) |
| 卖 | mài | (V) sell (7) |
| 慢 | màn | (SV) be slow (14) |
| 忙 | máng | (SV) be busy (7) |
| 毛 | -máo | (Cl) dimes (6) |
| 毛笔 | máobǐ | (N) writing brush (5/8) |
| <u>毛乐生</u> | <u>Máo Lèshēng</u> | (N) a personal name (8) |
| 毛衣 | máoyī | (N) sweater (Cl -件) (9) |
| 没关系 | méi guānxi | (Ex) never mind; it doesn't matter (7/16) |

| | | |
|---|---|---|
| 没问tí | méi wèntí | (Ex) not a problem (10) |
| 美国 | Měi.guó | (PW) America (10) |
| 妹妹 | mèimei | (N) younger sister (6) |
| 美思大学 | Měisī Dàxué | (PW) name of a university (11) |
| 没(有) | méi(.yǒu) | (V) not have; has not (8) |
| 没有 | méi.yǒu | (V) there isn't; there aren't (9) |
| 门 | mén | (N) door (16) |
| 门 | -mén | (Cl) (for a course taken at school) (10) |
| 米饭 | mǐfàn | (N) cooked rice (10) |
| 明白 | míngbai | (V) understand (8) |
| 明年 | míngnián | (TW) next year (13) |
| 名pái儿 | míngpáir | (N) famous brand; nameplate (16) |
| 明天 | míngtiān | (TW) tomorrow (12) |
| 名字 | míng.zì | (N) name (8) |

## N

| | | |
|---|---|---|
| 拿 | ná | (V) take; bring; pick up (11) |
| 那 | nà | (Pr) that (8) |
| 那 | nà | (Conj) in that case (14) |
| 男 | nán- | (Pre) male (human) (14) |
| 难 | nán | (SV) be difficult (14) |
| 南 | nán | (PS) the south (15) |
| 南京 | Nánjīng | (PW) a city in China (11) |
| 南京路 | Nánjīng Lù | (PW) name of a street (18) |
| 哪儿 | nǎr | (PW) where? (9) |
| 那儿 | nàr | (PW) there, that place (9) |
| 那么 | nèime (nàme) | (Adv) in that way, that (11) |
| 闹 | nào | (V) make noise; stir up trouble (20) |
| 呢 | ne | (P) (forms a reverse question) (5) |
| 呢 | ne | (P) (used at the end of a sentence for emphasis) (8) |
| 内衣 | nèiyī | (N) underwear (Cl -件) (9) |
| 能 | néng | (Aux) can (16) |
| 你 | nǐ | (Pr) you (singular) (5) |
| 年 | -nián | (TD) year (13) |
| 念书 | niàn shū | (VO) study (academically) (10) |
| 你们 | nǐmen | (Pr) you (plural) (5) |
| 牛奶 | niúnǎi | (N) milk (8) |
| 牛肉 | niúròu | (N) beef (10) |

| | | |
|---|---|---|
| 牛仔裤 | niúzǎikù | (N) denim jeans (Cl -条) (9/18) |
| 暖和 | nuǎnhuo | (SV) be (comfortably) warm (said of weather) (19) |
| 女 | nǚ- | (Pre) female (human) (16) |
| 女的 | nǚde | (N) woman, female (6/10) |
| 女儿 | nǚ'ér | (N) daughter (5) |

## P

| | | |
|---|---|---|
| 爬山 | pá shān | (VO) climb a mountain (15) |
| 胖 | pàng | (SV) be fat (of humans) (18) |
| 旁边儿 | páng.biānr | (PS/PW) the side (19) |
| 跑 | pǎo | (V) run (16) |
| 朋友 | péng.yǒu | (N) friend (8) |
| 便宜 | pián.yí | (SV) be cheap (6) |
| 啤酒 | píjiǔ | (N) beer (16) |
| 平常 | píngcháng | (Adv) usually (14) |
| 皮xié | píxié | (N) leather shoes (Cl -双) (8) |

## Q

| | | |
|---|---|---|
| 七 | qī | (Nu) seven (4) |
| 起 | -qǐ | (VC) afford to (16) |
| 千 | qiān | (Nu) thousand (5) |
| 前 | qián | (PS/PW) in front (11) |
| 钱 | qián | (N) money (12) |
| 浅 | qiǎn | (SV) be shallow; be light (14) |
| 铅笔 | qiānbǐ | (N) pencil (17) |
| 前边儿 | qián.biānr | (PS/PW) in front (9) |
| 前天 | qiántiān | (TW) the day before yesterday (14) |
| 钱希平 | Qián Xīpíng | (N) a personal name (15) |
| 汽车 | qìchē | (N) automobile (15) |
| 起床 | qǐ chuáng | (VO) get out of bed; get up (14) |
| 起来 | qǐlái | (V) rise (up); get up (15) |
| 请 | qǐng | (V) please; treat; hire; invite (8) |
| 清楚 | qīng.chǔ | (SV) be clear (16) |
| 请客 | qǐng kè | (VO) treat someone to food or entertainment (7) |
| 轻松 | qīngsōng | (SV) be relaxed (19) |
| 秋天 | qiūtiān | (TW) autumn, fall (13) |
| 去 | qù | (V) go to (a place) (8) |

| | | |
|---|---|---|
| 去年 | qùnián | (TW) last year (13) |
| 裙子 | qúnzi | (N) dress, skirt (Cl *-tiáo* 条) (14) |

## R

| | | |
|---|---|---|
| 然后 | ránhòu | (Conj) and then... (12) |
| 热 | rè | (SV) be hot (15) |
| 热闹 | rè.nào | (SV) be bustling (18) |
| 人 | rén | (N) person, human being (4) |
| 认识 | rènshi | (V) be acquainted with (9) |
| 日本 | Rìběn | (PW) Japan (4) |
| 日文 | Rìwén | (N) Japanese (language) (4) |
| 日语 | Rìyǔ | (N) Japanese (language) (5) |
| 容yì | róng.yì | (SV) be easy (8) |

## S

| | | |
|---|---|---|
| 三 | sān | (Nu) three (4) |
| 山 | shān | (N) hill; mountain (15) |
| 上 | shàng | (V) go or come up (15) |
| 上 | -shàng | (VC) come/go up (16) |
| 上班 | shàng bān | (VO) go to work (15) |
| 上边儿 | shàng.biānr | (PS) above (9) |
| 商场 | shāngchǎng | (PW) market; bazaar (14) |
| 商店 | shāngdiàn | (PW) shop; store (Cl-家) (9/14) |
| 上(个)月 | shàng(ge)yuè | (TW) last month (13) |
| 上海 | Shànghǎi | (PW) a city in eastern China (10) |
| 上街 | shàng jiē | (VO) go out (onto the city streets) (15) |
| 上课 | shàng kè | (VO) have class; attend class (10) |
| 上午 | shàngwǔ | (TW) in the morning (12) |
| 商先生 | Shāng Xiānshēng | (N) Mr. Shang (17) |
| 上学 | shàng xué | (VO) go to school (15) |
| 少 | shǎo | (SV) lack; be deficient; lose; be missing (16) |
| 谁 | shéi/shuí | (Pr) who (13) |
| 深 | shēn | (SV) be deep; be dark; be profound (14) |
| 生词 | shēngcí | (N) new words, new vocabulary (17) |
| 生气 | shēngqì | (SV) be angry (17) |
| 生日 | shēngrì | (N) birthday (13) |
| 生意 | shēng.yì | (N) (commercial) business (7) |
| 什么 | shénme | (QW) what (5) |
| 十 | shí | (Nu) ten (4) |

| | | |
|---|---|---|
| 是 | shì | (V) be, is, am, are (8) |
| 是 | shì | (Pat) (used to emphasize the doer, time, or place of an action) (15) |
| 事 | shì | (N) matter, affair (14) |
| 是……的 | shì…de | (Pat) (used to emphasize the doer, time or place of an action) (15) |
| 时间 | shíjiān | (N) time (17) |
| 时máo | shímáo | (SV) be fashionable (18) |
| 手 | shǒu | (N) hand (20) |
| 瘦 | shòu | (SV) be thin; be lean (18) |
| 手biǎo | shǒubiǎo | (N) watch (Cl -块) (9) |
| 手机 | shǒujī | (N) cell phone (12) |
| 书 | shū | (N) book (4) |
| 书店 | shūdiàn | (PW) bookshop (10/14) |
| 书fáng | shūfáng | (PW) den, (private) library (15) |
| 舒服 | shūfu | (SV) be comfortable (11) |
| 双 | -shuāng | (Cl) a pair of (8) |
| 水 | shuǐ | (N) water (12) |
| 睡 | shuì | (V) sleep (16) |
| 水果摊 | shuǐguǒtān | (PW) fruit stall (19) |
| 睡觉 | shuì jiào | (VO) sleep; "go to bed" (16) |
| 说 | shuō | (V) say, speak (5) |
| 说话 | shuō huà | (VO) speak (17) |
| 叔叔 | shūshu | (N) uncle (father's younger brother) (8) |
| 书桌 | shūzhuō | (N) desk (17) |
| 死 | -sǐ | (RVC) (indicates extremeness of state) (20) |
| 四 | sì | (Nu) four (4) |
| 送 | sòng | (V) escort; deliver; present; give (7) |
| 岁 | -suì | (Cl) age (15) |
| 虽然……可是…… | suīrán…kě.shì… | (Pat) although…however… (18) |
| 所以…… | suǒ.yǐ… | (Pat) therefore… (10/15) |
| 所有的 | suóyǒude | (N) every; all of something (17) |
| 宿舍 | sùshè | (PW) dormitory (20) |

## T

| | | |
|---|---|---|
| 他 | tā | (Pr) he, him (5) |
| 她 | tā | (Pr) she, her (7) |
| 太 | tài | (SV) overly, too (7) |
| 太太 | tàitai | (N) Mrs.; wife (5) |
| 他/她们 | tāmen | (Pr) they, them (6) |

| | | |
|---|---|---|
| 汤 | tāng | (N) soup (8) |
| 讨厌 | tǎoyàn | (SV) be a pain in the neck (20) |
| tè别 | tèbié | (SV) be special (14) |
| 疼 | téng | (V) feel pain (12) |
| 替 | tì | (CV) in place of (10) |
| 天 | -tiān | (TD) day (12) |
| 挑 | tiāo | (V) choose; select (19) |
| 条 | -tiáo | (Cl) (for things that are seen as long, narrow, and flexible) (11) |
| 听 | tīng | (V) listen (16) |
| 听说 | tīngshuō | (V) hear it said that... (13) |
| 同心街 | Tóngxīn Jiē | (PW) a street name (11) |
| 同学 | tóngxué | (N) fellow student, classmate (11) |
| 偷 | tōu | (V) steal (20) |
| 头 | tóu | (N) head (12) |
| 图书馆 | túshūguǎn | (PW) library (11) |

## V

| | | |
|---|---|---|
| V来V去 | V + lái + V + qù | (Pat) (indicates a thorough repetition of an action) (16) |
| (VO)V得...... | (VO)V de... | (Pat) (indicates customary manner or extent of an action) (14) |

## W

| | | |
|---|---|---|
| 外边儿 | wài.biānr | (PS/ PW) outside (11) |
| 外衣 | wàiyī | (N) jacket (Cl -件) (9/19) |
| 完 | -wán | (VC) finish, complete (16) |
| 万 | wàn | (N) a Chinese surname (Q) ten thousand (6) |
| 完全 | wánquán | (Adv) completely (18) |
| 晚 | wǎn | (SV) be late (12) |
| 晚饭 | wǎnfàn | (N) supper (8) |
| 玩儿 | wánr | (V) have a good time; play (13) |
| 晚上 | wǎnshang | (TW) in the evening (11) |
| 万文生 | Wàn Wénshēng | (N) a personal name (6) |
| 王 | Wáng | (N) a Chinese surname (4) |
| 往 | wàng | (CV) toward (11) |
| 王欢兰 | Wáng Huānlán | (N) a personal name (10) |
| 忘了 | wàngle | (V) forget (9) |
| 王太太 | Wáng Tàitai | (N) Mrs. Wang (5) |

| | | |
|---|---|---|
| 王先生 | Wáng Xiān.shēng | (N) Mr. Wang (5) |
| 王中书 | Wáng Zhōngshū | (N) a personal name (4) |
| 袜子 | wàzi | (N) socks (Cl -双, "pair"; -*zhī* 只, "single") (9) |
| 位 | wèi | (Cl) (polite, for persons) (10) |
| 为什么? | wèishénme? | (Adv) why? (9) |
| 文文 | Wénwen | (N) a personal name (5) |
| 问 | wèn | (V) ask (a question) (5) |
| 问lù | wèn lù | (VO) ask the way (11) |
| 问tí | wèntí | (N) question (10) |
| 我 | wǒ | (Pr) I, me (4) |
| 我们 | wǒmen | (Pr) we, us (6) |
| 五 | wǔ | (Nu) five (4) |
| 午饭 | wǔfàn | (N) lunch (7) |

## X

| | | |
|---|---|---|
| 下 | xià | (V) get off, disembark (12) |
| 下 | xià | (V) go or come down (15) |
| 下 | -xià | (VC) come/go down (16) |
| 下班 | xià bān | (VO) finish work (15) |
| 下边儿 | xià.biānr | (PS/PW) below (9) |
| 下个月 | xiàgeyuè | (TW) next month (15) |
| 下课 | xià kè | (VO) finish class (13) |
| 先 | xiān | (Adv) first (12) |
| 现成 | xiànchéng | (Attr) ready-made (17) |
| 先生 | xiān.shēng | (N) teacher; sir; Mr.; husband (5) |
| 现在 | xiànzài | (TW) presently, now (8/13) |
| 想 | xiǎng | (V) think; want to (7) |
| 箱子 | xiāngzi | (N) (large) box, trunk, chest (17) |
| 小 | xiǎo | (SV) be small, be minor (4) |
| 笑 | xiào | (V) laugh; smile; laugh at (10) |
| 小吃 | xiǎochī | (N) snack; refreshment; simple dish (7) |
| 小姐 | xiǎo.jiě | (N) young lady; Miss (10) |
| 小人书 | xiǎorénshū | (N) children's picture book (Cl -本) (6) |
| 小时 | xiǎoshí | (N) hour (19) |
| 小说 | xiǎoshūo | (N) fictional work (Cl -本) (5) |
| 小学 | xiǎoxué | (PW) elementary school (11) |
| 小学生 | xiǎoxué.shēng | (N) elementary school pupil (6/16) |
| xià天 | xiàtiān | (TW) summer (15) |
| 下午 | xiàwǔ | (TW) in the afternoon (12) |
| 下星期 | xiàxīngqī | (TW) next week (14) |

| | | |
|---|---|---|
| 下雪 | xià xuě | (VO) snow (15) |
| 下雨 | xià yǔ | (VO) rain (15) |
| 西边儿 | xī.biānr | (PS/PW) the west (9) |
| 写 | xiě | (V) write (17) |
| 写字 | xiě zì | (VO) write (17) |
| 谢里 | Xiè Lǐ | (N) a personal name (19) |
| 谢谢 | xièxie | (Ex) thank you (10) |
| 西瓜 | xīguā | (N) watermelon (19) |
| xǐ欢 | xǐ.huān | (V) like, prefer, enjoy, like to (8) |
| 新 | xīn | (SV) be new (15) |
| 信 | xìn | (N) letter (Cl -*fēng* 封) (10) |
| 醒 | xǐng | (V) wake (up) (16) |
| 姓 | xìng | (V) be surnamed (6) |
| 行李 | xínglǐ | (N) luggage (Cl -件) (17) |
| 星期 | xīngqī | (TW) week (13) |
| 星期日/天 | xīngqīrì/tiān | (TW) Sunday (13) |
| 兴趣 | xìng.qù | (N) interest (in something) (18) |
| 薪水 | xīnshuǐ | (N) salary (18) |
| 新西兰 | Xīnxīlán | (PW) New Zealand (4/6/19) |
| 信用kǎ | xìnyòngkǎ | (N) credit card (Cl -张) (20) |
| 兄弟姐妹 | xiōngdì-jiěmèi | (N) brothers and sisters; siblings (6) |
| 休息 | xiūxi | (V) rest (12) |
| 希望 | xīwàng | (V) hope, wish (13) |
| 学 | xué | (V) study; learn (10) |
| 学生 | xué.shēng | (N) student (11) |
| 学校 | xuéxiào | (PW) school (15) |
| 雪山城 | Xuéshānchéng | (PW) Snow City (19) |

## Y

| | | |
|---|---|---|
| 呀 | ya | (P) (tells listener he or she really should have known that) (9) |
| 眼睛 | yǎn.jīng | (N) eye (16) |
| 眼镜 | yǎnjìng | (N) eyeglasses (Cl -*fù* 副) (9/16) |
| 颜sè | yán.sè | (N) color (14) |
| 要 | yào | (V) want, want to (6) |
| 要 | yào | (Aux) going to; will; must; should (7) |
| 药 | yào | (N) medicine (12) |
| 要……了 | yào…le | (Pat) about to… (15) |
| 要是(的话)……就 | yào.shì (de huà)…jiù | (Pat) if…then (14) |
| 也 | yě | (Adv) also (4) |

| | | |
|---|---|---|
| 页 | -yè | (Cl) page (14) |
| 也许 | yěxǔ | (Adv) perhaps (15) |
| Y 分之 X | Y fēn zhī X | (Pat) (indicates X/Y fraction) (18) |
| 一 | yī, yì, yí | (Nu) one (4) |
| 一半 | yíbàn | (Q) half (6) |
| 一半 | yíbàn | (Q) half (6) |
| 一点儿 | yìdiǎnr | (Q) a bit, a little (7/12) |
| 一定 | yídìng | (Adv) definitely (10/12) |
| 衣服 | yīfu | (N) clothing (Cl -件) (9/14) |
| 一共 | yígòng | (Adv) altogether (6) |
| 以后 | yǐhòu | (TW) afterwards (13) |
| ……以后 | …yǐhòu | (Pat) after… (13) |
| 一会儿 | yìhuǐr | (TD) a while, a short time (20) |
| 一块儿 | yíkuàir | (Adv) together (9) |
| 应该 | yīnggāi | (Aux) ought to (20) |
| 英国 | Yīng.guó | (PW) England, United Kingdom (10) |
| 英文 | Yīngwén | (N) English (language) (4/10) |
| 英语 | Yīngyǔ | (N) English (language) (5/19) |
| 银行 | yínháng | (PW) bank (financial institution) (12) |
| 因为…… | yīn.wèi… | (Pat) because… (9) |
| 已经 | yǐjīng | (Adv) already (12) |
| 一……就…… | yī…jiù… | (Pat) as soon as (16) |
| 以前 | yǐqián | (TW) formerly, before (7) |
| ……以前 | …yíqián | (Pat) before… (13) |
| 医生 | yīshēng | (N) physician, doctor (12) |
| 意思 | yìsi | (N) meaning (17) |
| ……一下 | …yíxià | (Adv) a bit (after a verb) (17) |
| 一样 | yíyàng | (Adv) similarly (18) |
| 医院 | yīyuàn | (PW) hospital (12) |
| 一直 | yìzhí | (Adv) straight (11) |
| 用 | yòng | (CV) using; by means of (10) |
| 用 | yòng | (V) use (15) |
| 用功 | yònggōng | (SV) be diligent (13) |
| 有 | yǒu | (V) have, has (8) |
| 有 | yǒu | (V) there is, there are (9) |
| 又 | yòu | (Adv) once again (16) |
| 右边儿 | yòu.biānr | (PS/PW) the right (9) |
| 有的……有的 | yǒude…yǒude | (Pat) some…other (10) |
| 有空 | yǒu kòng | (VO) have free time (11/18) |
| 有名 | yǒumíng | (SV) be famous (9) |
| 有人 | yǒu rén | (Ph) somebody (8) |

| | | |
|---|---|---|
| 有意思 | yǒuyìsi | (SV) be interesting (8) |
| 又……又…… | yòu…yòu… | (P) both…and… (17) |
| 预备 | yùbei | (V) prepare (14) |
| 远 | yuǎn | (SV) be far (19) |
| 越……越…… | yuè…yuè… | (Pat) more and more (19) |

## Z

| | | |
|---|---|---|
| 再 | zài | (Adv) again; additionally (7) |
| 在 | zài | (CV) at, in (9) |
| 在 | zài | (V) be located at; be present (9) |
| 再 | zài | (Adv) and then (12) |
| 在 | zài | (Adv) be…ing (14) |
| 再见 | zàijiàn! | (Ex) good-bye, au revoir! (4) |
| 咱们 | zánmen | (Pr) we, us (inclusive of listener) (14) |
| 早 | zǎo | (SV) be early (15) |
| 早饭 | zǎofàn | (N) breakfast (8) |
| 早上 | zǎoshang | (TW) in the morning (12) |
| 杂志 | zázhì | (N) magazine (Cl -本 or -份) (9) |
| 怎么 | zěnme | (Adv) how? why? (11) |
| 怎么办? | zěnme bàn? | (Ex) what the heck do we do? (20) |
| 怎么了? | zěnme le? | (Ex) what's going on? what's the matter? (12) |
| 张 | -zhāng | (Cl) (for flat objects like tables, paper, paintings) (17) |
| 张伯伯 | Zhāng Bóbo | (N) Uncle Zhang (18) |
| 着 | -zháo | (VC) successfully complete (16) |
| 找 | zhǎo | (V) give change; look for (something) (9) |
| 着急 | zháojí | (SV) be anxious (19) |
| 着 | zhe | (P) (attached to verb to indicate action in progress) (10) |
| ……着(呢) | …zhe (ne) | (Pat) (description of a state) (11) |
| 这 | zhè | (Pr) this (8) |
| 这么 | zhème | (Adv) in this way; this (11) |
| 真 | zhēn | (Adv) really, truly (5) |
| 真气死人! | zhēn qìsǐ rén! | (Ex) how infuriating! (17) |
| 正(在)……(着)(呢) | zhèng(zài)…(zhe) (ne) | (Adv) right in the middle of… (11) |
| 这儿,这里 | zhèr, zhèlǐ | (PW) here, this place (13) |
| 支 | -zhī | (Cl) (for pens, pencils) (5) |
| 只 | zhǐ | (Adv) only, just (5) |
| 纸 | zhǐ | (N) paper (Cl -张) (17) |
| 知道 | zhī.dào | (V) know, know of, know that (7) |

| | | |
|---|---|---|
| 只要 | zhǐyào | (Conj) all you need to do is… (17) |
| 至少 | zhìshǎo | (Adv) at the very least (19) |
| 钟 | zhōng | (N) clock (time as measured in hours/ minutes) (13) |
| 中本一也 | Zhōngběn Yīyě | (N) a Japanese personal name (4) |
| 中国 | Zhōng.guó | (PW) China (4/9) |
| 中间 | zhōng.jiān | (PS) the middle (10/19) |
| 钟名然 | Zhōng Míngrán | (N) a personal name (19) |
| 钟头 | zhōng.tóu | (N) hour (14) |
| 中学 | zhōngxué | (PW) high school (11) |
| 中文 | Zhōngwén | (N) Chinese (language) (4) |
| 中午 | zhōngwǔ | (TW) noon (14) |
| 桌子 | zhuōzi | (N) table (16) |
| 住 | zhù | (V) reside (9) |
| 住 | -zhù | (VC) make secure or firm (16) |
| 抓 | zhuā | (V) grab; scratch; arrest (20) |
| 字 | zì | (N) (Chinese) character(s) (Cl -个) (6) |
| 自己 | zìjǐ | (Pr) self (19) |
| 仔细 | zǐxì | (Adv) careful (17) |
| 自行车 | zìxíngchē | (N) bicycle (Cl *-liàng* -辆) (6) |
| 走 | zǒu | (V) walk; go; move along; leave (11) |
| 最 | zuì | (Adv) most (12) |
| 做 | zuò | (V) do; take the role of (7) |
| 坐 | zuò | (V) sit; ride; take (a means of transportation) (11) |
| 左边儿 | zuǒ.biānr | (PS/PW) the left (11) |
| 做生意 | zuò shēng.yì | (VO) engage in commerce (18) |
| 昨天 | zuótiān | (TW) yesterday (12) |
| 作业 | zuòyè | (N) schoolwork; homework (13) |
| 左右 | zuǒyòu | (Adv) about, more or less (14) |
| 足球sài | zúqiúsài | (N) soccer match (20) |

# Alphabetized Character Index

| Pinyin | Character | Chapter | Radical | Traditional Character |
|---|---|---|---|---|
| **A** | | | | |
| ā | 阿 | 17 | 阝 | 阿 |
| á | 啊 | 16 | 口 | 啊 |
| āi | 哎 | 6 | 口 | 哎 |
| ài | 爱 | 15 | 爪 | 愛 |
| ān | 安 | 13 | 宀 | 安 |
| **B** | | | | |
| ba | 吧 | 8 | 口 | 吧 |
| bā | 八 | 4 | 八 | 八 |
| bǎ | 把 | 17 | 扌 | 把 |
| bái | 白 | 8 | 白 | 白 |
| bǎi | 百 | 5 | 一 | 百 |
| bān | 班 | 15 | 王 | 班 |
| bān | 搬 | 15 | 扌 | 搬 |
| bǎn | 板 | 9 | 木 | 板 |
| bàn | 半 | 6 | 八 | 半 |
| bàn | 办 | 20 | 力 | 辦 |
| bǎo | 饱 | 8 | 饣 | 飽 |
| bào | 报 | 9 | 扌 | 報 |
| bēi* | 杯 | 12 | 木 | 杯 |
| běi | 北 | 9 | 丨 | 北 |
| bèi | 备 | 14 | 田 | 備 |
| bèi* | 倍 | 18 | 亻 | 倍 |
| bèi | 被 | 20 | 衤 | 被 |

*An asterisk indicates that the character is bound and therefore cannot stand alone as an independent word.

| Pinyin | Character | Chapter | Radical | Traditional Character |
|---|---|---|---|---|
| běn* | 本 | 4 | 木 | 本 |
| bèn | 笨 | 8 | 竹 | 笨 |
| bǐ | 笔 | 8 | 竹 | 筆 |
| bǐ | 比 | 18 | 比 | 比 |
| bì* | 必 | 7 | 心 | 必 |
| biān | 边 | 9 | 辶 | 邊 |
| biàn/pián | 便 | 11 | 亻 | 便 |
| biàn* | 遍 | 17 | 辶 | 遍 |
| bié | 别 | 13 | 刂 | 別 |
| bīng | 冰 | 7 | 冫 | 冰 |
| bìng | 病 | 12 | 疒 | 病 |
| bó* | 伯 | 7 | 亻 | 伯 |
| bù | 不 | 4 | 一 | 不 |

## C

| Pinyin | Character | Chapter | Radical | Traditional Character |
|---|---|---|---|---|
| cái | 才 | 12 | 一 | 才 |
| cài | 菜 | 10 | 艹 | 菜 |
| cè* | 厕 | 15 | 厂 | 廁 |
| chā* | 叉 | 10 | 又 | 叉 |
| chá | 茶 | 10 | 艹 | 茶 |
| chà | 差 | 13 | 羊 | 差 |
| cháng | 常 | 13 | 巾 | 常 |
| cháng | 长 | 18 | 丿 | 長 |
| chǎng | 场 | 14 | 土 | 場 |
| chàng | 唱 | 20 | 口 | 唱 |
| chāo | 超 | 20 | 走 | 超 |
| chǎo | 炒 | 11 | 火 | 炒 |
| chǎo | 吵 | 16 | 口 | 吵 |
| chē | 车 | 6 | 车 | 車 |
| chèn* | 衬 | 9 | 衤 | 襯 |
| chéng | 城 | 9 | 土 | 城 |

| Pinyin | Character | Chapter | Radical | Traditional Character |
|---|---|---|---|---|
| chéng | 成 | 17 | 戈 | 成 |
| chī | 吃 | 7 | 口 | 吃 |
| chū | 出 | 15 | 山 | 出 |
| chú | 除 | 12 | 阝 | 除 |
| chú* | 厨 | 15 | 厂 | 廚 |
| chǔ* | 楚 | 16 | 木 | 楚 |
| chuān | 穿 | 18 | 穴 | 穿 |
| chuáng | 床 | 14 | 广 | 床 |
| chūn* | 春 | 13 | 日 | 春 |
| cí | 词 | 5 | 讠 | 詞 |
| cì* | 次 | 16 | 冫 | 次 |
| cóng | 从 | 11 | 人 | 從 |
| cuò | 错 | 13 | 钅 | 錯 |

**D**

| Pinyin | Character | Chapter | Radical | Traditional Character |
|---|---|---|---|---|
| dǎ | 打 | 10 | 扌 | 打 |
| dà | 大 | 4 | 大 | 大 |
| dài | 带 | 16 | 巾 | 帶 |
| dàn | 但 | 20 | 亻 | 但 |
| dāng | 当 | 13 | 小 | 當 |
| dāo | 刀 | 10 | 刀 | 刀 |
| dào | 道 | 7 | 辶 | 道 |
| dào | 到 | 13 | 刂 | 到 |
| de | 的 | 9 | 白 | 的 |
| de/děi | 得 | 14 | 彳 | 得 |
| de/dì | 地 | 13 | 土 | 地 |
| děi/de | 得 | 6 | 彳 | 得 |
| dēng | 灯 | 11 | 火 | 燈 |
| děng | 等 | 12 | 竹 | 等 |
| dì* | 弟 | 6 | 八 | 弟 |
| dì/de | 地 | 8 | 土 | 地 |

| Pinyin | Character | Chapter | Radical | Traditional Character |
|---|---|---|---|---|
| dì | 第 | 13 | 竹 | 第 |
| diǎn* | 典 | 6 | 八 | 典 |
| diǎn | 点 | 12 | 灬 | 點 |
| diàn | 电 | 6 | 曰 | 電 |
| diàn | 店 | 14 | 广 | 店 |
| dìng | 定 | 12 | 宀 | 定 |
| dōng | 东 | 7 | 一 | 東 |
| dōng | 冬 | 14 | 冫 | 冬 |
| dǒng | 懂 | 14 | 忄 | 懂 |
| dōu | 都 | 8 | 阝 | 都 |
| dǔ | 堵 | 19 | 土 | 堵 |
| dù* | 肚 | 12 | 月 | 肚 |
| dù* | 度 | 20 | 广 | 度 |
| duì | 对 | 8 | 又 | 對 |
| dùn* | 顿 | 14 | 页 | 頓 |
| duō | 多 | 11 | 夕 | 多 |
| duǒ* | 朵 | 16 | 木 | 朵 |

**E**

| Pinyin | Character | Chapter | Radical | Traditional Character |
|---|---|---|---|---|
| è | 饿 | 7 | 饣 | 餓 |
| ér* | 儿 | 5 | 儿 | 兒 |
| ér | 而 | 14 | 一 | 而 |
| ěr* | 耳 | 16 | 耳 | 耳 |
| èr | 二 | 4 | 二 | 二 |

**F**

| Pinyin | Character | Chapter | Radical | Traditional Character |
|---|---|---|---|---|
| fā | 发 | 12 | 又 | 發 |
| fǎ* | 法 | 8 | 氵 | 法 |
| fàn | 饭 | 7 | 饣 | 飯 |
| fāng | 方 | 9 | 方 | 方 |
| fàng | 放 | 17 | 攵 | 放 |
| fēi* | 啡 | 7 | 口 | 啡 |

| Pinyin | Character | Chapter | Radical | Traditional Character |
|---|---|---|---|---|
| fēi | 飞 | 17 | 乙 | 飛 |
| fēn | 分 | 6 | 八 | 分 |
| fěn | 粉 | 14 | 米 | 粉 |
| fèn* | 份 | 6 | 亻 | 份 |
| fēng | 风 | 15 | 风 | 風 |
| fú (noun)* | 服 | 11 | 月 | 服 |
| fù* | 父 | 6 | 父 | 父 |
| fù | 附 | 19 | 阝 | 附 |

## G

| Pinyin | Character | Chapter | Radical | Traditional Character |
|---|---|---|---|---|
| gāi | 该 | 20 | 讠 | 該 |
| gāng | 刚 | 16 | 刂 | 剛 |
| gāo | 高 | 9 | 亠 | 高 |
| gào | 告 | 6 | 口 | 告 |
| gē | 哥 | 6 | 口 | 哥 |
| gè* | 个 | 5 | 人 | 個 |
| gěi | 给 | 10 | 纟 | 給 |
| gēn | 跟 | 16 | 足 | 跟 |
| gèng | 更 | 18 | 一 | 更 |
| gōng* | 公 | 11 | 八 | 公 |
| gōng | 功 | 11 | 工 | 功 |
| gōng* | 工 | 19 | 工 | 工 |
| gòng* | 共 | 6 | 八 | 共 |
| gòu | 够 | 18 | 夕 | 夠 |
| gù* | 故 | 10 | 攵 | 故 |
| guā | 刮 | 15 | 刂 | 刮 |
| guā | 瓜 | 19 | 瓜 | 瓜 |
| guǎi | 拐 | 11 | 扌 | 拐 |
| guān | 关 | 7 | 八 | 關 |
| guǎn* | 馆 | 7 | 饣 | 館 |
| guì | 贵 | 18 | 贝 | 貴 |

| Pinyin | Character | Chapter | Radical | Traditional Character |
|---|---|---|---|---|
| guó | 国 | 8 | 口 | 國 |
| guǒ* | 果 | 19 | 木 | 果 |
| guò | 过 | 13 | 辶 | 過 |

**H**

| Pinyin | Character | Chapter | Radical | Traditional Character |
|---|---|---|---|---|
| hái/huán | 还 | 7 | 辶 | 還 |
| hái* | 孩 | 10 | 子 | 孩 |
| hǎi | 海 | 10 | 氵 | 海 |
| hài | 害 | 19 | 宀 | 害 |
| hán | 韩 | 14 | 十 | 韓 |
| hàn* | 汉 | 7 | 氵 | 漢 |
| hàn | 汗 | 9 | 氵 | 汗 |
| háng*/xíng | 行 | 12 | 彳 | 行 |
| hǎo | 好 | 6 | 女 | 好 |
| hào | 号 | 13 | 口 | 號 |
| hē | 喝 | 7 | 口 | 喝 |
| hé/huó | 和 | 11 | 禾 | 和 |
| hé | 河 | 18 | 氵 | 河 |
| hěn | 很 | 6 | 彳 | 很 |
| hóng | 红 | 14 | 纟 | 紅 |
| hòu* | 后 | 10 | 口 | 後 |
| hòu (time)* | 候 | 13 | 亻 | 候 |
| hū | 乎 | 18 | 丿 | 乎 |
| huā | 花 | 12 | 艹 | 花 |
| huá* | 华 | 17 | 十 | 華 |
| huà | 话 | 5 | 讠 | 話 |
| huà | 画 | 6 | 凵 | 畫 |
| huài | 坏 | 12 | 土 | 壞 |
| huán/hái | 还 | 17 | 辶 | 還 |
| huān* | 欢 | 8 | 又 | 歡 |
| huáng | 黄 | 14 | 艹 | 黄 |

| Pinyin | Character | Chapter | Radical | Traditional Character |
|---|---|---|---|---|
| huī | 灰 | 14 | 火 | 灰 |
| huí | 回 | 12 | 口 | 回 |
| huì | 会 | 5 | 人 | 會 |
| huó/hé | 和 | 19 | 禾 | 和 |
| huǒ | 火 | 11 | 火 | 火 |

## J

| Pinyin | Character | Chapter | Radical | Traditional Character |
|---|---|---|---|---|
| jī* | 机 | 10 | 木 | 機 |
| jí | 极 | 17 | 木 | 極 |
| jí | 急 | 19 | 心 | 急 |
| jí | 级 | 20 | 纟 | 級 |
| jǐ* | 几 | 5 | 几 | 幾 |
| jǐ | 挤 | 12 | 扌 | 擠 |
| jì | 记 | 17 | 讠 | 記 |
| jǐ* | 己 | 19 | 己 | 己 |
| jì* | 绩 | 18 | 纟 | 績 |
| jiā | 家 | 6 | 宀 | 家 |
| jiǎ | 假 | 19 | 亻 | 假 |
| jià (quarrel)* | 架 | 20 | 木 | 架 |
| jiān | 间 | 17 | 门 | 間 |
| jiàn | 见 | 4 | 见 | 見 |
| jiàn* | 件 | 9 | 亻 | 件 |
| jiāng | 江 | 18 | 氵 | 江 |
| jiǎng | 讲 | 16 | 讠 | 講 |
| jiāo | 教 | 10 | 攵 | 教 |
| jiǎo | 饺 | 17 | 饣 | 餃 |
| jiào | 叫 | 8 | 口 | 叫 |
| jiào* | 觉 | 16 | 见 | 覺 |
| jiào | 较 | 19 | 车 | 較 |
| jiē | 街 | 11 | 彳 | 街 |
| jiē | 接 | 20 | 扌 | 接 |

| Pinyin | Character | Chapter | Radical | Traditional Character |
|---|---|---|---|---|
| jiě | 姐 | 6 | 女 | 姐 |
| jiè* | 介 | 10 | 人 | 介 |
| jiè | 借 | 17 | 亻 | 借 |
| jīn | 今 | 12 | 人 | 今 |
| jīn* | 斤 | 20 | 斤 | 斤 |
| jìn | 进 | 15 | 辶 | 進 |
| jìn | 近 | 19 | 辶 | 近 |
| jīng* | 京 | 9 | 亠 | 京 |
| jīng | 经 | 12 | 纟 | 經 |
| jīng* | 睛 | 16 | 目 | 睛 |
| jǐng* | 景 | 19 | 日 | 景 |
| jìng* | 镜 | 16 | 钅 | 鏡 |
| jìng | 静 | 18 | 青 | 靜 |
| jiǔ | 九 | 4 | 丿 | 九 |
| jiǔ | 酒 | 7 | 氵 | 酒 |
| jiǔ | 久 | 12 | 丿 | 久 |
| jiù | 旧 | 8 | 日 | 舊 |
| jiù | 就 | 9 | 亠 | 就 |
| jù* | 具 | 15 | 八 | 具 |

**K**

| Pinyin | Character | Chapter | Radical | Traditional Character |
|---|---|---|---|---|
| kā* | 咖 | 7 | 口 | 咖 |
| kāi | 开 | 11 | 一 | 開 |
| kàn | 看 | 9 | 目 | 看 |
| kǎo | 考 | 10 | 十 | 考 |
| kě | 可 | 5 | 口 | 可 |
| kè | 客 | 7 | 宀 | 客 |
| kè | 课 | 10 | 讠 | 課 |
| kè | 刻 | 13 | 刂 | 刻 |
| kòng | 空 | 18 | 穴 | 空 |
| kǒu | 口 | 6 | 口 | 口 |

| Pinyin | Character | Chapter | Radical | Traditional Character |
|---|---|---|---|---|
| kū | 哭 | 20 | 口 | 哭 |
| kù* | 裤 | 18 | 衤 | 褲 |
| kuài | 快 | 7 | 忄 | 快 |
| kuài* | 块 | 8 | 土 | 塊 |
| kuài* | 筷 | 10 | 竹 | 筷 |

**L**

| Pinyin | Character | Chapter | Radical | Traditional Character |
|---|---|---|---|---|
| lā | 拉 | 20 | 扌 | 拉 |
| lái | 来 | 11 | 一 | 來 |
| lán | 兰 | 6 | 八 | 蘭 |
| lán | 蓝 | 14 | 艹 | 藍 |
| lǎo | 老 | 9 | 老 | 老 |
| le/liǎo | 了 | 7 | 乙 | 了 |
| lè | 乐 | 7 | 丿 | 樂 |
| lèi | 累 | 14 | 田 | 累 |
| lěng | 冷 | 15 | 冫 | 冷 |
| lǐ* | 里 | 13 | 里 | 裏 |
| lǐ | 李 | 17 | 木 | 李 |
| lì | 利 | 19 | 刂 | 利 |
| lián | 连 | 10 | 辶 | 連 |
| liàn | 练 | 13 | 纟 | 練 |
| liáng | 凉 | 17 | 冫 | 涼 |
| liǎng* | 两 | 5 | 一 | 兩 |
| liǎo/le | 了 | 17 | 乙 | 了 |
| lín* | 邻 | 16 | 阝 | 鄰 |
| liú | 流 | 20 | 氵 | 流 |
| liù | 六 | 9 | 亠 | 六 |
| lóu | 楼 | 14 | 木 | 樓 |
| lù | 路 | 18 | 足 | 路 |
| lǚ* | 旅 | 19 | 方 | 旅 |
| lǜ | 绿 | 14 | 纟 | 綠 |

| Pinyin | Character | Chapter | Radical | Traditional Character |
|---|---|---|---|---|
| **M** | | | | |
| ma | 吗 | 5 | 口 | 嗎 |
| mā | 妈 | 6 | 女 | 媽 |
| mǎ | 马 | 19 | 马 | 馬 |
| mǎi | 买 | 6 | 乙 | 買 |
| mài | 卖 | 7 | 十 | 賣 |
| màn | 慢 | 14 | 忄 | 慢 |
| máng | 忙 | 7 | 忄 | 忙 |
| máo | 毛 | 5 | 毛 | 毛 |
| me* | 么 | 5 | 厶 | 麼 |
| méi | 没 | 7 | 氵 | 沒 |
| měi | 美 | 10 | 羊 | 美 |
| mèi* | 妹 | 6 | 女 | 妹 |
| men* | 们 | 5 | 亻 | 們 |
| mén | 门 | 9 | 门 | 門 |
| mǐ | 米 | 10 | 米 | 米 |
| miàn | 面 | 13 | 一 | 面 |
| míng* | 名 | 8 | 口 | 名 |
| míng* | 明 | 8 | 日 | 明 |
| mǔ* | 母 | 6 | 母 | 母 |
| **N** | | | | |
| ná | 拿 | 11 | 人 | 拿 |
| nǎ | 哪 | 9 | 口 | 哪 |
| nà | 那 | 8 | 阝 | 那 |
| nǎi | 奶 | 8 | 女 | 奶 |
| nán | 南 | 11 | 十 | 南 |
| nán | 难 | 14 | 又 | 難 |
| nán* | 男 | 14 | 田 | 男 |
| nào | 闹 | 18 | 门 | 鬧 |
| ne | 呢 | 5 | 口 | 呢 |

| Pinyin | Character | Chapter | Radical | Traditional Character |
|---|---|---|---|---|
| nèi | 内 | 9 | 冂 | 內 |
| néng | 能 | 16 | 月 | 能 |
| nǐ | 你 | 5 | 亻 | 你 |
| nián | 年 | 13 | 丿 | 年 |
| niàn | 念 | 10 | 心 | 念 |
| niú | 牛 | 8 | 牛 | 牛 |
| nǚ* | 女 | 5 | 女 | 女 |
| nuǎn | 暖 | 19 | 日 | 暖 |

**P**

| Pinyin | Character | Chapter | Radical | Traditional Character |
|---|---|---|---|---|
| pá | 爬 | 15 | 爪 | 爬 |
| páng* | 旁 | 19 | 方 | 旁 |
| pàng | 胖 | 18 | 月 | 胖 |
| pǎo | 跑 | 16 | 足 | 跑 |
| péng* | 朋 | 8 | 月 | 朋 |
| pí* | 啤 | 16 | 口 | 啤 |
| pí | 皮 | 8 | 皮 | 皮 |
| pián*/biàn | 便 | 6 | 亻 | 便 |
| piào | 票 | 15 | 西 | 票 |
| píng | 平 | 14 | 一 | 平 |

**Q**

| Pinyin | Character | Chapter | Radical | Traditional Character |
|---|---|---|---|---|
| qī | 七 | 4 | 一 | 七 |
| qī* | 期 | 13 | 月 | 期 |
| qǐ | 起 | 14 | 走 | 起 |
| qì | 气 | 7 | 气 | 氣 |
| qì | 汽 | 11 | 氵 | 汽 |
| qiān | 千 | 5 | 十 | 千 |
| qiān | 铅 | 17 | 钅 | 鉛 |
| qián* | 前 | 7 | 八 | 前 |
| qián | 钱 | 12 | 钅 | 錢 |
| qiǎn | 浅 | 14 | 氵 | 淺 |

| Pinyin | Character | Chapter | Radical | Traditional Character |
|---|---|---|---|---|
| qiě | 且 | 20 | 一 | 且 |
| qīng | 清 | 16 | 氵 | 清 |
| qīng | 轻 | 19 | 车 | 輕 |
| qǐng | 请 | 7 | 讠 | 請 |
| qiū* | 秋 | 13 | 禾 | 秋 |
| qiú | 球 | 20 | 王 | 球 |
| quán | 全 | 18 | 人 | 全 |
| qù | 去 | 8 | 土 | 去 |
| qù* | 趣 | 18 | 走 | 趣 |
| qún* | 裙 | 14 | 衤 | 裙 |

**R**

| Pinyin | Character | Chapter | Radical | Traditional Character |
|---|---|---|---|---|
| rán* | 然 | 12 | 灬 | 然 |
| rè | 热 | 15 | 灬 | 熱 |
| rén | 人 | 4 | 人 | 人 |
| rèn | 认 | 9 | 讠 | 認 |
| rì* | 日 | 4 | 日 | 日 |
| róng* | 容 | 8 | 宀 | 容 |
| ròu | 肉 | 10 | 冂 | 肉 |

**S**

| Pinyin | Character | Chapter | Radical | Traditional Character |
|---|---|---|---|---|
| sān | 三 | 4 | 一 | 三 |
| shān* | 衫 | 9 | 衤 | 衫 |
| shān | 山 | 15 | 山 | 山 |
| shāng* | 商 | 9 | 亠 | 商 |
| shàng | 上 | 9 | 一 | 上 |
| shāo | 烧 | 12 | 火 | 燒 |
| shǎo | 少 | 13 | 小 | 少 |
| shào* | 绍 | 10 | 纟 | 紹 |
| shè* | 舍 | 20 | 人 | 舍 |
| shēn | 深 | 14 | 氵 | 深 |

| Pinyin | Character | Chapter | Radical | Traditional Character |
|---|---|---|---|---|
| shén* | 什 | 5 | 亻 | 甚 |
| shēng | 生 | 5 | 丿 | 生 |
| shéi/shuí | 谁 | 13 | 讠 | 誰 |
| shī* | 师 | 13 | 巾 | 師 |
| shí | 十 | 4 | 十 | 十 |
| shí | 时 | 13 | 日 | 時 |
| shǐ* | 始 | 12 | 女 | 始 |
| shì | 是 | 8 | 日 | 是 |
| shì | 识 | 9 | 讠 | 識 |
| shì | 事 | 10 | 一 | 事 |
| shì (noun)* | 试 | 10 | 讠 | 試 |
| shì* | 市 | 20 | 亠 | 市 |
| shǒu | 手 | 9 | 手 | 手 |
| shòu | 瘦 | 18 | 疒 | 瘦 |
| shū | 书 | 4 | 乙 | 書 |
| shū | 叔 | 8 | 又 | 叔 |
| shū* | 舒 | 11 | 人 | 舒 |
| shuāng* | 双 | 8 | 又 | 雙 |
| shuí/shéi | 谁 | 13 | 讠 | 誰 |
| shuǐ | 水 | 7 | 水 | 水 |
| shuì | 睡 | 16 | 目 | 睡 |
| shuō | 说 | 5 | 讠 | 說 |
| sī* | 思 | 8 | 心 | 思 |
| sǐ | 死 | 17 | 歹 | 死 |
| sì | 四 | 4 | 口 | 四 |
| sōng | 松 | 19 | 木 | 鬆 |
| sòng | 送 | 7 | 辶 | 送 |
| sù* | 诉 | 6 | 讠 | 訴 |
| sù* | 速 | 20 | 辶 | 速 |

| Pinyin | Character | Chapter | Radical | Traditional Character |
|---|---|---|---|---|
| sù* | 宿 | 20 | 宀 | 宿 |
| suī | 虽 | 18 | 口 | 雖 |
| suì* | 岁 | 15 | 山 | 歲 |
| suǒ* | 所 | 15 | 斤 | 所 |

**T**

| Pinyin | Character | Chapter | Radical | Traditional Character |
|---|---|---|---|---|
| tā | 他 | 5 | 亻 | 他 |
| tā | 她 | 6 | 女 | 她 |
| tài | 太 | 5 | 大 | 太 |
| tān (noun)* | 摊 | 19 | 扌 | 攤 |
| tāng | 汤 | 8 | 氵 | 湯 |
| tǎo | 讨 | 20 | 讠 | 討 |
| téng | 疼 | 12 | 疒 | 疼 |
| tī* | 梯 | 15 | 木 | 梯 |
| tì | 替 | 10 | 日 | 替 |
| tiān | 天 | 11 | 大 | 天 |
| tiāo | 挑 | 19 | 扌 | 挑 |
| tiáo* | 条 | 11 | 木 | 條 |
| tīng | 听 | 13 | 口 | 聽 |
| tīng* | 厅 | 15 | 厂 | 廳 |
| tóng* | 同 | 11 | 冂 | 同 |
| tōu | 偷 | 20 | 亻 | 偷 |
| tóu | 头 | 12 | 大 | 頭 |
| tú | 图 | 8 | 囗 | 圖 |

**W**

| Pinyin | Character | Chapter | Radical | Traditional Character |
|---|---|---|---|---|
| wà* | 袜 | 9 | 衤 | 襪 |
| wài* | 外 | 11 | 夕 | 外 |
| wán | 玩 | 13 | 王 | 玩 |
| wán | 完 | 16 | 宀 | 完 |
| wǎn | 晚 | 8 | 日 | 晚 |

| Pinyin | Character | Chapter | Radical | Traditional Character |
|---|---|---|---|---|
| wàn | 万 | 6 | 一 | 萬 |
| wáng | 王 | 4 | 王 | 王 |
| wàng | 忘 | 9 | 心 | 忘 |
| wàng | 往 | 11 | 彳 | 往 |
| wàng* | 望 | 13 | 月 | 望 |
| wèi | 为 | 9 | 丶 | 為 |
| wèi* | 位 | 10 | 亻 | 位 |
| wén* | 文 | 4 | 文 | 文 |
| wèn | 问 | 5 | 口 | 問 |
| wǒ | 我 | 4 | 戈 | 我 |
| wǔ | 五 | 4 | 一 | 五 |
| wǔ* | 午 | 7 | 丿 | 午 |

**X**

| Pinyin | Character | Chapter | Radical | Traditional Character |
|---|---|---|---|---|
| xī | 西 | 4 | 西 | 西 |
| xī* | 息 | 12 | 心 | 息 |
| xī* | 希 | 13 | 巾 | 希 |
| xí* | 习 | 13 | 乙 | 習 |
| xì* | 系 | 16 | 小 | 系 |
| xì | 细 | 17 | 纟 | 細 |
| xià | 下 | 9 | 一 | 下 |
| xiān | 先 | 5 | 儿 | 先 |
| xiàn* | 现 | 13 | 王 | 現 |
| xiāng* | 箱 | 17 | 竹 | 箱 |
| xiǎng | 想 | 7 | 心 | 想 |
| xiǎo | 小 | 4 | 小 | 小 |
| xiào | 笑 | 10 | 竹 | 笑 |
| xiào* | 校 | 15 | 木 | 校 |
| xiě | 写 | 17 | 冖 | 寫 |
| xiě/xuě | 血 | 20 | 血 | 血 |

| Pinyin | Character | Chapter | Radical | Traditional Character |
|---|---|---|---|---|
| xiè | 谢 | 10 | 讠 | 謝 |
| xīn | 心 | 11 | 心 | 心 |
| xīn | 新 | 15 | 斤 | 新 |
| xīn* | 薪 | 18 | 艹 | 薪 |
| xìn | 信 | 10 | 亻 | 信 |
| xīng | 星 | 13 | 日 | 星 |
| xíng/háng | 行 | 6 | 彳 | 行 |
| xǐng | 醒 | 16 | 酉 | 醒 |
| xìng | 姓 | 6 | 女 | 姓 |
| xìng* | 兴 | 13 | 八 | 興 |
| xiōng* | 兄 | 6 | 口 | 兄 |
| xiū* | 休 | 12 | 亻 | 休 |
| xǔ | 许 | 15 | 讠 | 許 |
| xué | 学 | 10 | 子 | 學 |
| xuě | 雪 | 15 | 雨 | 雪 |
| xuě/xiě | 血 | 20 | 血 | 血 |

**Y**

| Pinyin | Character | Chapter | Radical | Traditional Character |
|---|---|---|---|---|
| ya | 呀 | 6 | 口 | 呀 |
| yán* | 颜 | 14 | 页 | 顏 |
| yǎn | 眼 | 9 | 目 | 眼 |
| yàn* | 厌 | 20 | 厂 | 厭 |
| yàng* | 样 | 18 | 木 | 樣 |
| yào | 要 | 6 | 女 | 要 |
| yào | 药 | 12 | 艹 | 藥 |
| yě | 也 | 4 | 乙 | 也 |
| yè* | 业 | 13 | 业 | 業 |
| yè* | 页 | 14 | 页 | 頁 |
| yè | 夜 | 16 | 亠 | 夜 |
| yī | 一 | 4 | 一 | 一 |

| Pinyin | Character | Chapter | Radical | Traditional Character |
|---|---|---|---|---|
| yī* | 衣 | 9 | 衣 | 衣 |
| yī* | 医 | 12 | 匚 | 醫 |
| yí* | 宜 | 6 | 宀 | 宜 |
| yí | 姨 | 17 | 女 | 姨 |
| yǐ | 以 | 5 | 人 | 以 |
| yǐ* | 已 | 12 | 己 | 已 |
| yì* | 意 | 7 | 心 | 意 |
| yīn | 因 | 9 | 囗 | 因 |
| yín | 银 | 12 | 钅 | 銀 |
| yīng* | 英 | 10 | 艹 | 英 |
| yīng | 应 | 20 | 广 | 應 |
| yòng | 用 | 10 | 冂 | 用 |
| yóu | 游 | 19 | 氵 | 遊 |
| yǒu* | 友 | 8 | 又 | 友 |
| yǒu | 有 | 8 | 月 | 有 |
| yòu* | 右 | 9 | 口 | 右 |
| yòu | 又 | 16 | 又 | 又 |
| yǔ* | 语 | 5 | 讠 | 語 |
| yǔ | 雨 | 15 | 雨 | 雨 |
| yù* | 预 | 14 | 页 | 預 |
| yù* | 寓 | 15 | 宀 | 寓 |
| yuǎn | 远 | 19 | 辶 | 遠 |
| yuàn | 院 | 12 | 阝 | 院 |
| yuè | 月 | 13 | 月 | 月 |
| yuè (verb)* | 越 | 19 | 走 | 越 |

**Z**

| Pinyin | Character | Chapter | Radical | Traditional Character |
|---|---|---|---|---|
| zá | 杂 | 9 | 木 | 雜 |
| zǎi*/zǐ* | 仔 | 9 | 亻 | 仔 |
| zài | 再 | 4 | 一 | 再 |

| Pinyin | Character | Chapter | Radical | Traditional Character |
|---|---|---|---|---|
| zài | 在 | 8 | 土 | 在 |
| zán | 咱 | 14 | 口 | 咱 |
| zǎo | 早 | 8 | 日 | 早 |
| zěn* | 怎 | 11 | 心 | 怎 |
| zhàn | 站 | 19 | 立 | 站 |
| zhāng* | 张 | 17 | 弓 | 張 |
| zhǎo | 找 | 9 | 扌 | 找 |
| zhe* | 着 | 10 | 羊 | 著 |
| zhě* | 者 | 15 | 日 | 者 |
| zhè | 这 | 8 | 辶 | 這 |
| zhēn | 真 | 5 | 十 | 真 |
| zhèng | 正 | 11 | 一 | 正 |
| zhī* | 支 | 5 | 十 | 支 |
| zhī | 知 | 7 | 口 | 知 |
| zhī* | 之 | 18 | 丶 | 之 |
| zhí | 直 | 11 | 十 | 直 |
| zhǐ | 只 | 5 | 口 | 只 |
| zhǐ | 纸 | 17 | 纟 | 紙 |
| zhì* | 志 | 9 | 心 | 志 |
| zhì | 至 | 19 | 土 | 至 |
| zhōng | 中 | 4 | 丨 | 中 |
| zhōng | 钟 | 13 | 钅 | 鐘 |
| zhù | 住 | 9 | 亻 | 住 |
| zhuā | 抓 | 20 | 扌 | 抓 |
| zhuō* | 桌 | 15 | 木 | 桌 |
| zǐ*/zǎi* | 仔 | 17 | 亻 | 仔 |
| zì* | 子 | 5 | 子 | 子 |
| zì | 自 | 6 | 自 | 自 |
| zì | 字 | 6 | 宀 | 字 |

| Pinyin | Character | Chapter | Radical | Traditional Character |
|---|---|---|---|---|
| zǒu | 走 | 11 | 走 | 走 |
| zū | 租 | 11 | 禾 | 租 |
| zú* | 足 | 20 | 口 | 足 |
| zuì | 最 | 12 | 日 | 最 |
| zuó* | 昨 | 12 | 日 | 昨 |
| zuǒ | 左 | 11 | 工 | 左 |
| zuò | 做 | 7 | 亻 | 做 |
| zuò | 坐 | 11 | 土 | 坐 |
| zuò | 作 | 13 | 亻 | 作 |

# Radical Index

This list includes introduced radicals only.

| Radical | No. of Strokes | General Meaning | Independent Character? | Chapter First Introduced |
|---|---|---|---|---|
| 一 | 1 | one | Y | 4 |
| 丨 | 1 | (a vertical line) | N | 9 |
| 儿 | 2 | son | Y | 5 |
| 亻 | 2 | human | N | 5 |
| 讠 | 2 | speech | N | 5 |
| 人 | 2 | human | Y | 5 |
| 十 | 2 | ten | Y | 5 |
| 八 | 2 | eight | Y | 6 |
| 冫 | 2 | cold, ice | N | 7 |
| 又 | 2 | again, hand | Y | 8 |
| 阝 | 2 | ear | N | 8 |
| 亠 | 2 | coverage | N | 9 |
| 冂 | 2 | border | N | 10 |
| 刂 | 2 | knife | N | 13 |
| 厂 | 2 | factory, cover | Y | 15 |
| 冖 | 2 | cover | N | 17 |
| 口 | 3 | mouth | Y | 5 |
| 女 | 3 | female | Y | 6 |
| 宀 | 3 | roof | N | 6 |
| 彳 | 3 | double human | N | 6 |
| 忄 | 3 | heart, mind | N | 7 |
| 饣 | 3 | food | N | 7 |
| 氵 | 3 | water | N | 7 |
| 辶 | 3 | road, walking | N | 7 |

| Radical | No. of Strokes | General Meaning | Independent Character? | Chapter First Introduced |
|---|---|---|---|---|
| 口 | 3 | enclosure | Y | 8 |
| 土 | 3 | soil | Y | 8 |
| 扌 | 3 | hand | N | 9 |
| 子 | 3 | child | Y | 10 |
| 艹 | 3 | grass, plant | N | 10 |
| 纟 | 3 | silk | N | 10 |
| 工 | 3 | work | Y | 11 |
| 夕 | 3 | evening | Y | 11 |
| 匚 | 3 | ¾ enclosure | N | 12 |
| 巾 | 3 | towel | Y | 13 |
| 广 | 3 | extensive | Y | 14 |
| 山 | 3 | mountain | Y | 15 |
| 小 | 3 | little | Y | 13 |
| 门 | 3 | door | Y | 17 |
| 弓 | 3 | bow | Y | 17 |
| 心 | 4 | heart, mind | Y | 7 |
| 日 | 4 | sun | Y | 8 |
| 月 | 4 | moon, flesh | Y | 8 |
| 木 | 4 | wood, tree | Y | 9 |
| 攵 | 4 | culture, language | N | 10 |
| 火 | 4 | fire | Y | 11 |
| 灬 | 4 | fire | N | 12 |
| 王 | 4 | king, jade | Y | 13 |
| 斤 | 4 | ½ kilo, axe | Y | 15 |
| 爪 | 4 | paw | Y | 15 |
| 见 | 4 | see | Y | 16 |
| 贝 | 4 | shell, money | Y | 18 |
| 比 | 4 | compare | Y | 18 |
| 车 | 4 | vehicle | Y | 19 |

| Radical | No. of Strokes | General Meaning | Independent Character? | Chapter First Introduced |
|---|---|---|---|---|
| 方 | 4 | square, direction | Y | 19 |
| 白 | 5 | white, light | Y | 9 |
| 衤 | 5 | clothing | N | 9 |
| 目 | 5 | eye | Y | 9 |
| 禾 | 5 | grain | Y | 11 |
| 疒 | 5 | illness, disease | N | 12 |
| 钅 | 5 | metal, money | N | 12 |
| 田 | 5 | field | Y | 14 |
| 穴 | 5 | cave, hole | Y | 18 |
| 立 | 5 | stand | Y | 19 |
| 竹 | 6 | bamboo | Y | 8 |
| 羊 | 6 | goat | Y | 10 |
| 米 | 6 | rice | Y | 14 |
| 页 | 6 | page | Y | 14 |
| 西 | 6 | west | Y | 15 |
| 走 | 7 | walk | Y | 14 |
| 酉 | 7 | wine | Y | 16 |
| 足 | 7 | foot | Y | 16 |
| 雨 | 8 | rain | Y | 15 |
| 青 | 8 | glassy green | Y | 18 |

# Character Index by Radical Stroke Count

| Radical | Character | Pinyin | No. of Strokes | Chapter First Appears | Traditional Character |
|---|---|---|---|---|---|
| 丶 | 之 | zhī | 3 | 18 | 之 |
| 丶 | 为 | wèi | 4 | 9 | 為 |
| 一 | 一 | yī | 1 | 4 | 一 |
| 一 | 七 | qī | 2 | 4 | 七 |
| 一 | 三 | sān | 3 | 4 | 三 |
| 一 | 万 | wàn | 3 | 6 | 萬 |
| 一 | 上 | shàng | 3 | 9 | 上 |
| 一 | 下 | xià | 3 | 9 | 下 |
| 一 | 才 | cái | 3 | 12 | 才 |
| 一 | 五 | wǔ | 4 | 4 | 五 |
| 一 | 不 | bù | 4 | 4 | 不 |
| 一 | 开 | kāi | 4 | 11 | 開 |
| 一 | 正 | zhèng | 5 | 11 | 正 |
| 一 | 且 | qiě | 5 | 20 | 且 |
| 一 | 平 | píng | 5 | 14 | 平 |
| 一 | 再 | zài | 6 | 4 | 再 |
| 一 | 百 | bǎi | 6 | 5 | 百 |
| 一 | 东 | dōng | 6 | 7 | 東 |
| 一 | 而 | ér | 6 | 14 | 而 |
| 一 | 两 | liǎng | 7 | 5 | 兩 |
| 一 | 来 | lái | 7 | 11 | 來 |
| 一 | 更 | gèng | 7 | 18 | 更 |
| 一 | 事 | shì | 8 | 10 | 事 |
| 一 | 面 | miàn | 9 | 13 | 面 |

| Radical | Character | Pinyin | No. of Strokes | Chapter First Appears | Traditional Character |
|---|---|---|---|---|---|
| 丨 | 中 | zhōng | 4 | 4 | 中 |
| 丨 | 北 | běi | 5 | 9 | 北 |
| 丿 | 九 | jiǔ | 2 | 4 | 九 |
| 丿 | 久 | jiǔ | 3 | 12 | 久 |
| 丿 | 午 | wǔ | 4 | 7 | 午 |
| 丿 | 生 | shēng | 5 | 5 | 生 |
| 丿 | 乐 | lè | 5 | 7 | 樂 |
| 丿 | 乎 | hū | 5 | 18 | 乎 |
| 丿 | 长 | cháng | 5 | 18 | 長 |
| 丿 | 年 | nián | 6 | 13 | 年 |
| 乙 | 了 | le/liǎo | 2 | 7 | 了 |
| 乙 | 也 | yě | 3 | 4 | 也 |
| 乙 | 习 | xí | 3 | 13 | 習 |
| 乙 | 飞 | fēi | 3 | 17 | 飛 |
| 乙 | 书 | shū | 4 | 4 | 書 |
| 乙 | 买 | mǎi | 6 | 6 | 買 |
| 二 | 二 | èr | 2 | 4 | 二 |
| 亠 | 六 | liù | 4 | 9 | 六 |
| 亠 | 市 | shì | 5 | 20 | 市 |
| 亠 | 京 | jīng | 8 | 9 | 京 |
| 亠 | 夜 | yè | 8 | 16 | 夜 |
| 亠 | 高 | gāo | 10 | 9 | 高 |
| 亠 | 商 | shāng | 11 | 9 | 商 |
| 亠 | 就 | jiù | 12 | 9 | 就 |
| 冫 | 冬 | dōng | 5 | 14 | 冬 |
| 冫 | 冰 | bīng | 6 | 7 | 冰 |
| 冫 | 次 | cì | 6 | 16 | 次 |
| 冫 | 冷 | lěng | 7 | 15 | 冷 |
| 冫 | 凉 | liáng | 10 | 17 | 涼 |
| 冖 | 写 | xiě | 5 | 17 | 寫 |

| Radical | Character | Pinyin | No. of Strokes | Chapter First Appears | Traditional Character |
|---|---|---|---|---|---|
| 讠 | 认 | rèn | 4 | 9 | 認 |
| 讠 | 记 | jì | 5 | 17 | 記 |
| 讠 | 讨 | tǎo | 5 | 20 | 討 |
| 讠 | 许 | xǔ | 6 | 15 | 許 |
| 讠 | 讲 | jiǎng | 6 | 16 | 講 |
| 讠 | 词 | cí | 7 | 5 | 詞 |
| 讠 | 诉 | sù | 7 | 6 | 訴 |
| 讠 | 识 | shì | 7 | 9 | 識 |
| 讠 | 话 | huà | 8 | 5 | 話 |
| 讠 | 试 | shì | 8 | 10 | 試 |
| 讠 | 该 | gāi | 8 | 20 | 該 |
| 讠 | 说 | shuō | 9 | 5 | 說 |
| 讠 | 语 | yǔ | 9 | 5 | 語 |
| 讠 | 请 | qǐng | 10 | 7 | 請 |
| 讠 | 课 | kè | 10 | 10 | 課 |
| 讠 | 谁 | shéi/shuí | 11 | 13 | 誰 |
| 讠 | 谢 | xiè | 12 | 10 | 謝 |
| 十 | 十 | shí | 2 | 4 | 十 |
| 十 | 千 | qiān | 3 | 5 | 千 |
| 十 | 支 | zhī | 4 | 5 | 支 |
| 十 | 考 | kǎo | 6 | 10 | 考 |
| 十 | 华 | huá | 6 | 17 | 華 |
| 十 | 卖 | mài | 8 | 7 | 賣 |
| 十 | 直 | zhí | 8 | 11 | 直 |
| 十 | 南 | nán | 9 | 11 | 南 |
| 十 | 真 | zhēn | 10 | 5 | 真 |
| 十 | 韩 | hán | 12 | 14 | 韓 |
| 厂 | 厅 | tīng | 4 | 15 | 廳 |
| 厂 | 厌 | yàn | 6 | 20 | 厭 |
| 厂 | 厕 | cè | 8 | 15 | 廁 |

| Radical | Character | Pinyin | No. of Strokes | Chapter First Appears | Traditional Character |
|---|---|---|---|---|---|
| 厂 | 厨 | chú | 12 | 15 | 廚 |
| 匚 | 医 | yī | 7 | 12 | 醫 |
| 刂 | 刚 | gāng | 6 | 16 | 剛 |
| 刂 | 别 | bié | 7 | 13 | 別 |
| 刂 | 利 | lì | 7 | 19 | 利 |
| 刂 | 刻 | kè | 8 | 13 | 刻 |
| 刂 | 到 | dào | 8 | 13 | 到 |
| 刂 | 刮 | guā | 8 | 15 | 刮 |
| 冂 | 内 | nèi | 4 | 9 | 內 |
| 冂 | 用 | yòng | 5 | 10 | 用 |
| 冂 | 肉 | ròu | 6 | 10 | 肉 |
| 冂 | 同 | tóng | 6 | 11 | 同 |
| 八 | 八 | bā | 2 | 4 | 八 |
| 八 | 分 | fēn | 4 | 6 | 分 |
| 八 | 公 | gōng | 4 | 11 | 公 |
| 八 | 兰 | lán | 5 | 6 | 蘭 |
| 八 | 半 | bàn | 5 | 6 | 半 |
| 八 | 共 | gòng | 6 | 6 | 共 |
| 八 | 关 | guān | 6 | 7 | 關 |
| 八 | 兴 | xìng | 6 | 13 | 興 |
| 八 | 典 | diǎn | 7 | 6 | 典 |
| 八 | 弟 | dì | 7 | 6 | 弟 |
| 八 | 具 | jù | 8 | 15 | 具 |
| 八 | 前 | qián | 9 | 7 | 前 |
| 人 | 人 | rén | 2 | 4 | 人 |
| 人 | 个 | gè | 3 | 5 | 個 |
| 人 | 介 | jiè | 4 | 10 | 介 |
| 人 | 以 | yǐ | 4 | 5 | 以 |
| 人 | 从 | cóng | 4 | 11 | 從 |
| 人 | 今 | jīn | 4 | 12 | 今 |

| Radical | Character | Pinyin | No. of Strokes | Chapter First Appears | Traditional Character |
|---|---|---|---|---|---|
| 人 | 会 | huì | 6 | 5 | 會 |
| 人 | 全 | quān | 6 | 18 | 全 |
| 人 | 舍 | shè | 8 | 20 | 舍 |
| 人 | 拿 | ná | 10 | 11 | 拿 |
| 人 | 舒 | shū | 12 | 11 | 舒 |
| 亻 | 们 | men | 4 | 5 | 們 |
| 亻 | 什 | shén | 4 | 5 | 什 |
| 亻 | 他 | tā | 5 | 5 | 他 |
| 亻 | 仔 | zǎi/zǐ | 5 | 9 | 仔 |
| 亻 | 份 | fèn | 6 | 6 | 份 |
| 亻 | 住 | zhù | 7 | 9 | 住 |
| 亻 | 件 | jiàn | 6 | 9 | 件 |
| 亻 | 休 | xiū | 6 | 12 | 休 |
| 亻 | 你 | nǐ | 7 | 5 | 你 |
| 亻 | 伯 | bó | 7 | 7 | 伯 |
| 亻 | 位 | wèi | 7 | 10 | 位 |
| 亻 | 作 | zuò | 7 | 13 | 作 |
| 亻 | 但 | dàn | 7 | 20 | 但 |
| 亻 | 便 | pián/biàn | 9 | 6 | 便 |
| 亻 | 信 | xìn | 9 | 10 | 信 |
| 亻 | 候 | hòu | 10 | 13 | 候 |
| 亻 | 借 | jiè | 10 | 17 | 借 |
| 亻 | 倍 | bèi | 10 | 18 | 倍 |
| 亻 | 做 | zuò | 11 | 7 | 做 |
| 亻 | 假 | jiǎ | 11 | 19 | 假 |
| 亻 | 偷 | tōu | 11 | 20 | 偷 |
| 几 | 几 | jǐ | 2 | 5 | 幾 |
| 儿 | 儿 | ér | 2 | 5 | 兒 |
| 儿 | 先 | xiān | 6 | 5 | 先 |
| 厶 | 么 | me | 3 | 5 | 麼 |

| Radical | Character | Pinyin | No. of Strokes | Chapter First Appears | Traditional Character |
|---|---|---|---|---|---|
| 又 | 又 | yòu | 2 | 16 | 又 |
| 又 | 叉 | chā | 3 | 10 | 叉 |
| 又 | 双 | shuāng | 4 | 8 | 雙 |
| 又 | 友 | yǒu | 4 | 8 | 友 |
| 又 | 对 | duì | 5 | 8 | 對 |
| 又 | 发 | fā | 5 | 12 | 發 |
| 又 | 欢 | huān | 6 | 8 | 歡 |
| 又 | 叔 | shū | 8 | 8 | 叔 |
| 又 | 难 | nán | 10 | 14 | 難 |
| 阝 | 那 | nà | 6 | 8 | 那 |
| 阝 | 邻 | lín | 7 | 16 | 鄰 |
| 阝 | 阿 | ā | 7 | 17 | 阿 |
| 阝 | 附 | fù | 7 | 19 | 附 |
| 阝 | 除 | chú | 9 | 12 | 除 |
| 阝 | 院 | yuàn | 9 | 12 | 院 |
| 阝 | 都 | dōu | 10 | 8 | 都 |
| 凵 | 画 | huà | 8 | 6 | 畫 |
| 刀 | 刀 | dāo | 2 | 10 | 刀 |
| 力 | 办 | bàn | 4 | 20 | 辦 |
| 氵 | 汉 | hàn | 5 | 7 | 漢 |
| 氵 | 汤 | tāng | 6 | 8 | 湯 |
| 氵 | 汗 | hàn | 6 | 9 | 汗 |
| 氵 | 江 | jiāng | 6 | 18 | 江 |
| 氵 | 没 | méi | 7 | 7 | 沒 |
| 氵 | 汽 | qì | 7 | 11 | 汽 |
| 氵 | 法 | fǎ | 8 | 8 | 法 |
| 氵 | 浅 | qiǎn | 8 | 14 | 淺 |
| 氵 | 河 | hé | 8 | 18 | 河 |
| 氵 | 酒 | jiǔ | 10 | 7 | 酒 |
| 氵 | 海 | hǎi | 10 | 10 | 海 |

| Radical | Character | Pinyin | No. of Strokes | Chapter First Appears | Traditional Character |
|---|---|---|---|---|---|
| 氵 | 流 | liú | 10 | 20 | 流 |
| 氵 | 深 | shēn | 11 | 14 | 深 |
| 氵 | 清 | qīng | 11 | 16 | 清 |
| 氵 | 游 | yóu | 12 | 19 | 遊 |
| 忄 | 快 | kuài | 7 | 7 | 快 |
| 忄 | 忙 | máng | 6 | 7 | 忙 |
| 忄 | 慢 | màn | 14 | 14 | 慢 |
| 忄 | 懂 | dǒng | 15 | 14 | 懂 |
| 宀 | 字 | zì | 6 | 6 | 字 |
| 宀 | 安 | ān | 6 | 13 | 安 |
| 宀 | 完 | wán | 7 | 16 | 完 |
| 宀 | 宜 | yí | 8 | 6 | 宜 |
| 宀 | 定 | dìng | 8 | 12 | 定 |
| 宀 | 客 | kè | 9 | 7 | 客 |
| 宀 | 家 | jiā | 10 | 6 | 家 |
| 宀 | 容 | róng | 10 | 8 | 容 |
| 宀 | 害 | hài | 10 | 19 | 害 |
| 宀 | 宿 | sù | 11 | 20 | 宿 |
| 宀 | 寓 | yù | 12 | 15 | 寓 |
| 广 | 床 | chuán | 7 | 14 | 床 |
| 广 | 应 | yīng | 7 | 20 | 應 |
| 广 | 店 | diàn | 8 | 14 | 店 |
| 广 | 度 | dù | 9 | 20 | 度 |
| 门 | 门 | mén | 3 | 9 | 門 |
| 门 | 间 | jiān | 7 | 17 | 間 |
| 门 | 闹 | nào | 8 | 18 | 鬧 |
| 辶 | 边 | biān | 5 | 9 | 邊 |
| 辶 | 过 | guò | 6 | 13 | 過 |
| 辶 | 还 | hái/huán | 7 | 7 | 還 |
| 辶 | 这 | zhè | 7 | 8 | 這 |

| Radical | Character | Pinyin | No. of Strokes | Chapter First Appears | Traditional Character |
|---|---|---|---|---|---|
| 辶 | 连 | lián | 7 | 10 | 連 |
| 辶 | 进 | jìn | 7 | 15 | 進 |
| 辶 | 远 | yuǎn | 7 | 19 | 遠 |
| 辶 | 近 | jìn | 7 | 19 | 近 |
| 辶 | 送 | sòng | 9 | 7 | 送 |
| 辶 | 速 | sù | 10 | 20 | 速 |
| 辶 | 道 | dào | 12 | 7 | 道 |
| 辶 | 遍 | biàn | 12 | 17 | 遍 |
| 扌 | 打 | dǎ | 5 | 10 | 打 |
| 扌 | 找 | zhǎo | 7 | 9 | 找 |
| 扌 | 报 | bào | 7 | 9 | 報 |
| 扌 | 把 | bǎ | 7 | 17 | 把 |
| 扌 | 抓 | zhuā | 7 | 20 | 抓 |
| 扌 | 拐 | guǎi | 8 | 11 | 拐 |
| 扌 | 拉 | lā | 8 | 20 | 拉 |
| 扌 | 挤 | jǐ | 9 | 12 | 擠 |
| 扌 | 挑 | tiāo | 9 | 19 | 挑 |
| 扌 | 接 | jiē | 11 | 20 | 接 |
| 扌 | 搬 | bān | 13 | 15 | 搬 |
| 扌 | 摊 | tān | 13 | 19 | 攤 |
| 工 | 工 | gōng | 3 | 19 | 工 |
| 工 | 功 | gōng | 5 | 11 | 功 |
| 工 | 左 | zuǒ | 5 | 11 | 左 |
| 土 | 去 | qù | 5 | 8 | 去 |
| 土 | 地 | de/dì | 6 | 8 | 地 |
| 土 | 在 | zài | 6 | 8 | 在 |
| 土 | 块 | kuài | 7 | 8 | 塊 |
| 土 | 场 | chǎng | 6 | 14 | 場 |
| 土 | 至 | zhì | 6 | 19 | 至 |
| 土 | 坐 | zuò | 7 | 11 | 坐 |

| Radical | Character | Pinyin | No. of Strokes | Chapter First Appears | Traditional Character |
|---|---|---|---|---|---|
| 土 | 坏 | huài | 7 | 12 | 壞 |
| 土 | 城 | chéng | 9 | 9 | 城 |
| 土 | 堵 | dǔ | 11 | 19 | 堵 |
| 艹 | 花 | huā | 7 | 12 | 花 |
| 艹 | 英 | yīng | 8 | 10 | 英 |
| 艹 | 茶 | chá | 9 | 10 | 茶 |
| 艹 | 药 | yào | 9 | 12 | 藥 |
| 艹 | 菜 | cài | 11 | 10 | 菜 |
| 艹 | 黄 | huáng | 11 | 14 | 黃 |
| 艹 | 蓝 | lán | 13 | 14 | 藍 |
| 艹 | 薪 | xīn | 16 | 18 | 薪 |
| 大 | 大 | dà | 3 | 4 | 大 |
| 大 | 太 | tài | 4 | 5 | 太 |
| 大 | 天 | tiān | 4 | 11 | 天 |
| 大 | 头 | tóu | 5 | 12 | 頭 |
| 小 | 小 | xiǎo | 3 | 4 | 小 |
| 小 | 少 | shǎo | 4 | 13 | 少 |
| 小 | 当 | dāng | 6 | 13 | 當 |
| 小 | 系 | xì | 7 | 16 | 系 |
| 口 | 口 | kǒu | 3 | 6 | 口 |
| 口 | 只 | zhǐ | 5 | 5 | 只 |
| 口 | 可 | kě | 5 | 5 | 可 |
| 口 | 兄 | xiōng | 5 | 6 | 兄 |
| 口 | 叫 | jiào | 5 | 8 | 叫 |
| 口 | 右 | yòu | 5 | 9 | 右 |
| 口 | 号 | hào | 5 | 13 | 號 |
| 口 | 问 | wèn | 6 | 5 | 問 |
| 口 | 吗 | ma | 6 | 5 | 嗎 |
| 口 | 告 | gào | 6 | 6 | 告 |
| 口 | 吃 | chī | 6 | 7 | 吃 |

| Radical | Character | Pinyin | No. of Strokes | Chapter First Appears | Traditional Character |
|---|---|---|---|---|---|
| 口 | 名 | míng | 6 | 8 | 名 |
| 口 | 后 | hòu | 6 | 10 | 後 |
| 口 | 回 | huí | 6 | 12 | 回 |
| 口 | 呀 | ya | 7 | 6 | 呀 |
| 口 | 吧 | ba | 7 | 8 | 吧 |
| 口 | 听 | tīng | 7 | 13 | 聽 |
| 口 | 吵 | chǎo | 7 | 16 | 吵 |
| 口 | 足 | zú | 7 | 20 | 足 |
| 口 | 呢 | ne | 8 | 5 | 呢 |
| 口 | 哎 | āi | 8 | 6 | 哎 |
| 口 | 知 | zhī | 8 | 7 | 知 |
| 口 | 咖 | kā | 8 | 7 | 咖 |
| 口 | 哥 | gē | 10 | 6 | 哥 |
| 口 | 哪 | nǎ | 9 | 9 | 哪 |
| 口 | 咱 | zán | 9 | 14 | 咱 |
| 口 | 虽 | suī | 9 | 18 | 雖 |
| 口 | 啊 | á | 10 | 16 | 啊 |
| 口 | 哭 | kū | 10 | 20 | 哭 |
| 口 | 啡 | fēi | 11 | 7 | 啡 |
| 口 | 啤 | pí | 11 | 16 | 啤 |
| 口 | 唱 | chàng | 11 | 20 | 唱 |
| 口 | 喝 | hē | 12 | 7 | 喝 |
| 囗 | 四 | sì | 5 | 4 | 四 |
| 囗 | 因 | yīn | 6 | 9 | 因 |
| 囗 | 国 | guó | 8 | 8 | 國 |
| 囗 | 图 | tú | 8 | 8 | 圖 |
| 巾 | 师 | shī | 6 | 13 | 師 |
| 巾 | 希 | xī | 7 | 13 | 希 |
| 巾 | 常 | cháng | 11 | 13 | 常 |
| 巾 | 带 | dài | 9 | 16 | 帶 |

| Radical | Character | Pinyin | No. of Strokes | Chapter First Appears | Traditional Character |
|---|---|---|---|---|---|
| 山 | 山 | shān | 3 | 15 | 山 |
| 山 | 出 | chū | 5 | 15 | 出 |
| 山 | 岁 | suì | 6 | 15 | 歲 |
| 彳 | 行 | xíng/háng | 6 | 6 | 行 |
| 彳 | 往 | wàng | 8 | 11 | 往 |
| 彳 | 很 | hěn | 9 | 6 | 很 |
| 彳 | 得 | de/děi | 11 | 6 | 得 |
| 彳 | 街 | jiē | 12 | 11 | 街 |
| 夕 | 外 | wài | 5 | 11 | 外 |
| 夕 | 多 | duō | 6 | 11 | 多 |
| 夕 | 够 | gòu | 11 | 18 | 夠 |
| 饣 | 饭 | fàn | 7 | 7 | 飯 |
| 饣 | 饱 | bǎo | 8 | 8 | 飽 |
| 饣 | 饺 | jiǎo | 9 | 17 | 餃 |
| 饣 | 饿 | è | 10 | 7 | 餓 |
| 饣 | 馆 | guǎn | 11 | 7 | 館 |
| 己 | 已 | yǐ | 3 | 12 | 已 |
| 己 | 己 | jǐ | 3 | 19 | 己 |
| 弓 | 张 | zhāng | 8 | 17 | 張 |
| 子 | 子 | zì | 3 | 5 | 子 |
| 子 | 学 | xué | 8 | 10 | 學 |
| 子 | 孩 | hái | 9 | 10 | 孩 |
| 女 | 女 | nǚ | 3 | 5 | 女 |
| 女 | 她 | tā | 6 | 6 | 她 |
| 女 | 奶 | nǎi | 5 | 8 | 奶 |
| 女 | 妈 | mā | 6 | 6 | 媽 |
| 女 | 好 | hǎo | 6 | 6 | 好 |
| 女 | 妹 | mèi | 8 | 6 | 妹 |
| 女 | 姐 | jiě | 8 | 6 | 姐 |
| 女 | 姓 | xìng | 8 | 6 | 姓 |

| Radical | Character | Pinyin | No. of Strokes | Chapter First Appears | Traditional Character |
|---|---|---|---|---|---|
| 女 | 始 | shǐ | 8 | 12 | 始 |
| 女 | 要 | yào | 9 | 6 | 要 |
| 女 | 姨 | yí | 9 | 17 | 姨 |
| 纟 | 红 | hóng | 6 | 14 | 紅 |
| 纟 | 纸 | zhǐ | 7 | 17 | 紙 |
| 纟 | 级 | jí | 7 | 20 | 級 |
| 纟 | 绍 | shào | 8 | 10 | 紹 |
| 纟 | 经 | jīng | 8 | 12 | 經 |
| 纟 | 练 | liàn | 8 | 13 | 練 |
| 纟 | 细 | xì | 8 | 17 | 細 |
| 纟 | 给 | gěi | 9 | 10 | 給 |
| 纟 | 绿 | lǜ | 11 | 14 | 綠 |
| 纟 | 绩 | jì | 11 | 18 | 績 |
| 马 | 马 | mǎ | 3 | 19 | 馬 |
| 灬 | 点 | diǎn | 9 | 12 | 點 |
| 灬 | 热 | rè | 10 | 15 | 熱 |
| 灬 | 然 | rán | 12 | 12 | 然 |
| 文 | 文 | wén | 4 | 4 | 文 |
| 方 | 方 | fāng | 4 | 9 | 方 |
| 方 | 旁 | páng | 10 | 19 | 旁 |
| 方 | 旅 | lǚ | 10 | 19 | 旅 |
| 火 | 火 | huǒ | 4 | 11 | 火 |
| 火 | 灯 | dēng | 6 | 11 | 燈 |
| 火 | 灰 | huī | 6 | 14 | 灰 |
| 火 | 炒 | chǎo | 8 | 11 | 炒 |
| 火 | 烧 | shāo | 10 | 12 | 燒 |
| 心 | 心 | xīn | 4 | 11 | 心 |
| 心 | 必 | bì | 5 | 7 | 必 |
| 心 | 忘 | wàng | 7 | 9 | 忘 |
| 心 | 志 | zhì | 7 | 9 | 志 |

| Radical | Character | Pinyin | No. of Strokes | Chapter First Appears | Traditional Character |
|---|---|---|---|---|---|
| 心 | 念 | niàn | 8 | 10 | 念 |
| 心 | 怎 | zěn | 9 | 11 | 怎 |
| 心 | 思 | sī | 9 | 8 | 思 |
| 心 | 急 | jí | 9 | 19 | 急 |
| 心 | 息 | xī | 10 | 12 | 息 |
| 心 | 想 | xiǎng | 13 | 7 | 想 |
| 心 | 意 | yì | 13 | 7 | 意 |
| 王 | 王 | wáng | 4 | 4 | 王 |
| 王 | 现 | xiàn | 8 | 13 | 現 |
| 王 | 玩 | wán | 8 | 13 | 玩 |
| 王 | 班 | bān | 10 | 15 | 班 |
| 王 | 球 | qiú | 11 | 20 | 球 |
| 木 | 本 | běn | 5 | 4 | 本 |
| 木 | 机 | jī | 5 | 10 | 機 |
| 木 | 杂 | zá | 6 | 9 | 雜 |
| 木 | 朵 | duǒ | 6 | 16 | 朵 |
| 木 | 条 | tiáo | 7 | 11 | 條 |
| 木 | 李 | lǐ | 7 | 17 | 李 |
| 木 | 板 | bǎn | 8 | 9 | 板 |
| 木 | 杯 | bēi | 8 | 12 | 杯 |
| 木 | 极 | jí | 8 | 17 | 極 |
| 木 | 松 | sōng | 8 | 19 | 松 |
| 木 | 果 | guǒ | 8 | 19 | 果 |
| 木 | 架 | jià | 9 | 20 | 架 |
| 木 | 校 | xiào | 10 | 15 | 校 |
| 木 | 桌 | zhuō | 10 | 15 | 桌 |
| 木 | 样 | yàng | 10 | 18 | 樣 |
| 木 | 梯 | tī | 11 | 15 | 梯 |
| 木 | 楼 | lóu | 13 | 14 | 樓 |
| 木 | 楚 | chǔ | 13 | 16 | 楚 |

| Radical | Character | Pinyin | No. of Strokes | Chapter First Appears | Traditional Character |
|---|---|---|---|---|---|
| 歹 | 死 | sǐ | 6 | 17 | 死 |
| 车 | 车 | chē | 4 | 6 | 車 |
| 车 | 轻 | qīng | 9 | 19 | 輕 |
| 车 | 较 | jiào | 10 | 19 | 較 |
| 戈 | 成 | chéng | 6 | 17 | 成 |
| 戈 | 我 | wǒ | 7 | 4 | 我 |
| 比 | 比 | bǐ | 4 | 18 | 比 |
| 日 | 日 | rì | 4 | 4 | 日 |
| 日 | 电 | diàn | 5 | 6 | 電 |
| 日 | 旧 | jiù | 5 | 8 | 舊 |
| 日 | 早 | zǎo | 6 | 8 | 早 |
| 日 | 时 | shí | 7 | 13 | 時 |
| 日 | 明 | míng | 8 | 8 | 明 |
| 日 | 者 | zhě | 8 | 15 | 者 |
| 日 | 是 | shì | 9 | 8 | 是 |
| 日 | 昨 | zuó | 9 | 12 | 昨 |
| 日 | 春 | chūn | 9 | 13 | 春 |
| 日 | 星 | xīng | 9 | 13 | 星 |
| 日 | 晚 | wǎn | 12 | 8 | 晚 |
| 日 | 替 | tì | 12 | 10 | 替 |
| 日 | 最 | zuì | 12 | 12 | 最 |
| 日 | 景 | jǐng | 12 | 19 | 景 |
| 日 | 暖 | nuǎn | 13 | 19 | 暖 |
| 水 | 水 | shuǐ | 4 | 7 | 水 |
| 贝 | 贵 | guì | 9 | 18 | 貴 |
| 见 | 见 | jiàn | 4 | 4 | 見 |
| 见 | 觉 | jiào | 9 | 16 | 覺 |
| 父 | 父 | fù | 4 | 6 | 父 |
| 牛 | 牛 | niú | 4 | 8 | 牛 |
| 手 | 手 | shǒu | 4 | 9 | 手 |

| Radical | Character | Pinyin | No. of Strokes | Chapter First Appears | Traditional Character |
|---|---|---|---|---|---|
| 毛 | 毛 | máo | 4 | 5 | 毛 |
| 气 | 气 | qì | 4 | 7 | 氣 |
| 攵 | 放 | fàng | 8 | 17 | 放 |
| 攵 | 故 | gù | 9 | 10 | 故 |
| 攵 | 教 | jiāo | 11 | 10 | 教 |
| 斤 | 斤 | jīn | 4 | 20 | 斤 |
| 斤 | 所 | suǒ | 8 | 15 | 所 |
| 斤 | 新 | xīn | 13 | 15 | 新 |
| 爪 | 爬 | pá | 8 | 15 | 爬 |
| 爪 | 爱 | ài | 10 | 15 | 愛 |
| 月 | 月 | yuè | 4 | 13 | 月 |
| 月 | 有 | yǒu | 6 | 8 | 有 |
| 月 | 肚 | dù | 7 | 12 | 肚 |
| 月 | 朋 | péng | 8 | 8 | 朋 |
| 月 | 服 | fú | 8 | 11 | 服 |
| 月 | 胖 | pàng | 9 | 18 | 胖 |
| 月 | 能 | néng | 10 | 16 | 能 |
| 月 | 望 | wàng | 11 | 13 | 望 |
| 月 | 期 | qī | 12 | 13 | 期 |
| 风 | 风 | fēng | 4 | 15 | 風 |
| 母 | 母 | mǔ | 5 | 6 | 母 |
| 穴 | 空 | kòng | 8 | 18 | 空 |
| 穴 | 穿 | chuān | 9 | 18 | 穿 |
| 立 | 站 | zhàn | 10 | 19 | 站 |
| 疒 | 病 | bìng | 10 | 12 | 病 |
| 疒 | 疼 | téng | 10 | 12 | 疼 |
| 疒 | 瘦 | shòu | 14 | 18 | 瘦 |
| 衤 | 衫 | shān | 8 | 9 | 衫 |
| 衤 | 衬 | chèn | 8 | 9 | 襯 |
| 衤 | 袜 | wà | 10 | 9 | 襪 |

| Radical | Character | Pinyin | No. of Strokes | Chapter First Appears | Traditional Character |
|---|---|---|---|---|---|
| 衤 | 被 | bèi | 10 | 20 | 被 |
| 衤 | 裙 | qún | 12 | 14 | 裙 |
| 衤 | 裤 | kù | 12 | 18 | 褲 |
| 业 | 业 | yè | 5 | 13 | 業 |
| 目 | 看 | kàn | 9 | 9 | 看 |
| 目 | 眼 | yǎn | 11 | 9 | 眼 |
| 目 | 睡 | shuì | 13 | 16 | 睡 |
| 目 | 睛 | jīng | 13 | 16 | 睛 |
| 田 | 男 | nán | 7 | 14 | 男 |
| 田 | 备 | bèi | 8 | 14 | 備 |
| 田 | 累 | lèi | 11 | 14 | 累 |
| 钅 | 钟 | zhōng | 9 | 13 | 鐘 |
| 钅 | 钱 | qián | 10 | 12 | 錢 |
| 钅 | 铅 | qiān | 10 | 17 | 鉛 |
| 钅 | 银 | yín | 11 | 12 | 銀 |
| 钅 | 错 | cuò | 13 | 13 | 錯 |
| 钅 | 镜 | jìng | 16 | 16 | 鏡 |
| 禾 | 和 | hé/huó | 8 | 11 | 和 |
| 禾 | 秋 | qiū | 9 | 13 | 秋 |
| 禾 | 租 | zū | 10 | 11 | 租 |
| 白 | 白 | bái | 5 | 8 | 白 |
| 白 | 的 | de | 8 | 9 | 的 |
| 瓜 | 瓜 | guā | 5 | 19 | 瓜 |
| 皮 | 皮 | pí | 5 | 8 | 皮 |
| 衣 | 衣 | yī | 6 | 9 | 衣 |
| 羊 | 美 | měi | 9 | 10 | 美 |
| 羊 | 差 | chà | 9 | 13 | 差 |
| 羊 | 着 | zhe | 11 | 10 | 著 |
| 米 | 米 | mǐ | 6 | 10 | 米 |
| 米 | 粉 | fěn | 10 | 14 | 粉 |

| Radical | Character | Pinyin | No. of Strokes | Chapter First Appears | Traditional Character |
|---|---|---|---|---|---|
| 老 | 老 | lǎo | 6 | 9 | 老 |
| 耳 | 耳 | ěr | 6 | 16 | 耳 |
| 西 | 西 | xī | 6 | 4 | 西 |
| 西 | 票 | piào | 11 | 15 | 票 |
| 页 | 页 | yè | 6 | 14 | 頁 |
| 页 | 预 | yù | 10 | 14 | 預 |
| 页 | 顿 | dùn | 10 | 14 | 頓 |
| 页 | 颜 | yán | 15 | 14 | 顏 |
| 竹 | 笔 | bǐ | 10 | 8 | 筆 |
| 竹 | 笑 | xiào | 10 | 10 | 笑 |
| 竹 | 笨 | bèn | 11 | 8 | 笨 |
| 竹 | 第 | dì | 11 | 13 | 第 |
| 竹 | 等 | děng | 12 | 12 | 等 |
| 竹 | 筷 | kuài | 13 | 10 | 筷 |
| 竹 | 箱 | xiāng | 15 | 17 | 箱 |
| 自 | 自 | zì | 6 | 6 | 自 |
| 血 | 血 | xiě/xuě | 6 | 20 | 血 |
| 走 | 走 | zǒu | 7 | 11 | 走 |
| 走 | 起 | qǐ | 10 | 14 | 起 |
| 走 | 越 | yuè | 12 | 19 | 越 |
| 走 | 超 | chāo | 12 | 20 | 超 |
| 走 | 趣 | qù | 15 | 18 | 趣 |
| 酉 | 醒 | xǐng | 16 | 16 | 醒 |
| 里 | 里 | lǐ | 7 | 13 | 裏 |
| 足 | 跑 | pǎo | 12 | 16 | 跑 |
| 足 | 跟 | gēn | 13 | 16 | 跟 |
| 足 | 路 | lù | 13 | 18 | 路 |
| 青 | 静 | jìng | 14 | 18 | 靜 |
| 雨 | 雨 | yǔ | 8 | 15 | 雨 |
| 雨 | 雪 | xuě | 11 | 15 | 雪 |

# Simplified versus Traditional Character Comparison

| Simplified Radical | Simplified Character | Traditional Character | Pinyin | No. of Strokes (Simplified) | No. of Strokes (Traditional) | Chapter First Introduced |
|---|---|---|---|---|---|---|
| 丶 | 之 | 之 | zhī | 3 | 3 | 18 |
| 丶 | 为 | 為 | wèi | 4 | 9 | 9 |
| 一 | 一 | 一 | yī | 1 | 1 | 4 |
| 一 | 七 | 七 | qī | 2 | 2 | 4 |
| 一 | 三 | 三 | sān | 3 | 3 | 4 |
| 一 | 万 | 萬 | wàn | 3 | 12 | 6 |
| 一 | 上 | 上 | shàng | 3 | 3 | 9 |
| 一 | 下 | 下 | xià | 3 | 3 | 9 |
| 一 | 才 | 才 | cái | 3 | 3 | 12 |
| 一 | 五 | 五 | wǔ | 4 | 4 | 4 |
| 一 | 不 | 不 | bù | 4 | 4 | 4 |
| 一 | 开 | 開 | kāi | 4 | 12 | 11 |
| 一 | 正 | 正 | zhèng | 5 | 5 | 11 |
| 一 | 且 | 且 | qiě | 5 | 5 | 20 |
| 一 | 平 | 平 | píng | 5 | 5 | 14 |
| 一 | 再 | 再 | zài | 6 | 6 | 4 |
| 一 | 百 | 百 | bǎi | 6 | 6 | 5 |
| 一 | 东 | 東 | dōng | 6 | 8 | 7 |
| 一 | 而 | 而 | ér | 6 | 6 | 14 |
| 一 | 两 | 兩 | liǎng | 7 | 8 | 5 |
| 一 | 来 | 來 | lái | 7 | 8 | 11 |
| 一 | 更 | 更 | gèng | 7 | 7 | 18 |
| 一 | 事 | 事 | shì | 8 | 8 | 10 |
| 一 | 面 | 面 | miàn | 9 | 9 | 13 |

| Simplified Radical | Simplified Character | Traditional Character | Pinyin | No. of Strokes (Simplified) | No. of Strokes (Traditional) | Chapter First Introduced |
|---|---|---|---|---|---|---|
| 丨 | 中 | 中 | zhōng | 4 | 4 | 4 |
| 丨 | 北 | 北 | běi | 5 | 5 | 9 |
| 丿 | 九 | 九 | jiǔ | 2 | 2 | 4 |
| 丿 | 久 | 久 | jiǔ | 3 | 3 | 12 |
| 丿 | 午 | 午 | wǔ | 4 | 4 | 7 |
| 丿 | 生 | 生 | shēng | 5 | 5 | 5 |
| 丿 | 乐 | 樂 | lè | 5 | 15 | 7 |
| 丿 | 乎 | 乎 | hū | 5 | 5 | 18 |
| 丿 | 长 | 長 | cháng | 5 | 8 | 18 |
| 丿 | 年 | 年 | nián | 6 | 6 | 13 |
| 乙 | 了 | 了 | le/liǎo | 2 | 2 | 7 |
| 乙 | 也 | 也 | yě | 3 | 3 | 4 |
| 乙 | 习 | 習 | xí | 3 | 11 | 13 |
| 乙 | 飞 | 飛 | fēi | 3 | 9 | 17 |
| 乙 | 书 | 書 | shū | 4 | 10 | 4 |
| 乙 | 买 | 買 | mǎi | 6 | 12 | 6 |
| 二 | 二 | 二 | èr | 2 | 2 | 4 |
| 亠 | 六 | 六 | liù | 4 | 4 | 9 |
| 亠 | 市 | 市 | shì | 5 | 5 | 20 |
| 亠 | 京 | 京 | jīng | 8 | 8 | 9 |
| 亠 | 夜 | 夜 | yè | 8 | 8 | 16 |
| 亠 | 高 | 高 | gāo | 10 | 10 | 9 |
| 亠 | 商 | 商 | shāng | 11 | 11 | 9 |
| 亠 | 就 | 就 | jiù | 12 | 12 | 9 |
| 冫 | 冬 | 冬 | dōng | 5 | 5 | 14 |
| 冫 | 冰 | 冰 | bīng | 6 | 6 | 7 |
| 冫 | 次 | 次 | cì | 6 | 6 | 16 |
| 冫 | 冷 | 冷 | lěng | 7 | 7 | 15 |
| 冫 | 凉 | 涼 | liáng | 10 | 11 | 17 |

| Simplified Radical | Simplified Character | Traditional Character | Pinyin | No. of Strokes (Simplified) | No. of Strokes (Traditional) | Chapter First Introduced |
|---|---|---|---|---|---|---|
| 冖 | 写 | 寫 | xiě | 5 | 15 | 17 |
| 讠 | 认 | 認 | rèn | 4 | 14 | 9 |
| 讠 | 记 | 記 | jì | 5 | 10 | 17 |
| 讠 | 讨 | 討 | tǎo | 5 | 10 | 20 |
| 讠 | 许 | 許 | xǔ | 6 | 11 | 15 |
| 讠 | 讲 | 講 | jiǎng | 6 | 17 | 16 |
| 讠 | 词 | 詞 | cí | 7 | 12 | 5 |
| 讠 | 诉 | 訴 | sù | 7 | 12 | 6 |
| 讠 | 识 | 識 | shì | 7 | 19 | 9 |
| 讠 | 话 | 話 | huà | 8 | 13 | 5 |
| 讠 | 试 | 試 | shì | 8 | 13 | 10 |
| 讠 | 该 | 該 | gāi | 8 | 13 | 20 |
| 讠 | 说 | 說 | shuō | 9 | 14 | 5 |
| 讠 | 语 | 語 | yǔ | 9 | 14 | 5 |
| 讠 | 请 | 請 | qǐng | 10 | 15 | 7 |
| 讠 | 课 | 課 | kè | 10 | 15 | 10 |
| 讠 | 谁 | 誰 | shéi/shuí | 11 | 16 | 13 |
| 讠 | 谢 | 謝 | xiè | 12 | 17 | 10 |
| 十 | 十 | 十 | shí | 2 | 2 | 4 |
| 十 | 千 | 千 | qiān | 3 | 3 | 5 |
| 十 | 支 | 支 | zhī | 4 | 4 | 5 |
| 十 | 考 | 考 | kǎo | 6 | 6 | 10 |
| 十 | 华 | 華 | huá | 6 | 10 | 17 |
| 十 | 卖 | 賣 | mài | 8 | 15 | 7 |
| 十 | 直 | 直 | zhí | 8 | 8 | 11 |
| 十 | 南 | 南 | nán | 9 | 9 | 11 |
| 十 | 真 | 真 | zhēn | 10 | 10 | 5 |
| 十 | 韩 | 韓 | hán | 12 | 18 | 14 |
| 厂 | 厅 | 廳 | tīng | 4 | 25 | 15 |

| Simplified Radical | Simplified Character | Traditional Character | Pinyin | No. of Strokes (Simplified) | No. of Strokes (Traditional) | Chapter First Introduced |
|---|---|---|---|---|---|---|
| 厂 | 厌 | 厭 | yàn | 6 | 14 | 20 |
| 厂 | 厕 | 廁 | cè | 8 | 12 | 15 |
| 厂 | 厨 | 廚 | chú | 12 | 13 | 15 |
| 匚 | 医 | 醫 | yī | 7 | 18 | 12 |
| 刂 | 刚 | 剛 | gāng | 6 | 10 | 16 |
| 刂 | 别 | 別 | bié | 7 | 7 | 13 |
| 刂 | 利 | 利 | lì | 7 | 7 | 19 |
| 刂 | 刻 | 刻 | kè | 8 | 8 | 13 |
| 刂 | 到 | 到 | dào | 8 | 8 | 13 |
| 刂 | 刮 | 刮 | guā | 8 | 8 | 15 |
| 冂 | 内 | 內 | nèi | 4 | 4 | 9 |
| 冂 | 用 | 用 | yòng | 5 | 5 | 10 |
| 冂 | 肉 | 肉 | ròu | 6 | 6 | 10 |
| 冂 | 同 | 同 | tóng | 6 | 6 | 11 |
| 八 | 八 | 八 | bā | 2 | 2 | 4 |
| 八 | 分 | 分 | fēn | 4 | 4 | 6 |
| 八 | 公 | 公 | gōng | 4 | 4 | 11 |
| 八 | 兰 | 蘭 | lán | 5 | 19 | 6 |
| 八 | 半 | 半 | bàn | 5 | 5 | 6 |
| 八 | 共 | 共 | gòng | 6 | 6 | 6 |
| 八 | 关 | 關 | guān | 6 | 19 | 7 |
| 八 | 兴 | 興 | xìng | 6 | 14 | 13 |
| 八 | 典 | 典 | diǎn | 7 | 7 | 6 |
| 八 | 弟 | 弟 | dì | 7 | 7 | 6 |
| 八 | 具 | 具 | jù | 8 | 8 | 15 |
| 八 | 前 | 前 | qián | 9 | 9 | 7 |
| 人 | 人 | 人 | rén | 2 | 2 | 4 |
| 人 | 个 | 個 | gè | 3 | 10 | 5 |
| 人 | 介 | 介 | jiè | 4 | 4 | 10 |

| Simplified Radical | Simplified Character | Traditional Character | Pinyin | No. of Strokes (Simplified) | No. of Strokes (Traditional) | Chapter First Introduced |
|---|---|---|---|---|---|---|
| 人 | 以 | 以 | yǐ | 4 | 4 | 5 |
| 人 | 从 | 從 | cóng | 4 | 11 | 11 |
| 人 | 今 | 今 | jīn | 4 | 4 | 12 |
| 人 | 会 | 會 | huì | 6 | 13 | 5 |
| 人 | 全 | 全 | quān | 6 | 6 | 18 |
| 人 | 舍 | 舍 | shè | 8 | 8 | 20 |
| 人 | 拿 | 拿 | ná | 10 | 10 | 11 |
| 人 | 舒 | 舒 | shū | 12 | 12 | 11 |
| 亻 | 们 | 們 | men | 4 | 10 | 5 |
| 亻 | 什 | 什 | shén | 4 | 4 | 5 |
| 亻 | 他 | 他 | tā | 5 | 5 | 5 |
| 亻 | 仔 | 仔 | zǎi/zǐ | 5 | 5 | 9 |
| 亻 | 份 | 份 | fèn | 6 | 6 | 6 |
| 亻 | 住 | 住 | zhù | 7 | 7 | 9 |
| 亻 | 件 | 件 | jiàn | 6 | 6 | 9 |
| 亻 | 休 | 休 | xiū | 6 | 6 | 12 |
| 亻 | 你 | 你 | nǐ | 7 | 7 | 5 |
| 亻 | 伯 | 伯 | bó | 7 | 7 | 7 |
| 亻 | 位 | 位 | wèi | 7 | 7 | 10 |
| 亻 | 作 | 作 | zuò | 7 | 7 | 13 |
| 亻 | 但 | 但 | dàn | 7 | 7 | 20 |
| 亻 | 便 | 便 | pián/biàn | 9 | 9 | 6 |
| 亻 | 信 | 信 | xìn | 9 | 9 | 10 |
| 亻 | 候 | 候 | hòu | 10 | 10 | 13 |
| 亻 | 借 | 借 | jiè | 10 | 10 | 17 |
| 亻 | 倍 | 倍 | bèi | 10 | 10 | 18 |
| 亻 | 做 | 做 | zuò | 11 | 11 | 7 |
| 亻 | 假 | 假 | jiǎ | 11 | 11 | 19 |
| 亻 | 偷 | 偷 | tōu | 11 | 11 | 20 |

| Simplified Radical | Simplified Character | Traditional Character | Pinyin | No. of Strokes (Simplified) | No. of Strokes (Traditional) | Chapter First Introduced |
|---|---|---|---|---|---|---|
| 几 | 几 | 幾 | jǐ | 2 | 12 | 5 |
| 儿 | 儿 | 兒 | ér | 2 | 8 | 5 |
| 儿 | 先 | 先 | xiān | 6 | 6 | 5 |
| 厶 | 么 | 麼 | me | 3 | 14 | 5 |
| 又 | 又 | 又 | yòu | 2 | 2 | 16 |
| 又 | 叉 | 叉 | chā | 3 | 3 | 10 |
| 又 | 双 | 雙 | shuāng | 4 | 18 | 8 |
| 又 | 友 | 友 | yǒu | 4 | 4 | 8 |
| 又 | 对 | 對 | duì | 5 | 14 | 8 |
| 又 | 发 | 發 | fā | 5 | 12 | 12 |
| 又 | 欢 | 歡 | huān | 6 | 21 | 8 |
| 又 | 叔 | 叔 | shū | 8 | 8 | 8 |
| 又 | 难 | 難 | nán | 10 | 19 | 14 |
| 阝 | 那 | 那 | nà | 6 | 6 | 8 |
| 阝 | 邻 | 鄰 | lín | 7 | 14 | 16 |
| 阝 | 阿 | 阿 | ā | 7 | 7 | 17 |
| 阝 | 附 | 附 | fù | 7 | 7 | 19 |
| 阝 | 除 | 除 | chú | 9 | 9 | 12 |
| 阝 | 院 | 院 | yuàn | 9 | 9 | 12 |
| 阝 | 都 | 都 | dōu | 10 | 10 | 8 |
| 凵 | 画 | 畫 | huà | 8 | 12 | 6 |
| 刀 | 刀 | 刀 | dāo | 2 | 2 | 10 |
| 力 | 办 | 辦 | bàn | 4 | 16 | 20 |
| 氵 | 汉 | 漢 | hàn | 5 | 14 | 7 |
| 氵 | 汤 | 湯 | tāng | 6 | 12 | 8 |
| 氵 | 汗 | 汗 | hàn | 6 | 6 | 9 |
| 氵 | 江 | 江 | jiāng | 6 | 6 | 18 |
| 氵 | 没 | 沒 | méi | 7 | 7 | 7 |
| 氵 | 汽 | 汽 | qì | 7 | 7 | 11 |

| Simplified Radical | Simplified Character | Traditional Character | Pinyin | No. of Strokes (Simplified) | No. of Strokes (Traditional) | Chapter First Introduced |
|---|---|---|---|---|---|---|
| 氵 | 法 | 法 | fǎ | 8 | 8 | 8 |
| 氵 | 浅 | 淺 | qiǎn | 8 | 11 | 14 |
| 氵 | 河 | 河 | hé | 8 | 8 | 18 |
| 氵 | 酒 | 酒 | jiǔ | 10 | 10 | 7 |
| 氵 | 海 | 海 | hǎi | 10 | 10 | 10 |
| 氵 | 流 | 流 | liú | 10 | 10 | 20 |
| 氵 | 深 | 深 | shēn | 11 | 11 | 14 |
| 氵 | 清 | 清 | qīng | 11 | 11 | 16 |
| 氵 | 游 | 遊 | yóu | 12 | 12 | 19 |
| 忄 | 快 | 快 | kuài | 7 | 7 | 7 |
| 忄 | 忙 | 忙 | máng | 6 | 6 | 7 |
| 忄 | 慢 | 慢 | màn | 14 | 14 | 14 |
| 忄 | 懂 | 懂 | dǒng | 15 | 15 | 14 |
| 宀 | 字 | 字 | zì | 6 | 6 | 6 |
| 宀 | 安 | 安 | ān | 6 | 6 | 13 |
| 宀 | 完 | 完 | wán | 7 | 7 | 16 |
| 宀 | 宜 | 宜 | yí | 8 | 8 | 6 |
| 宀 | 定 | 定 | dìng | 8 | 8 | 12 |
| 宀 | 客 | 客 | kè | 9 | 9 | 7 |
| 宀 | 家 | 家 | jiā | 10 | 10 | 6 |
| 宀 | 容 | 容 | róng | 10 | 10 | 8 |
| 宀 | 害 | 害 | hài | 10 | 10 | 19 |
| 宀 | 宿 | 宿 | sù | 11 | 11 | 20 |
| 宀 | 寓 | 寓 | yù | 12 | 12 | 15 |
| 广 | 床 | 床 | chuán | 7 | 7 | 14 |
| 广 | 应 | 應 | yīng | 7 | 17 | 20 |
| 广 | 店 | 店 | diàn | 8 | 8 | 14 |
| 广 | 度 | 度 | dù | 9 | 9 | 20 |
| 门 | 门 | 門 | mén | 3 | 8 | 9 |

| Simplified Radical | Simplified Character | Traditional Character | Pinyin | No. of Strokes (Simplified) | No. of Strokes (Traditional) | Chapter First Introduced |
|---|---|---|---|---|---|---|
| 门 | 间 | 間 | jiān | 7 | 12 | 17 |
| 门 | 闹 | 鬧 | nào | 8 | 13 | 18 |
| 辶 | 边 | 邊 | biān | 5 | 18 | 9 |
| 辶 | 过 | 過 | guò | 6 | 12 | 13 |
| 辶 | 还 | 還 | hái/huán | 7 | 16 | 7 |
| 辶 | 这 | 這 | zhè | 7 | 10 | 8 |
| 辶 | 连 | 連 | lián | 7 | 10 | 10 |
| 辶 | 进 | 進 | jìn | 7 | 11 | 15 |
| 辶 | 远 | 遠 | yuǎn | 7 | 13 | 19 |
| 辶 | 近 | 近 | jìn | 7 | 7 | 19 |
| 辶 | 送 | 送 | sòng | 9 | 9 | 7 |
| 辶 | 速 | 速 | sù | 10 | 10 | 20 |
| 辶 | 道 | 道 | dào | 12 | 12 | 7 |
| 辶 | 遍 | 遍 | biàn | 12 | 12 | 17 |
| 扌 | 打 | 打 | dǎ | 5 | 5 | 10 |
| 扌 | 找 | 找 | zhǎo | 7 | 7 | 9 |
| 扌 | 报 | 報 | bào | 7 | 12 | 9 |
| 扌 | 把 | 把 | bǎ | 7 | 7 | 17 |
| 扌 | 抓 | 抓 | zhuā | 7 | 7 | 20 |
| 扌 | 拐 | 拐 | guǎi | 8 | 8 | 11 |
| 扌 | 拉 | 拉 | lā | 8 | 8 | 20 |
| 扌 | 挤 | 擠 | jǐ | 9 | 17 | 12 |
| 扌 | 挑 | 挑 | tiāo | 9 | 9 | 19 |
| 扌 | 接 | 接 | jiē | 11 | 11 | 20 |
| 扌 | 搬 | 搬 | bān | 13 | 13 | 15 |
| 扌 | 摊 | 攤 | tān | 13 | 22 | 19 |
| 工 | 工 | 工 | gōng | 3 | 3 | 19 |
| 工 | 功 | 功 | gōng | 5 | 5 | 11 |
| 工 | 左 | 左 | zuǒ | 5 | 5 | 11 |

| Simplified Radical | Simplified Character | Traditional Character | Pinyin | No. of Strokes (Simplified) | No. of Strokes (Traditional) | Chapter First Introduced |
|---|---|---|---|---|---|---|
| 土 | 去 | 去 | qù | 5 | 5 | 8 |
| 土 | 地 | 地 | de/dì | 6 | 6 | 8 |
| 土 | 在 | 在 | zài | 6 | 6 | 8 |
| 土 | 块 | 塊 | kuài | 7 | 12 | 8 |
| 土 | 场 | 場 | chǎng | 6 | 12 | 14 |
| 土 | 至 | 至 | zhì | 6 | 6 | 19 |
| 土 | 坐 | 坐 | zuò | 7 | 7 | 11 |
| 土 | 坏 | 壞 | huài | 7 | 18 | 12 |
| 土 | 城 | 城 | chéng | 9 | 9 | 9 |
| 土 | 堵 | 堵 | dǔ | 11 | 11 | 19 |
| 艹 | 花 | 花 | huā | 7 | 7 | 12 |
| 艹 | 英 | 英 | yīng | 8 | 8 | 10 |
| 艹 | 茶 | 茶 | chá | 9 | 9 | 10 |
| 艹 | 药 | 藥 | yào | 9 | 18 | 12 |
| 艹 | 菜 | 菜 | cài | 11 | 11 | 10 |
| 艹 | 黄 | 黃 | huáng | 11 | 11 | 14 |
| 艹 | 蓝 | 藍 | lán | 13 | 18 | 14 |
| 艹 | 薪 | 薪 | xīn | 16 | 16 | 18 |
| 大 | 大 | 大 | dà | 3 | 3 | 4 |
| 大 | 太 | 太 | tài | 4 | 4 | 5 |
| 大 | 天 | 天 | tiān | 4 | 4 | 11 |
| 大 | 头 | 頭 | tóu | 5 | 16 | 12 |
| 小 | 小 | 小 | xiǎo | 3 | 3 | 4 |
| 小 | 少 | 少 | shǎo | 4 | 4 | 13 |
| 小 | 当 | 當 | dāng | 6 | 13 | 13 |
| 小 | 系 | 系 | xì | 7 | 7 | 16 |
| 口 | 口 | 口 | kǒu | 3 | 3 | 6 |
| 口 | 只 | 只 | zhǐ | 5 | 5 | 5 |
| 口 | 可 | 可 | kě | 5 | 5 | 5 |

| Simplified Radical | Simplified Character | Traditional Character | Pinyin | No. of Strokes (Simplified) | No. of Strokes (Traditional) | Chapter First Introduced |
|---|---|---|---|---|---|---|
| 口 | 兄 | 兄 | xiōng | 5 | 5 | 6 |
| 口 | 叫 | 叫 | jiào | 5 | 5 | 8 |
| 口 | 右 | 右 | yòu | 5 | 5 | 9 |
| 口 | 号 | 號 | hào | 5 | 13 | 13 |
| 口 | 问 | 問 | wèn | 6 | 11 | 5 |
| 口 | 吗 | 嗎 | ma | 6 | 13 | 5 |
| 口 | 告 | 告 | gào | 6 | 6 | 6 |
| 口 | 吃 | 吃 | chī | 6 | 6 | 7 |
| 口 | 名 | 名 | míng | 6 | 6 | 8 |
| 口 | 后 | 後 | hòu | 6 | 9 | 10 |
| 口 | 回 | 回 | huí | 6 | 6 | 12 |
| 口 | 呀 | 呀 | ya | 7 | 7 | 6 |
| 口 | 吧 | 吧 | ba | 7 | 7 | 8 |
| 口 | 听 | 聽 | tīng | 7 | 22 | 13 |
| 口 | 吵 | 吵 | chǎo | 7 | 7 | 16 |
| 口 | 足 | 足 | zú | 7 | 7 | 20 |
| 口 | 呢 | 呢 | ne | 8 | 8 | 5 |
| 口 | 哎 | 哎 | āi | 8 | 8 | 6 |
| 口 | 知 | 知 | zhī | 8 | 8 | 7 |
| 口 | 咖 | 咖 | kā | 8 | 8 | 7 |
| 口 | 哥 | 哥 | gē | 10 | 10 | 6 |
| 口 | 哪 | 哪 | nǎ | 9 | 9 | 9 |
| 口 | 咱 | 咱 | zán | 9 | 9 | 14 |
| 口 | 虽 | 雖 | suī | 9 | 17 | 18 |
| 口 | 啊 | 啊 | á | 10 | 10 | 16 |
| 口 | 哭 | 哭 | kū | 10 | 10 | 20 |
| 口 | 啡 | 啡 | fēi | 11 | 11 | 7 |
| 口 | 啤 | 啤 | pí | 11 | 11 | 16 |
| 口 | 唱 | 唱 | chàng | 11 | 11 | 20 |

| Simplified Radical | Simplified Character | Traditional Character | Pinyin | No. of Strokes (Simplified) | No. of Strokes (Traditional) | Chapter First Introduced |
|---|---|---|---|---|---|---|
| 口 | 喝 | 喝 | hē | 12 | 12 | 7 |
| 囗 | 四 | 四 | sì | 5 | 5 | 4 |
| 囗 | 因 | 因 | yīn | 6 | 6 | 9 |
| 囗 | 国 | 國 | guó | 8 | 11 | 8 |
| 囗 | 图 | 圖 | tú | 8 | 14 | 8 |
| 巾 | 师 | 師 | shī | 6 | 10 | 13 |
| 巾 | 希 | 希 | xī | 7 | 7 | 13 |
| 巾 | 常 | 常 | cháng | 11 | 11 | 13 |
| 巾 | 带 | 帶 | dài | 9 | 9 | 16 |
| 山 | 山 | 山 | shān | 3 | 3 | 15 |
| 山 | 出 | 出 | chū | 5 | 5 | 15 |
| 山 | 岁 | 歲 | suì | 6 | 13 | 15 |
| 彳 | 行 | 行 | xíng/háng | 6 | 6 | 6 |
| 彳 | 往 | 往 | wàng | 8 | 8 | 11 |
| 彳 | 很 | 很 | hěn | 9 | 9 | 6 |
| 彳 | 得 | 得 | de/děi | 11 | 11 | 6 |
| 彳 | 街 | 街 | jiē | 12 | 12 | 11 |
| 夕 | 外 | 外 | wài | 5 | 5 | 11 |
| 夕 | 多 | 多 | duō | 6 | 6 | 11 |
| 夕 | 够 | 夠 | gòu | 11 | 11 | 18 |
| 饣 | 饭 | 飯 | fàn | 7 | 12 | 7 |
| 饣 | 饱 | 飽 | bǎo | 8 | 13 | 8 |
| 饣 | 饺 | 餃 | jiǎo | 9 | 14 | 17 |
| 饣 | 饿 | 餓 | è | 10 | 15 | 7 |
| 饣 | 馆 | 館 | guǎn | 11 | 16 | 7 |
| 己 | 已 | 已 | yǐ | 3 | 3 | 12 |
| 己 | 己 | 己 | jǐ | 3 | 3 | 19 |
| 弓 | 张 | 張 | zhāng | 8 | 11 | 17 |
| 子 | 子 | 子 | zì | 3 | 3 | 5 |

| Simplified Radical | Simplified Character | Traditional Character | Pinyin | No. of Strokes (Simplified) | No. of Strokes (Traditional) | Chapter First Introduced |
|---|---|---|---|---|---|---|
| 子 | 学 | 學 | xué | 8 | 16 | 10 |
| 子 | 孩 | 孩 | hái | 9 | 9 | 10 |
| 女 | 女 | 女 | nǚ | 3 | 3 | 5 |
| 女 | 她 | 她 | tā | 6 | 6 | 6 |
| 女 | 奶 | 奶 | nǎi | 5 | 5 | 8 |
| 女 | 妈 | 媽 | mā | 6 | 13 | 6 |
| 女 | 好 | 好 | hǎo | 6 | 6 | 6 |
| 女 | 妹 | 妹 | mèi | 8 | 8 | 6 |
| 女 | 姐 | 姐 | jiě | 8 | 8 | 6 |
| 女 | 姓 | 姓 | xìng | 8 | 8 | 6 |
| 女 | 始 | 始 | shǐ | 8 | 8 | 12 |
| 女 | 要 | 要 | yào | 9 | 9 | 6 |
| 女 | 姨 | 姨 | yí | 9 | 9 | 17 |
| 纟 | 红 | 紅 | hóng | 6 | 9 | 14 |
| 纟 | 纸 | 紙 | zhǐ | 7 | 10 | 17 |
| 纟 | 级 | 級 | jí | 7 | 10 | 20 |
| 纟 | 绍 | 紹 | shào | 8 | 11 | 10 |
| 纟 | 经 | 經 | jīng | 8 | 13 | 12 |
| 纟 | 练 | 練 | liàn | 8 | 15 | 13 |
| 纟 | 细 | 細 | xì | 8 | 11 | 17 |
| 纟 | 给 | 給 | gěi | 9 | 12 | 10 |
| 纟 | 绿 | 綠 | lǜ | 11 | 14 | 14 |
| 纟 | 绩 | 績 | jì | 11 | 17 | 18 |
| 马 | 马 | 馬 | mǎ | 3 | 10 | 19 |
| 灬 | 点 | 點 | diǎn | 9 | 17 | 12 |
| 灬 | 热 | 熱 | rè | 10 | 15 | 15 |
| 灬 | 然 | 然 | rán | 12 | 12 | 12 |
| 文 | 文 | 文 | wén | 4 | 4 | 4 |
| 方 | 方 | 方 | fāng | 4 | 4 | 9 |

| Simplified Radical | Simplified Character | Traditional Character | Pinyin | No. of Strokes (Simplified) | No. of Strokes (Traditional) | Chapter First Introduced |
|---|---|---|---|---|---|---|
| 方 | 旁 | 旁 | páng | 10 | 10 | 19 |
| 方 | 旅 | 旅 | lǚ | 10 | 10 | 19 |
| 火 | 火 | 火 | huǒ | 4 | 4 | 11 |
| 火 | 灯 | 燈 | dēng | 6 | 16 | 11 |
| 火 | 灰 | 灰 | huī | 6 | 6 | 14 |
| 火 | 炒 | 炒 | chǎo | 8 | 8 | 11 |
| 火 | 烧 | 燒 | shāo | 10 | 16 | 12 |
| 心 | 心 | 心 | xīn | 4 | 4 | 11 |
| 心 | 必 | 必 | bì | 5 | 5 | 7 |
| 心 | 忘 | 忘 | wàng | 7 | 7 | 9 |
| 心 | 志 | 志 | zhì | 7 | 7 | 9 |
| 心 | 念 | 念 | niàn | 8 | 8 | 10 |
| 心 | 怎 | 怎 | zěn | 9 | 9 | 11 |
| 心 | 思 | 思 | sī | 9 | 9 | 8 |
| 心 | 急 | 急 | jí | 9 | 9 | 19 |
| 心 | 息 | 息 | xī | 10 | 10 | 12 |
| 心 | 想 | 想 | xiǎng | 13 | 13 | 7 |
| 心 | 意 | 意 | yì | 13 | 13 | 7 |
| 王 | 王 | 王 | wáng | 4 | 4 | 4 |
| 王 | 现 | 現 | xiàn | 8 | 11 | 13 |
| 王 | 玩 | 玩 | wán | 8 | 8 | 13 |
| 王 | 班 | 班 | bān | 10 | 10 | 15 |
| 王 | 球 | 球 | qiú | 11 | 11 | 20 |
| 木 | 本 | 本 | běn | 5 | 5 | 4 |
| 木 | 机 | 機 | jī | 5 | 16 | 10 |
| 木 | 杂 | 雜 | zá | 6 | 18 | 9 |
| 木 | 朵 | 朵 | duǒ | 6 | 6 | 16 |
| 木 | 条 | 條 | tiáo | 7 | 10 | 11 |
| 木 | 李 | 李 | lǐ | 7 | 7 | 17 |

| Simplified Radical | Simplified Character | Traditional Character | Pinyin | No. of Strokes (Simplified) | No. of Strokes (Traditional) | Chapter First Introduced |
|---|---|---|---|---|---|---|
| 木 | 板 | 板 | bǎn | 8 | 8 | 9 |
| 木 | 杯 | 杯 | bēi | 8 | 8 | 12 |
| 木 | 极 | 極 | jí | 8 | 12 | 17 |
| 木 | 松 | 松 | sōng | 8 | 8 | 19 |
| 木 | 果 | 果 | guǒ | 8 | 8 | 19 |
| 木 | 架 | 架 | jià | 9 | 9 | 20 |
| 木 | 校 | 校 | xiào | 10 | 10 | 15 |
| 木 | 桌 | 桌 | zhuō | 10 | 10 | 15 |
| 木 | 样 | 樣 | yàng | 10 | 15 | 18 |
| 木 | 梯 | 梯 | tī | 11 | 11 | 15 |
| 木 | 楼 | 樓 | lóu | 13 | 15 | 14 |
| 木 | 楚 | 楚 | chǔ | 13 | 13 | 16 |
| 歹 | 死 | 死 | sǐ | 6 | 6 | 17 |
| 车 | 车 | 車 | chē | 4 | 7 | 6 |
| 车 | 轻 | 輕 | qīng | 9 | 14 | 19 |
| 车 | 较 | 較 | jiào | 10 | 13 | 19 |
| 戈 | 成 | 成 | chéng | 6 | 6 | 17 |
| 戈 | 我 | 我 | wǒ | 7 | 7 | 4 |
| 比 | 比 | 比 | bǐ | 4 | 4 | 18 |
| 日 | 日 | 日 | rì | 4 | 4 | 4 |
| 日 | 电 | 電 | diàn | 5 | 13 | 6 |
| 日 | 旧 | 舊 | jiù | 5 | 18 | 8 |
| 日 | 早 | 早 | zǎo | 6 | 6 | 8 |
| 日 | 时 | 時 | shí | 7 | 10 | 13 |
| 日 | 明 | 明 | míng | 8 | 8 | 8 |
| 日 | 者 | 者 | zhě | 8 | 8 | 15 |
| 日 | 是 | 是 | shì | 9 | 9 | 8 |
| 日 | 昨 | 昨 | zuó | 9 | 9 | 12 |
| 日 | 春 | 春 | chūn | 9 | 9 | 13 |

| Simplified Radical | Simplified Character | Traditional Character | Pinyin | No. of Strokes (Simplified) | No. of Strokes (Traditional) | Chapter First Introduced |
|---|---|---|---|---|---|---|
| 日 | 星 | 星 | xīng | 9 | 9 | 13 |
| 日 | 晚 | 晚 | wǎn | 12 | 12 | 8 |
| 日 | 替 | 替 | tì | 12 | 12 | 10 |
| 日 | 最 | 最 | zuì | 12 | 12 | 12 |
| 日 | 景 | 景 | jǐng | 12 | 12 | 19 |
| 日 | 暖 | 暖 | nuǎn | 13 | 13 | 19 |
| 水 | 水 | 水 | shuǐ | 4 | 4 | 7 |
| 贝 | 贵 | 貴 | guì | 9 | 12 | 18 |
| 见 | 见 | 見 | jiàn | 4 | 7 | 4 |
| 见 | 觉 | 覺 | jiào | 9 | 20 | 16 |
| 父 | 父 | 父 | fù | 4 | 4 | 6 |
| 牛 | 牛 | 牛 | niú | 4 | 4 | 8 |
| 手 | 手 | 手 | shǒu | 4 | 4 | 9 |
| 毛 | 毛 | 毛 | máo | 4 | 4 | 5 |
| 气 | 气 | 氣 | qì | 4 | 10 | 7 |
| 攵 | 放 | 放 | fàng | 8 | 8 | 17 |
| 攵 | 故 | 故 | gù | 9 | 9 | 10 |
| 攵 | 教 | 教 | jiāo | 11 | 11 | 10 |
| 斤 | 斤 | 斤 | jīn | 4 | 4 | 20 |
| 斤 | 所 | 所 | suǒ | 8 | 8 | 15 |
| 斤 | 新 | 新 | xīn | 13 | 13 | 15 |
| 爪 | 爬 | 爬 | pá | 8 | 8 | 15 |
| 爪 | 爱 | 愛 | ài | 10 | 13 | 15 |
| 月 | 月 | 月 | yuè | 4 | 4 | 13 |
| 月 | 有 | 有 | yǒu | 6 | 6 | 8 |
| 月 | 肚 | 肚 | dù | 7 | 7 | 12 |
| 月 | 朋 | 朋 | péng | 8 | 8 | 8 |
| 月 | 服 | 服 | fú | 8 | 8 | 11 |
| 月 | 胖 | 胖 | pàng | 9 | 9 | 18 |

| Simplified Radical | Simplified Character | Traditional Character | Pinyin | No. of Strokes (Simplified) | No. of Strokes (Traditional) | Chapter First Introduced |
|---|---|---|---|---|---|---|
| 月 | 能 | 能 | néng | 10 | 10 | 16 |
| 月 | 望 | 望 | wàng | 11 | 11 | 13 |
| 月 | 期 | 期 | qī | 12 | 12 | 13 |
| 风 | 风 | 風 | fēng | 4 | 9 | 15 |
| 母 | 母 | 母 | mǔ | 5 | 5 | 6 |
| 穴 | 空 | 空 | kòng | 8 | 8 | 18 |
| 穴 | 穿 | 穿 | chuān | 9 | 9 | 18 |
| 立 | 站 | 站 | zhàn | 10 | 10 | 19 |
| 疒 | 病 | 病 | bìng | 10 | 10 | 12 |
| 疒 | 疼 | 疼 | téng | 10 | 10 | 12 |
| 疒 | 瘦 | 瘦 | shòu | 14 | 14 | 18 |
| 衤 | 衫 | 衫 | shān | 8 | 8 | 9 |
| 衤 | 衬 | 襯 | chèn | 8 | 21 | 9 |
| 衤 | 袜 | 襪 | wà | 10 | 19 | 9 |
| 衤 | 被 | 被 | bèi | 10 | 10 | 20 |
| 衤 | 裙 | 裙 | qún | 12 | 12 | 14 |
| 衤 | 裤 | 褲 | kù | 12 | 15 | 18 |
| 业 | 业 | 業 | yè | 5 | 13 | 13 |
| 目 | 看 | 看 | kàn | 9 | 9 | 9 |
| 目 | 眼 | 眼 | yǎn | 11 | 11 | 9 |
| 目 | 睡 | 睡 | shuì | 13 | 13 | 16 |
| 目 | 睛 | 睛 | jīng | 13 | 13 | 16 |
| 田 | 男 | 男 | nán | 7 | 7 | 14 |
| 田 | 备 | 備 | bèi | 8 | 12 | 14 |
| 田 | 累 | 累 | lèi | 11 | 11 | 14 |
| 钅 | 钟 | 鐘 | zhōng | 9 | 20 | 13 |
| 钅 | 钱 | 錢 | qián | 10 | 16 | 12 |
| 钅 | 铅 | 鉛 | qiān | 10 | 13 | 17 |
| 钅 | 银 | 銀 | yín | 11 | 14 | 12 |

| Simplified Radical | Simplified Character | Traditional Character | Pinyin | No. of Strokes (Simplified) | No. of Strokes (Traditional) | Chapter First Introduced |
|---|---|---|---|---|---|---|
| 钅 | 错 | 錯 | cuò | 13 | 16 | 13 |
| 钅 | 镜 | 鏡 | jìng | 16 | 19 | 16 |
| 禾 | 和 | 和 | hé/huó | 8 | 8 | 11 |
| 禾 | 秋 | 秋 | qiū | 9 | 9 | 13 |
| 禾 | 租 | 租 | zū | 10 | 10 | 11 |
| 白 | 白 | 白 | bái | 5 | 5 | 8 |
| 白 | 的 | 的 | de | 8 | 8 | 9 |
| 瓜 | 瓜 | 瓜 | guā | 5 | 5 | 19 |
| 皮 | 皮 | 皮 | pí | 5 | 5 | 8 |
| 衣 | 衣 | 衣 | yī | 6 | 6 | 9 |
| 羊 | 美 | 美 | měi | 9 | 9 | 10 |
| 羊 | 差 | 差 | chà | 9 | 9 | 13 |
| 羊 | 着 | 著 | zhe | 11 | 11 | 10 |
| 米 | 米 | 米 | mǐ | 6 | 6 | 10 |
| 米 | 粉 | 粉 | fěn | 10 | 10 | 14 |
| 老 | 老 | 老 | lǎo | 6 | 6 | 9 |
| 耳 | 耳 | 耳 | ěr | 6 | 6 | 16 |
| 西 | 西 | 西 | xī | 6 | 6 | 4 |
| 西 | 票 | 票 | piào | 11 | 11 | 15 |
| 页 | 页 | 頁 | yè | 6 | 9 | 14 |
| 页 | 预 | 預 | yù | 10 | 13 | 14 |
| 页 | 顿 | 頓 | dùn | 10 | 13 | 14 |
| 页 | 颜 | 顏 | yán | 15 | 18 | 14 |
| 竹 | 笔 | 筆 | bǐ | 10 | 12 | 8 |
| 竹 | 笑 | 笑 | xiào | 10 | 10 | 10 |
| 竹 | 笨 | 笨 | bèn | 11 | 11 | 8 |
| 竹 | 第 | 第 | dì | 11 | 11 | 13 |
| 竹 | 等 | 等 | děng | 12 | 12 | 12 |
| 竹 | 筷 | 筷 | kuài | 13 | 13 | 10 |

| Simplified Radical | Simplified Character | Traditional Character | Pinyin | No. of Strokes (Simplified) | No. of Strokes (Traditional) | Chapter First Introduced |
|---|---|---|---|---|---|---|
| 竹 | 箱 | 箱 | xiāng | 15 | 15 | 17 |
| 自 | 自 | 自 | zì | 6 | 6 | 6 |
| 血 | 血 | 血 | xiě/xuě | 6 | 6 | 20 |
| 走 | 走 | 走 | zǒu | 7 | 7 | 11 |
| 走 | 起 | 起 | qǐ | 10 | 10 | 14 |
| 走 | 越 | 越 | yuè | 12 | 12 | 19 |
| 走 | 超 | 超 | chāo | 12 | 12 | 20 |
| 走 | 趣 | 趣 | qù | 15 | 15 | 18 |
| 酉 | 醒 | 醒 | xǐng | 16 | 16 | 16 |
| 里 | 里 | 裏 | lǐ | 7 | 13 | 13 |
| 足 | 跑 | 跑 | pǎo | 12 | 12 | 16 |
| 足 | 跟 | 跟 | gēn | 13 | 13 | 16 |
| 足 | 路 | 路 | lù | 13 | 13 | 18 |
| 青 | 静 | 靜 | jìng | 14 | 16 | 18 |
| 雨 | 雨 | 雨 | yǔ | 8 | 8 | 15 |
| 雨 | 雪 | 雪 | xuě | 11 | 11 | 15 |

# Passages in English

## Chapter 4

### Text 1

I read books, and I also buy books. I have Chinese books—one, two three, four, five. I also have Japanese books—six, seven, eight, nine, ten. My books are not large, nor are they small. Do you have Chinese books or Japanese books?

### Text 2

He is Chinese and is called Wang Zhongshu. You are not Chinese, and I am not Chinese either. You are a New Zealander, and I am Japanese. My family name is Nakamoto, and my personal name is Kazuya. He speaks Chinese, you speak English, and I speak Japanese. You study Chinese, and so do I. See you.

## Chapter 5

### Text 1

Mr. Wang has 1,254 books. He has Chinese books, English books, and even Japanese books. He asked Wenwen what books she has and how many she has. Wenwen only has a few English works of fiction. Mr. Wang said that Wenwen could read his Chinese books. However, Wenwen doesn't understand Chinese. Wenwen can't speak Chinese and can't read it either. Wenwen can only say, "Hello! Good-bye." Mr. Wang gave Wenwen a Chinese-English dictionary. He said that he could teach Wenwen Chinese. Wenwen wants to study Chinese.

### Text 2

I am a New Zealander. I can speak English and Japanese. I can also write a few Chinese characters. I teach Mrs. Wang's son and daughter to speak Japanese. Mrs. Wang gave me three brush pens. I asked her, "Can you teach me to write with a brush pen?" She said, "Sure." She's really good. And what about you? Do you want to learn how to write with a brush pen? I can give you two.

## Chapter 6

### Text 1

My good friend Wensheng's family name is Wan. There are altogether eight people in his family—his father, mother, an older sister, two younger sisters, an older brother, a younger brother, and Wensheng. Half of the siblings are male and half are female. His older sister has four Japanese dictionaries, two Chinese illustrated periodicals, and three New Zealand works of fiction. Both of his younger sisters are elementary school students, and they don't like to read fiction. They want to read children's picture books. They say that children's picture books have very interesting stories, and there aren't many words either. Neither Wensheng nor his younger brother likes to read books. They want to watch TV. They say that TV is very interesting to watch.

### Text 2

Neither my older sister nor I have a bicycle. I must buy one. Bicycles are RMB740.95 each, neither expensive nor cheap. My older sister also wants to buy one. How much altogether are two? Tell me, OK? Oh my! Altogether it's RMB1,481.90. No way. We only have RMB1,000 and can only buy one. My parents have a lot of money. They have tens of thousands of dollars. They said they could give us two bicycles. My parents are really good!

## Chapter 7

It is about the time for lunch. I'm really hungry but don't want to cook. I'd like to go to a Chinese restaurant for some simple dishes and then have a bit to drink. Simple Chinese dishes are quite delicious but are not easy to make. Lanlan says that she is also very hungry and that she also wants to go to eat lunch. However, she wants to eat Japanese food and drink ice water and Coca Cola. Lanlan's uncle and aunt are the proprietors of a Japanese restaurant. Their business is very brisk, and their customers are also numerous. The dishes made by their restaurant are very delicious. However, their coffee isn't good-tasting. They used to sell liquor, but now they don't. Lanlan even says that her uncle won't take our money, as he really likes to treat people to a meal. We needn't be over-polite or give him anything. It doesn't matter. (After all), he is Lanlan's uncle. However, her uncle likes to speak Chinese. When we go to his restaurant, we'll have to speak Chinese. That's great! I can speak a little Chinese, and I also like to speak Chinese. I can even write a few Chinese characters.

## Chapter 8

This is my good friend. His name is Mao Lesheng. Xiao Mao is French. He is really interesting, as he likes buying authentic French things. That pair of French leather shoes he wears is very expensive, more than $400 a pair. I only buy cheap leather shoes. All of my old leather shoes are only $80 a pair. Some people say that Mao Lesheng is quite clever, but I say that he is really stupid. Look, he wears expensive French leather shoes but has no money left to buy something to eat. He no longer eats breakfast and just drinks milk. And he no longer eats lunch either and just drinks a bit of soup. It's really not easy not to eat. I asked him if he was hungry or not, and he said it's not a problem. I really don't get it. He cannot not eat, right? I'd like to treat him to dinner. He really likes authentic French things, but he doesn't like to eat French food. That's right, he likes eating Chinese food. I'll invite Xiao Mao to go to my uncle's Chinese restaurant for dinner. Xiao Mao is too hungry. He hasn't eaten breakfast or lunch and only eats dinner. He says that the dishes made by that restaurant are outstandingly delicious. He is no longer hungry and is full now. My uncle even gave Xiao Mao a Chinese writing brush and a Chinese atlas.

## Chapter 9

There is a famous store downtown. It sells many things. Upstairs they sell clothing and (leather) shoes. There are shirts, T-shirts, jackets, underwear, sweaters, and denim jeans. The things are all very cheap. Look, is this sweater I am wearing beautiful? It was only $40. That's not expensive, eh. The socks and shoes sold there are also very good-looking. Downstairs to the east of the main entrance they sell watches and eyeglasses. The watches there are not cheap—more than $1,000 each; the eyeglasses are also quite expensive—more than $600 a pair. That store does not have cheap watches or eyeglasses. Don't buy watches there, and don't buy eyeglasses there either. To the west of the main entrance they sell books, newspapers, magazines, writing implements, illustrated periodicals, and maps. They are all Chinese. In front of the main entrance they sell things to eat and drink. Do you want to go there to shop? Do you want to drink cold milk or soda pop? Oh my! I forgot to inform you where the store is located. It is on Beijing Street. It's not difficult to find. The proprietor of the shop is surnamed Fang. He is called Fang Yisi. He is quite tall. I know him. He lives to the right of our place. His house is quite large. There are four rooms upstairs and two rooms downstairs. Fang Laoban and the (other) people in his family are all very busy, and so they are very infrequently at home. I like going to shop at his store very much. Why? Because the things he sells are very good. Do you know where I want to go now? I want to go to Fang Laoban's store. Do you want to go with me?

## Chapter 10

Gao Xiaomei is American. She lives on Shanghai Road, between a bookstore and a coffee shop. Before, her children were small and she had to be at home to look after the kids, so she didn't have an opportunity to study Chinese and could only speak English. Now her four kids are all older so she can now go study. Before, Mrs. Gao couldn't write even a single Chinese character. Now she is a university student and studies Chinese and French. Chinese is not easy, (as) the teacher teaches in Chinese all the time, and the Chinese books are all written in Chinese. It is almost exam time, and Mrs. Gao is really busy. She has exams in two classes, Chinese and French. She doesn't even cook anymore. The adults and kids all go to the restaurant behind their house to eat dinner. She says that she will soon be taking exams, so she has to read more than ten books. Some are Chinese books, and some are French books. Mrs. Gao has a friend named Wang Huanlan. She is female. Among Mrs. Gao's friends, only Wang Hanlan is Chinese. Miss Wang lives to the north of Mrs. Gao. Mrs. Gao can use Chinese to phone Wang Huanglan. Wang Huanlan also uses Chinese to speak with Mrs. Gao and tells her Chinese stories. Wang Huanlan can use a brush pen to write Chinese characters. She writes Chinese letters to the Chinese teacher with a brush pen for Mrs. Gao. Mrs. Gao is also very good to Huanlan, inviting her for a meal at a Chinese restaurant. Wang Huanlan has taught Mrs. Gao how to use chopsticks to eat rice. She even introduces (special) Chinese tea to her. Mrs. Gao makes English tea for Wang Huanlan, and teaches her how to use a knife and fork to eat beef. They laugh together as they eat and drink tea. Mrs. Gao thinks it is really great to have a Chinese friend. She'll have no trouble with the exam. She really has to thank Wang Huanlan.

## Chapter 11

Bai Jingyi is my middle school classmate and is now a student at Meisi University. He is very bright and his homework is quite good. But he doesn't know how to drive a car and goes everywhere by bicycle. He says riding a bus is very cheap, but too many people ride the bus. It's too uncomfortable. Taking a taxi is very convenient and comfortable, but it is not cheap. Therefore, he goes everywhere by bicycle.

Bai Jingyi phoned me at night. I was just reading. I said I was free. Come on over to my place for a chat and some drinks. He said great, but he didn't know how to get to my place. I told him that my home is on Tongxin Street, and there was a train station on its left. Just keep on going straight from the train station, and there is my house. To the right of my home is a primary school and to the left is a library. There's a light on outside of the library, so it's not hard to find. Bai Jingyi rode from this street to that street asking directions, but no one knew where Tongxin Street was. Bai Jingyi then stopped riding his bicycle and took a taxi to come to my home. I asked him why he didn't buy a map book. Looking for the street while holding the map book would be (so much) easier. He's really stupid, not the least bit smart.

That night Bai Jingyi and I drank Chinese liquor and chatted. My wife made us many small Shanghai snacks and Nanjing stir-fried dishes. Bai Jingyi said that because there are such delicious dishes and such tasty spirits, he likes coming to drink and shoot the breeze with me very much.

## Chapter 12

I dislike going to see a doctor the most. You have to spend a lot of money, and (even) if you take medicine, you won't necessarily get better. But this morning I went to the hospital to see a doctor.

Yesterday Bai Jingyi came looking for me to shoot the breeze, and we drank a lot of alcohol and ate a lot of delicious things. That night I become uncomfortable. I had a headache and my stomach hurt. I was uncomfortable everywhere.

My wife said, "This isn't good. You're sick." She first gave me a glass of water to drink, and then she gave me some medicine to take. However, I was still uncomfortable everywhere. I thought, "Before when I drank I was never uncomfortable. What's going on today?" My wife said that night I drank too much and ate too many things. It's the case that I ate to the point of getting sick. Therefore I'm uncomfortable. My wife said, "It's too late tonight. Why don't you drink a glass of water and take a rest. Tomorrow you must go see my classmate's elder brother, Dr. Gao."

This morning I still had a headache. I didn't want to eat anything, so I went to see the doctor.

I took a bus to the hospital from the bus stop in front of my home. It was very crowded on the bus. There was no place to sit. I got off at Beijing Road. The hospital was to the left of the Bank of China. Dr. Gao is a famous doctor of this hospital. The people inside the hospital who had come to see a doctor were very numerous. I waited a very long time before I could be seen. Dr. Gao said that I didn't have a fever, that my sickness wasn't a big problem, that it didn't matter. He told me that for a few days I shouldn't eat meat and I shouldn't drink alcohol. Besides drinking water or soup I could only eat rice. He wanted me to return home, rest well and take medicine. This afternoon I took some medicine and also had some soup. Now I am already better. I don't know whether Lao Bai also got sick. I still haven't phoned him. He is not at home now. I have to ring his mobile.

## Chapter 13

In the autumn of last year, Fang Meichun and her classmates came to Beijing to study Chinese. Before coming to Beijing they had already studied a year of Chinese. Before, none of them had ever come to China. The day after arriving in Beijing, they started classes. With the exception of Saturday and Sunday they have classes every day. From 8:10 a.m. until 11:30 they have Chinese language class, and from 1:45 p.m. until 4:00 p.m. they have (language) practice class. After class they still have to do a lot of homework. They all love going to the library best to do homework, because it's very quiet there. Each and every student is very diligent and is very busy every day.

When they get to Saturday and Sunday, everyone is very happy. They can stay at home and chat or cook. Or they can also go see a movie, go shopping, or (just go out and) have fun. Before coming to Beijing Fang Meichun had never cooked. Now everyone says that the Chinese fried rice she cooks is delicious. She often invites classmates and teachers to come over here to eat. Everyone likes to eat her Chinese fried rice. Meichun rang her mother, saying that when she returns home in the spring of next year she plans to make fried rice for her. The twentieth of last month, a Sunday, was her birthday. Her boyfriend Haiming said that because it was her birthday she shouldn't cook at home. (Therefore) Haiming invited Meichun and friends to go have dinner at a good restaurant. He had heard that the new English restaurant across from the bank was quite good, both inside and out (lit. "outside and in"). He hoped to go there, and Meichun said of course they could go. However, an English restaurant certainly doesn't have fried rice. Meichun took a lot of fried rice to the restaurant. Practically all of Meichun's classmates and friends had arrived. Do you know how many of them altogether? Over twenty! They even invited the English boss to come eat with them. Haiming happily said, "This is really great. I have never before eaten Chinese fried rice at an English restaurant." The English boss went on to say that after this he wanted to learn from Meichun how to cook Chinese fried rice.

## Chapter 14

The day before yesterday was a Saturday, and at around 9:00 in the morning, Fang Meichun still had not gotten out of bed, her boyfriend Haiming phoned her. He said that he wanted to invite her to go downtown for some fun. He said that he'd wait for her at the main entrance to the large department store downtown at around 10:00. From where Fang Meichun lives to where the large department store is located takes about an hour. If there are many people on the street and lots of traffic, then it takes more than an hour. Right after Fang Meichun got up, she went out the door without even eating breakfast. She first rode the bus downtown and then walked to the department store. When she got off the bus, it was already five minutes before 10:00. She thought, "Oh no, I'm late. Haiming is certainly already waiting for me at the entrance to the department store. I'll have to walk quickly (lit. 'a bit quicker [than normal]')." It normally takes Meichun fifteen minutes to walk from the bus stop to the department store, but that day she walked quickly and got to the department store at just 10:05. Haiming was already there and had been waiting for quite a while, having arrived at just 9:45. Haiming asked Meichun where she wanted to go. She said, "It's almost winter. I'd like to buy a skirt to wear in winter." They then went to the second floor (of the department store), where there were many beautiful clothes, including very many skirts of all colors—red ones, pink ones, grey ones, yellow ones, light blue ones, white ones, and dark green ones. Haiming asked Meichun which color dress she liked. She said, "With this many colors I don't know which one I like." Haiming said, "In that case why don't you simply try them on one at a time and see which one looks the most beautiful on you." Meichun tried on quite a few, taking more than an hour, but she didn't like even one of them. "Some are bad-looking, and some are too expensive." She said, "I'm hungry. I didn't eat breakfast, and it's almost noon. Why don't we go to that famous Korean restaurant and have some lunch. After lunch we can go to some other department stores to have a look." Haiming said, "You go by yourself. I'll be reading in the café in front. After you have bought your skirt, come look for me."

Meichun went to three department stores, and none of them had a skirt she liked, so she went to the café to look for Haiming. He was drinking coffee and reading. He reads very quickly, so he had already read several dozen pages. He really didn't understand why buying a skirt could be this difficult. Everything else Meichun does she does quickly. It is only shopping where she is especially slow.

Meichun said, "I'm exhausted. Let's go home and come again tomorrow." Haiming unhappily said, "I won't be coming tomorrow after all. I have to prepare for next week's test. We didn't come out today to go shopping, and we didn't come out today to read. Rather, we were supposed to have fun. If you hadn't gone to buy a skirt, then we'd still have had some time to go have fun. In the future, if you want to go shopping, don't come looking for me. Look for someone else to go with you, OK?"

## Chapter 15

Qian Xiping has been living on the east side of the city for seven years. The day after tomorrow he is moving. This is because starting this year he has been teaching at a new school, and this school is located on the south side of the city. Driving a car from the east side of the city to the south side takes an hour and a half. Where they are (now) is very hot in summer and very cold in winter. It even often snows. In the spring if the wind isn't blowing, then it is raining. It is really inconvenient to go outside. Every day the round trip bus ticket is seven or eight dollars, not cheap at all. Qian Xiping's wife said that they certainly had to move to the south side of the city.

Qian Xiping's new home is located in an apartment building on the third floor. Their new house is very large: four bedrooms, a study, a living room, a dining room, and beyond that a very large kitchen and two bathrooms. Inside the apartment building is an elevator, but their family ordinarily won't be using it, as they are only on the third floor and don't have to use it. It is just fine to go up and down using the stairs. The house on the south side of the city is really expensive. It cost 560,000 of Qian Xiping's dollars.

They're about to move to their new house and Qian Xiping still needs to buy a lot of furniture. His parents, older brother, and older sister all think that because he has bought a house, perhaps he has run out of money. Therefore everyone wants to buy some furniture to give to him. Next month is his fortieth birthday and the new furniture is his birthday present. The furniture is all very beautiful, and the piece that Qian Xiping likes the best is the dining table given to him by his older sister. It is made in Japan.

After he moves into his new home Qian Xiping will no longer need to travel to and from work by bus. It is also very convenient for his children to go to school and for his wife to go out and shop. Behind is the city's highest mountain, South Mountain. He can take the children mountain climbing on Saturdays and Sundays. The children all love mountain climbing. He does not need to get up early every morning. In the afternoon after work, he can walk home in just ten minutes! While his wife cooks dinner, he can either play with the children or have a rest. In the evening he can return home this early, so everyone in the family is very happy.

## Chapter 16

After Qian Xiping moved into his new home, he invited some twenty-odd friends to go to his home for a meal. His wife busied herself with this for three days and made more than ten different dishes. Qian Xiping additionally bought quite a lot of alcohol. There was white wine, red wine, rice wine, and of course there was famous brand beer. Both children ran back and forth moving things. Qian Xiping has one son and one daughter. The son is thirteen years old now and just started middle school last year. The daughter is just eight years old this year and is a primary school student. At around five o'clock in the afternoon all of the guests arrived. Upon entering, Qian Xiping's old classmate Huang Jiashen loudly said, "Ah, Xiping, Look at you! You're able to live in this good a house. I don't know when I'll ever have this much money to afford to buy this nice a house. What about the kids? Come, come, come. These are the presents for you." Every time Jiashen comes to their house, he always brings presents for the kids of things they like and plays with them. This time he gave them a novel each. The kids also really like Jiashen. Because Jiashen wears glasses, the kids call him Uncle Glasses.

Qian Xiping invited the guests to eat the food prepared by his wife. Mrs. Qian's dishes are very authentic, as quite a number (of the dishes) can't be found in restaurants. Everyone drank quite a bit of alcohol, Jiashen likes to drink too much. That day, he drank more than any of the other guests and couldn't hold the chopsticks firmly. His wife said to him, "I think you've drunk quite a bit and can't drink anymore." However, he said, "It doesn't matter. I can still drink quite a number more glasses of booze. Look, my eyes can still see very clearly. I can see the food on top of the dining table. My ears can still hear very clearly what you are saying. Come, come. Let's drink! Let's drink! Oh, the lovely drink." Qian Xiping said, "Yes, yes, yes. Everybody, continue to eat, eat a bit more, drink a bit more. Don't stand on ceremony. Our neighbors are out. Do not worry about the noise."

Twenty-plus friends ate and drank, and after finishing the meal, they chatted again. And it wasn't until midnight that everybody finally returned home to sleep. However, the next morning nobody could get up. When Jiashen woke up, it was already 2:00 in the afternoon.

## Chapter 17

Mr. Shang is a New Zealand Chinese. He only began to study Chinese when he was sixty. He is very hard-working, but he can never learn it well, cannot memorize the new vocabulary. He says that it is too much, too difficult to have to remember more than fifty new vocabulary items each week. Teenagers and twenty-year-olds can't remember this many words—how is he supposed to remember them!

Every morning he gets up and then both memorizes new vocabulary and practices writing Chinese characters. He carefully writes down the characters he has already studied on (a piece of) paper. As soon as he has some free time, he takes the paper out and has a look. He also puts the characters on the desk next to his bed. Before going to sleep at night, he looks at them a few times and has a look at them (again) after he wakes up. He says all he has to do is study every day, and he can certainly learn Chinese well and can memorize the new words.

Mr. Shang was considering going to China next year to see his mother's ninety-something-year-old sister. It has already been more than fifty years since he last saw her.

In Mr. Shang's house there were Chinese characters here and Chinese characters there. His wife said to his friends that she couldn't read Chinese characters and that as soon as she saw one she got angry. The rooms upstairs and downstairs were just filled with characters. It really got her angry. Last year she also began studying Chinese. Mr. and Mrs. Shang went to the library together to borrow books and to return books. In less than half a year they were already able to say quite a bit of Chinese and had learned quite a large number of Chinese characters. They also learned how to make Chinese dumplings. They thought about it over and over again. "Why do we have to wait until next year before we go to China? Why not go now? It is autumn now and Beijing is very cool. Once in China we can practice Chinese very thoroughly and eat ready-made Chinese dumplings."

Last month Mr. and Mrs. Shang brought with them a large suitcase containing all of their Chinese books and other luggage and went to China.

After they got off the airplane, Mr. Shang used Chinese to speak with a young woman at the airport. He was extremely tense. The young woman couldn't understand his Chinese. Mr. Shang then used a pencil to write down on a piece of paper, "Search, think, sell Chinese self liquor. Do you buy here?" That young women looked at what he had written for a long time, but she still could not understand what he meant. Do you know why? Mr. Shang had written the character " I" as " search," "white" as "self," and additionally had written the character "buy" as "sell" and "sell" as "buy." Do you think that the young woman could understand what Mr. Shang had written?

## Chapter 18

I live on Nanjing Street. Nanjing Street is very quiet. It is not the least bit noisy, and it is not bustling either. Right across from our house is a very small store selling clothing. Of the two bosses of that store, one is surnamed Chang and the other is surnamed Zhang. I call them Uncle Chang and Uncle Zhang. When I have free time, I often go there for fun.

Uncle Chang is very tall and is also very thin. He originally lived north of the Yellow River. Uncle Zhang is not as tall as Uncle Chang, and he is neither fat nor thin. In the past he lived south of the

Yangtze River. Uncle Zhang said that the Yangtze River is longer than the Yellow River, while Uncle Chang said that the Yangtze and Yellow Rivers are equally long. I said, "I know (the answer). Our teacher said that the Yangtze River is longer than the Yellow River." Uncle Zhang heard this and was very happy.

Both Uncle Chang and Uncle Zhang are fifty-something. Neither of them is particularly interested in doing business. But they are especially interested in making clothing, as all of the clothing in their store is made by them. The clothing sold in their shop is both comfortable and inexpensive, but it is not fashionable enough. They say that although the clothing sold in other stores is fashionable, it is almost twice as expensive as theirs, so only rich people can afford it.

Both of my parents are teachers. Their salaries are not very high. However, my score on last month's test was especially high. (Therefore) they bought a couple of pairs of famous-maker jeans for me. This pair of pants I am wearing now is 33 percent more expensive than the most expensive pair of pants selling in Uncle Chang's store. Uncle Zhang asked me why I didn't buy my pants in their store. I said that this pair of pants I am wearing is completely different from the pants that they sell in their store. My pants are both fashionable and come from a famous maker. This pair I am wearing now still isn't my most expensive pair. I still have another pair that is even more expensive than this one.

## Chapter 19

Zhong Mingran left Beijing in February of this year and came to New Zealand to study English. After arriving in New Zealand, he has been living at my house. Zhong Mingran is very studious, (so over) these (past) several months he has come to speak English extremely well. Because he is so nervous every day (about his study), he hasn't the time to go anywhere to have some fun.

He has heard that the scenery around Snowy Mountain Town is very beautiful, and he really wants to go travel there. Since finishing his exams, he has been relatively free and wants to relax a bit, so he gave his classmate Xie Li a phone call. Xie Li is French and found a job over the vacation in Snowy Mountain Town. (Therefore) he said he could take Zhong Mingran to Snowy Mountain Town for some fun. Zhong Mingran heard this and was very happy.

In July it is winter in New Zealand, so Snowy Mountain Town is very cold. Therefore they had to bring a bit more clothing with them (than usual). Isn't that the truth! On TV, they said that when it snows in Snowy Mountain Town, all the roads are white, and that perhaps you won't feel warm enough wearing just two sweaters and a jacket. The more Zhong Mingran watched the news, the colder he felt, so he immediately went out and bought an overcoat.

Snowy Mountain Town is very far from my home, altogether more than 700 kilometers, and there's even a big river in between (the two places). Do you know how long it takes to get to Snowy Mountain Town by train? At the very least it takes six hours. It is really not close at all. It is (also) much colder there than here. Although it doesn't get too windy, it still does snow. The scenery of Snowy Mountain Town is particularly beautiful, so large numbers of foreigners like to travel to Snowy Mountain Town.

After Zhong Mingran and Xie Li got to Snowy Mountain Town, they came out of the train station and immediately took a taxi to their hotel. The hotel is not far away, but there were lots of cars on the road, and lots of students came here over their break to have fun, so the traffic jams were horrific. They didn't arrive at their hotel until very late. The next day Zhong Mingran got up very early. However, the previous night Xie Li had gone drinking with his friends, so he went to sleep fairly late. Zhong Mingran thought that maybe Xie Li couldn't get up so early, so he went out by himself to have some fun. After Xie Li woke up, he couldn't find Zhong Mingran and became very worried. He put on his coat and immediately went to search for Zhong Mingran. He knew that Zhong Mingran loves most to eat watermelon, so he went to a fruit stall near the hotel to look for him. Would you look at that! Zhong Mingran was right there by the stall, carefully choosing a watermelon.

## Chapter 20

Mrs. Jiang knew that Jiang Xingcheng wasn't going to work in the afternoon, so because he was free she asked him to go to the nearby supermarket to buy a few things for her. She said that it is almost vacation time, and she'd like to take the kids away over the vacation, so she wants to buy some things to eat, to drink, for them to use, and so on, but naturally he should buy several catties of ready-made Chinese dumplings. While out shopping (for her), Mrs. Jiang also wanted him (to keep a sharp eye on his wallet so as) not to have the money and credit cards stolen. Jiang Xingcheng had barely gone out the door when his wife called out to him to stop, telling him that on the way home from going shopping he should get off the expressway and go to school to pick up the kids. Jiang Xingcheng unhappily said, "I got it. What a pain!"

Two hours later Jiang Xingcheng returned home with four kids. The kids were both noisy and loud, and Jiang Xingcheng wanted them to quiet down a bit. Not only did they not listen to him, but they (actually) became noisier and noisier. His oldest daughter walked in the door and immediately wanted to sing karaoke. His second daughter wanted to phone classmates, and his youngest daughter was fighting with his young son, and he started to cry. His hand had been scratched open by his older sister, and it had started to bleed. His second daughter was also angry. Jiang Xingcheng said that having four kids at home was a real racket, and that all of them should go live in the school dorm. However, what was he going to do after the start of vacation with the kids at home every day? He should simply go to work every day. Not being at home is the best solution.